PONDERING THE
PERMANENT THINGS

THOMAS HOWARD

Pondering the Permanent Things

Reflections on Faith, Art, and Culture

Compiled by
Keith Call

IGNATIUS PRESS   SAN FRANCISCO

Photograph of Thomas Howard

Cover design by Riz Boncan Marsella

© 2023 by Ignatius Press, San Francisco
All rights reserved
ISBN 978-1-62164-638-9 (PB)
ISBN 978-1-64229-277-0 (eBook)
Library of Congress Catalogue number 2023932337
Printed in the United States of America ∞

CONTENTS

FOREWORD

When my twelve-year-old son won a batting title in Little League baseball, his coach told him at the end of the season that next year he would be ready to move up to the next level, Little League's "majors". But instead of rejoicing, he was full of worry. Asked why, he replied, "I'm not big enough yet to play at Fenway Park with guys like Carl Yastrzemski!"

That's how I felt when I first met Tom Howard. I had not yet published anything, and he had written *Christ the Tiger*, which I had read in awe, struck by passages like this one, which I deem worthy to be compared to Augustine's *Confessions*:

> I announce to you what is guessed at in all the phenomena of your world. You see the grain of wheat shrivel and break open and die, but you expect a crop. I tell you of the Springtime of which all springtimes speak. I tell you of the world for which this world groans and toward which it strains. I tell you that beyond the awful borders imposed by time and space and contingency, there lies what you seek.... For I announce to you redemption. Behold I make all things new. Behold I do what cannot be done. I restore the years that the locusts and worms have eaten. I restore the years which you have drooped away upon your crutches and in your wheelchair. I restore the symphonies and operas which your deaf ears have never heard, and the snowy massif your blind eyes have never seen, and the freedom lost to you through plunder, and the identity lost to you because of calumny and the failure

9

of justice; and I restore the good which your own foolish mistakes have cheated you of. And I bring you to the Love of which all other loves speak, the Love which is joy and beauty, and which you have sought in a thousand streets and for which you have wept and clawed your pillow.

We met on the same panel discussion at a local university. Knowing how common the name Howard is, when I was introduced to him I assumed that this was another Tom Howard. How could they have put this Yastrzemski on the same panel with a Little Leaguer? When he revealed his identity, I was too embarrassed to say another word.

Our next meeting was at a C.S. Lewis conference at the Benedictine monastery in Valyermo, California, in the high Mojave desert. All the participants were asked with which character in the Chronicles of Narnia they most identified. Tom and I were the only two who picked Puddleglum. I later discovered that the license plates on his two cars spelled out "Alas" and "Alack".

Tom had the best of both worlds: he laughed joyfully at his own pessimism. He was deeply happy, rejoicing in almost everything (including both animals and angels) but not the modern desacralized world, "The Waste Land". (I am not absolutely sure he was not an angel in disguise; their disguises are remarkably convincing.) Like Tolkien, he was a pessimist by temperament and an optimist by conviction, a pessimist by observation and an optimist by faith.

Before both he and Sheldon Vanauken (author of *A Severe Mercy*, another book I dare to compare with the *Confessions*) became Catholics, the three of us met for about six glorious hours at the Portsmouth Abbey digs of Dom Julian Stead, who dared to label us "The Little Inklings". Tom and Van both confessed they were considering swimming the Tiber, and Julian prophesied that "the only uncertain thing is who will go first." He turned to me and asked, "Which do you think it will be?" I replied: "Let's look at the data." I asked both Tom and Van, "What would you do if you knew you would die tomorrow?" Van instantly answered: "Call a priest." Tom said, "I'd have to think and pray about it first." I completed the prophecy: "You first," I said to Van, "and you next," to Tom.

The prophecies all came true. When Tom did become a Catholic, he did me the astonishing honor of asking me to be his godfather. Van did the same. Grace is always undeserved.

Tom and I created the "Saint Socrates Society" (named after Erasmus' famous prayer, "Saint Socrates, pray for us"), which met monthly at his gracious-in-every-way house for a decade or two. Evangelicals from Gordon College & Seminary and Catholics from Boston College honestly, passionately, intelligently, critically, and respectfully listened to and learned from each other.

When Tom "poped", Gordon decided that a line must be drawn in the sand. Although a rabbi and an Orthodox priest had been visiting professors there years before and although I, as a Catholic, was teaching part-time there, Gordon's authorities politely called the two of us into a meeting and explained that they had to let us go because we could not have signed the college's "statement of faith" in good conscience since it included the statement that the Bible "contains everything we need to know that is necessary for salvation" and that "we are saved by grace, not by the works of the law." We protested that Catholics believe these things, too, but it fell on deaf ears. My loss was minor, but Tom lost his whole job and many of his Evangelical friends. He was chairman of the English Department and the most famous, beloved, and sought-out professor on campus. Yet, honorable gentleman that he was, he refused to sue or even argue. He stoutly maintained that the college had a right to define its identity, and he honored that principle.

It was a move up, not down, for he moved to Saint John's Seminary to teach future priests. He was there for another decade or two, when the seminary was at its lowest point. He complained to me that students would come to him for spiritual advice because they were not sure that many of the clergy who were teaching them really believed the Faith they were paid to teach. Things have improved vastly there since then, and Tom certainly had something to do with that.

ᕀ ᕀ ᕀ

The articles in this anthology are from both before and after his conversion, and they show the continuity between the "before" and the "after". They all manifest the same "Tomistic" vision of a world full of awe, adoration, authority; beauty, courage, charity, chastity, courtesy, concreteness, duty, discipline, dignity, femininity, fidelity, glory, grace, gratitude, hierarchy, holiness, humility, heroism, honor, imagination, incarnation, ineffability, innocence, joy, masculinity, myth, manners, majesty, nobility, obedience, piety, purity, paradox, sacrifice, solemnity, sublimity, splendor, sacramentality, sanctity, and wonder. Tom not only admired, praised, and wrote eloquently about these "old" values, he also embodied them. We meet in this book not only the ideas but the person. For me to read these typical writings of Tom and to hear his voice in them is almost a foretaste of the resurrection.

Alas and alack for us, Tom has left us for a world where all these values still live, eternally, while meanwhile here below all these things are draining away from our not only post-Christian but Christophobic culture as we stumble and lurch toward the *Brave New World, That Hideous Strength*, and *The Abolition of Man*. Utilitarianism, materialism, collectivism, sterility, reductionism, relativism, subjectivism, mechanism, hubris, Gnosticism, artificiality, economism, abnormality, totalitarianism, self indulgence, cynicism, nihilism, sophism, propaganda, boredom, debauchery, ideologism, abstraction, technologism, transhumanism—throughout our culture the works of hell are replacing the works of heaven. If you are not a Puddleglum today, you are blinkered or blind. And if you are a "culture junky", if culture is your god, you are doomed. But even so, we have hope and good cheer because we reread and believe paragraphs like the one I compared to Augustine's *Confessions*. One of Tom's favorite lines, from a Cavalier poet, was "Man, please thy Maker and be merry / And for this world give not a cherry."

And yet Tom was in love with the world and its beauty and its art. Most of these essays and articles are about the rich and paradoxical relationship between the two things Tom loved most: Christ and culture, holiness and art. Beauty, like truth, was to be loved for its own sake; yet our hope and our salvation is not the glory of great culture but the glory of God. He loved and embodied great charm and grace and gentlemanliness, but he also embodied something of another order: great faith, hope, and charity.

❧ ❧ ❧

Tom's masterpiece is *Chance or the Dance?* It is the single best and most beautiful book contrasting the mediaeval and the modern, the Christian and the post-Christian, world views that I have ever read. His books on Charles Williams, C. S. Lewis, and T. S. Eliot are very close behind.

In fact, almost everything his words touch turns to gold. He is our Chrysostom, the golden-tongued. It is not likely that we shall see his like again.

Peter Kreeft

Art as Incarnation

I shall blame the title and hence the topic on the powers that be; but the title that was given to me in a letter is non-negotiable, and that is "Art as Incarnation". As it happens, that title does indeed suggest an area about which I think almost without stopping, along with the topic of death. I find my reveries running in these directions. What I would like to do in our time together is to reflect on this topic, not just in a general sort of way, which of course would be impossible to do.

This is sort of an inside speech, I might say. We are at Wheaton College, which does indeed represent one of the major streams in Christendom. It has been an institution where the Christian faith has been celebrated, taught, defended, and articulated in a certain way with a particular clarity. Besides that, Wheaton College and the conferences it sponsors, even the summer schools, have addressed themselves to some of these questions, particularly about art and the arts. Wheaton has been a bellwether in the whole enterprise of writers' conferences, approached from a Christian point of view. So I would like to address myself to some of the questions that arise when you try to think about the phenomenon of art from an evangelical Christian point of view.

Immediately that locates the discussion. I would like to lead up to that by offering some comments about art itself.

Lecture given in a slightly different form at Wheaton College, 1984.

Very often you find well-intentioned, earnest, thinking Christian people attempting to find a warrant for the artistic enterprise of writing, painting, sculpture, or whatever else, by leafing through the Bible; and they will light upon Leviticus or Exodus, which spell out all the superb work that went into the Tabernacle. Indeed, a great deal of exquisite craftsmanship went into the Tabernacle. And there you have it. You see, God likes beauty. That is true. I am not leading up to disagreeing with that, by the way. And then a number of texts from the Prophets speak of beauty or elegant workmanship or God's handiwork, and so on. It's thin-going when you get to the New Testament if you are trying to find texts to encourage the artistic enterprise, but they can be found. I am trying to think what they might be, but there are some. In any event, if indeed the attempt is to find a warrant to launch people on the artistic enterprise from specific scriptural texts, that is the easiest thing in the world to do.

The reason for that, it seems to me, is the same reason that we would have to use if we were looking for scriptural texts encouraging us to sleep at night or eat our meals, and so on. We do not need scriptural texts to encourage us to do what we are made to do. We do not need to be told in the Bible to eat enough food to keep going. We will eat. That is the kind of creature we are. We will play. That is the kind of creature we are. We will celebrate. We will ceremonialize. That is the kind of creature we are. We will sleep periodically. That is the kind of creature we are. We do not need a particular or special divine injunction to cause us to do the thing which is in our very nature. I think it is for this reason, frankly, that we neither find nor need to find any articulated biblical rationale for the artistic enterprise. It is coterminate with what we are. It is coeval with what we are. It is part of the warp and woof of the fabric of our being. We are that kind of creature. We are makers.

You need only poke through anthropology and archaeology, and what you find when you dig up this or that mound is the stuff that people made, shards and Hittite tablets and pediments from buildings and so on. They were always making something, and a great many of the things that they made do not have a very functional purpose. You can poke around among the Anglo-Saxon remnants and find all this marvelous gold and enameled jewelry. Those were hard days. Those were long, bitter winters. You had Norsemen sailing across the North Sea with fire and sword, scouring the land. They did not have a whole lot of leisure, and yet they kept making this exquisite jewelry. It seems we cannot be stopped from doing this sort of thing. It does not matter if Attila the Hun is at the gate, we keep on singing and dancing and making things and telling stories. Art is what we do. This is the kind of creature we are. There is no question about it, and we do not need to be divinely enjoined to do it. We are already divinely enjoined by our creation. Now let's say art is what we do and what we are going to do, willy-nilly. You won't stop us from doing it.

And let me re-emphasize, or place a different emphasis, on that phrase "art is what we do." Art is what *we* do, we being human beings. It is what we do about our experience, which is—this is not a definition of art, but is one way of coming at or looking at the phenomena—what we do about our experience that is, shall we say, "non-utilitarian" or "non-necessary". There is a sort of practical, pragmatic, or technological accounting for things, which would of course exclude artistic activity. When I say it is what we do about our experiences that is non-utilitarian or non-necessary, I mean as opposed to what we have to do. For instance, if we are cold, we must find firewood somewhere to get warm. The whole world of science and technology represents the fruit of our intelligence being brought to bear on our experience and doing something about it. If you need to go across the river, build a bridge. One way is to throw a log across. If it is the Hudson River and there is much traffic, you need more than a log, so eventually you construct the George Washington Bridge.

This is the realm of science and technology, and so on. That is one of the sets of things we do about our experience that is what I would call utilitarian. It has a manifest fruit that shows up in making life easier, more livable, more defensible, whatever you want to call it. The whole world, legislation, politics, economics, and so on, is conducted according to our experiences. If there are too many people in our city, we must get them one-way streets. We must paint yellow lines down the middle and install red and green lights if we cannot move all these people through the intersection. So let's pass some laws. We cannot have everybody lifting things out of each other's houses, so we say, "Don't steal." This is what we do in a utilitarian way about our experience. The world of behavioral science is a whole region representing "what we do about our experience". People are in trouble. They need help. Here is a person who is very confused, so send him off to a counselor. That is one of the things we do about our experience. Of course, the region that we are talking about, that comes under the great rubric called art, by which I include all that is non-utilitarian or non-necessary, comprises sculpture, dance, painting, singing, narrative, poetry, and architecture. This region of activity is an interesting index.

I return to my emphasis on the personal pronoun "we". It is about what we do about our experience that is apparently non-utilitarian or non-necessary. It is about what we do about our experience, as opposed to the creatures who stand on both sides of us in the created order. That is to say, we are here in the created order, and we have our friends the dogs, who are near at hand. We and the dogs go through many of the same sets of experiences. We get hungry, dogs get hungry. We get sleepy, dogs get sleepy. We get frustrated, dogs get frustrated. Shut a door in a dog's face, and he is rather disappointed about it. A dog hopes he is going to gnaw a lovely dog bone, and it turns out to be for somebody else, so he stops wagging his tail. Down it goes, wagging more and more feebly. He thinks he is going to ride in the car, and off you go, and there he is. Dogs get embarrassed. Dogs hop up on the sofa, knowing they are not supposed to be on it, and they look distinctly sheepish. They possess a great array of emotional nuances, besides being hungry and sleepy and all of that. But no dog has ever done anything about it. No dog has ever written so much as a letter, let alone a sonnet, epic, or lyric, nothing about his frustration, disappointment, love, and so on. Dogs die, but you never see a procession of dogs moving slowly down the street. They do nothing at all about that. There are no dog obsequies, no dog requiems, no nothing. We are the ones who mourn the loss of dogs, which is all by way of saying, we mortal men and women not only go through the experiences that other creatures do, we apparently must do something about it.

We need to re-go-through experience. We need to re-create experience. We need to re-evoke and re-invoke these experiences of ours. That is indeed at least part of, not the whole of, this enterprise we call art. Every story that has ever been told, every drama that has ever been written, every song that has ever been sung, every painting that has ever been painted, every sculpture that has ever been sculpted, every monument that has ever been erected is a case in point of us attempting to give our experience back to ourselves of having gone through that experience. It is a memorial, a re-telling, a re-shaping, an attempt somehow to cope with, or respond to, or give shape to, the raw business of experience. We do not seem able merely to "go through" experience. We are the kind of creature who must do something about it, must articulate it one way or another. This is the experience we call art. The most obvious thing about art is that when the activity has reached its fruition, when you have completed the poem, sonata, narrative, or sculpture, there is something solid, something tangible, visible, or audible. The most obvious case in point would be something like the Ecstasy of Saint Teresa or David or the Venus de Milo. Generation after generation, century after century, there it sits. Why is that? What is that shape of sculpture doing there? What is evoked?

My daughter joined an art history tour to Rome, Venice, and Florence. She returned absolutely dazzled and swept away. She was telling us about an experience at Saint Peter's in Rome. She had studied all about what was where, but she had forgotten that the Pietà was in Saint Peter's; and when she strolled around one of those immense columns, there it was. She found herself pale, overwhelmed at just the shape of the surface of the marble. Of course, the joker in the pack is that the shape of the surface of the marble evokes ... what? The entirety of the human mystery. Here is the Mother. Here is the dead God, if you will. Here is all of maternity and filial piety and everything else in that shape, and there is no difference, or you cannot unscramble the difference, between the shape of the marble and that which it evokes. No one needs to scotch tape a little placard onto the thing, declaring, "My dear, you must understand that this is about grief." It is there, expressed in the Pietà.

You walk into Chartres Cathedral, another kind of a monument. On one accounting it represents an immense amount of wasted space. It is difficult to justify all those square yards of material. It is a very inefficient building indeed. Nowadays, of course, the mayor of the town of Chartres could say, "We are wasting all this space. We could build fifteen floors in here, moving in typists and computers and everything, and use the space much more efficiently." Those arches are a colossal monstrosity, a grotesque weight, aren't they? Yet what are they for? What does that shape articulate? What is it about? We want to leave it alone. We do not want to change one stone.

You stumble across an icon, it need not be very big, 5 × 7 or so, of the Mother and Child. So what about a mother and her child? I see them every day in the park, mothers and children all over the place. Yet what do you see in the icon of the Mother and Child? A whole universe, not just of piety, but a vision, a dogma, a whole Byzantine sensibility. Everything is there in that visible, tangible artifact, if you will. When the artistic enterprise has reached its fruition, you have something tangible or visible or audible, or all three, there. Now when we come to the question of narrative and poetry, it raises some interesting questions. Where does a sonnet exist? Is it in the ink and paper? Is it in the mind of Petrarch or Dante or whomever? Does it come into being when you are sitting in your chair reading it? Does it come into being when you read it out loud? Where does the sonnet exist? I do not think anybody can answer that question.

The sonnet is not a sonnet unless at some point or other it hails us physically, it smites our eardrums or eyes or whatever. Music partakes of that same mystery. Where is music? It exists like a plane exists in time as well as space. There is no such thing as a stationary plane. It is always

moving. Where is that plane? What was the plane a second ago is not the same plane now. It is the same thing
with music. Where is a Mozart horn concerto? Is it in
the curls of the French horn? Is it in the mind of Dennis
Brain as he plays the French horn? Is it in Mozart's imagination? He is dead in his coffin. Where is his concerto?
Is it in your eardrums? Where is it? No one can say, but
nonetheless it exists only insofar as at some point or other
it is or becomes audible. What about dance? Where does
choreography exist? I find myself fascinated by that question. I keep asking ballet dancers, "What is the notation
for choreography?" None of them is ever able to tell me
how George Balanchine writes these things down. Where
does dance exist? It exists in time as well as in space and
in body. There is no such thing as a dance with no body
involved. You cannot have a spiritual dance. The Dance
of the Hours is a lovely idea, but we must see somebody
dance to see the Dance of the Hours.

The most obvious thing about art is that it exists in the
physical realm, the visible, the audible, the tangible. Now
this making something visible and tangible and audible out
of our experience is what we do, we being you and I, we
mortal human beings. What we do with our experiences,
what we do about our experiences, they cannot seem to
stop us doing it. Aristotle pointed this out. The poet is
a poeta, a maker. That is what the word poetry means.
Poetry is a thing made; and this activity that we call art,
we can call poetry if we want. It is ceaseless, it is focal, it is
central, it is quintessential to us. It is heroic. We keep on
doing it, even with Attila the Hun after us, and it seems
to be some sort of index to what we are as opposed to the
dogs, who do not do anything about it. I often find myself
mulling over the question (just for the purposes of speculation) of angelic art. I am a great fan of angels and art, but

I do not think that the angels produce any art. You say, "Yes, they do. They sing angelic music." But I think that angelic music is not what you think of as music. I do not think that they write down any chorales, if there is indeed angelic music.

But I think it is synonymous with the music of the spheres. There is an immediacy. I think it is virtually inconceivable that there is a shelf of angelic music sitting somewhere that can be reproduced tomorrow. As far as we know from glimpses in Scripture and Church Tradition, the angels are pure intellect. T. S. Eliot said that humans cannot bear too much reality, but angels are able to bear much reality. The Doctors tell us that at least the seraphim, not the lower orders, are able to gaze directly upon the divine reality. The music there must be the product of the moment, if we can speak that way about it. Of course, the angels do not fashion sculpture or paintings, no memorializing of anything. Why? Because there is no sequence with them. Art, among other things, does indeed exist in time. It is a tragic witness to sequence, if it is nothing else. That is to say, it is in some sense our attempt, desperate in certain situations, to erect the fugitive.

The narrative tells the story over again. Tell us about the Battle of Baldwin again. We want to hear it. Tell us about the Battle of Brunanburh. Tell us the Song of Roland. For the umpteenth time, we want to hear it. What does art do? It memorializes, it arrests, it catches what is otherwise merely fugitive, merely ephemeral, merely fleeting. Of course, your experience and mine of the passing of time is tragic. We do not like to see things drain off into the sand. We would like to be able to arrest things. Even that stone jar Keats liked does not move. What does he like about it? It was as if the figures on the jar had arrested the moment just before the moment of ecstasy, which is even better than the moment of ecstasy, because he still had it coming. He envied those fawns and satyrs on there. You lucky guys, it will never fade away for you. For the rest of time, you will know this glorious anticipation, whereas for the rest of us, experience comes, goes, and there we are, left empty-handed. We are terribly aware that time is the agent of tragedy. It is the dimension of loss. Our experience comes, and it goes.

Art at least is part of our attempt to arrest it in visible, audible, and tangible terms. We cannot do it with mere thought. Why? Because we are flesh and blood creatures. We are that maddening sort of creature which Hamlet ruminated about. We possess these angelic, godlike imaginations, and yet here we are in these bodies. But more than the dogs, we worry about things. We feel the shaft of immortality coming at us. We find that we are mere, shall I say, flesh and blood creatures. Our experience comes to us physically, our experience of bliss, ecstasy, yearning, grief, loss, and so on. It comes to us via our senses, and we shape it physically. We shape all of our experience physically. Anybody who has ever loved anybody else has given a physical shape to affection. You do not say, "Well, I have already expressed to you the fact that I care for you." Sooner or later, you want to hold her hand. You want to put an arm around him. You want to seal the thing with a kiss.

Why? Milton has some very funny passages about the methods by which angels love each other. I think it is among the least successful parts of *Paradise Lost*. Far be it from me to take a view on that, but I do not think he brought it off. However it is that angels express their love, we want to touch and kiss the other person. For spouses or anybody who has been madly in love with somebody, it will not do to say, "You know that last Wednesday I told you that I love you." It is still true, but as Julie Andrews sang, "Never do I ever want to hear another word." Show me. We need to register and shape and feel our experience physically. Every gesture you have ever made, the nod of your head, a smile, a wave of your hand, a kiss, a hug, an embrace, these are the indexes of our physicality. All ceremony, all slow processions, all fast processions, all victory parades, all liturgies, these arise from what we are. We do not have to be taught to do this. We try to shape our experience physically.

Now, bringing it closer to the actual enterprise of art, any of you who have ever tried to write a story or poem, or tried to paint a picture or do choreography, one of the things you struggle with, as Eliot describes in *The Four Quartets*, is that you want to get the thing you are making to answer as nearly as you can to the thing or the experience that you bespeak or evoke. What I am talking about here is this old, vexed question of form and meaning. And you know that I would be speaking falsely if I said, "Do you have a good idea for a story? Well, think of a story that will sort of carry that idea and attach that idea onto the story." Anybody who teaches or writes fiction will say that is a recipe for disaster. You do not have a narrative here and a meaning there and somehow try to make them jibe with each other. The narrative is the meaning. The meaning is not something you can pull out with tweezers and say, "Now there, dear, is what the story really means." Your poet or writer of fiction would say, "Well, no, that really does not do justice to what's going on." So the form and meaning, if we can use the terms at all, must be one seamless fabric. The artistic enterprise endeavors desperately to achieve that integrity, that seamlessness of fabric. There are obvious examples.

For instance, I often think of George Herbert, who wrote a couple of shaped poems. One is called "Easter

Wings", which has a humorous element in it. It is a wonderful poem, by the way, about the spiritual life. The
first line goes, "Lord, who createdst man in wealth and
store...." The lines get thinner and thinner. Because of
sin, we became, as a little line in the middle of the second
verse, says, "... most thinne ..." It is very good theology
and very good spirituality and jolly good poetry, but Herbert did not write many poems like that. It is a gimmick.
You cannot do it too often. It's like a dog walking on its
hind legs. But you can do it, and the shape, sound, and
meaning of the poem are all woven into a seamless fabric.
I often think of a Hemingway short story, about four pages
long, called "Hills Like White Elephants". It is "nothing at
all" except two people (I don't think we ever learn their
names) sitting at a little table in a railroad depot in Spain,
waiting for the train. But eventually, just through their
typical monosyllabic Hemingway comments, you not only
find out that there is an immediate drama here, but you
discover what kind of people they are.

But it is not the kind of story where you can underline
anything, any more than you can underline special lines in
a T. S. Eliot poem. To do that would be to dismantle the
thing. It's the whole fabric. All this is by way of saying,
of course, that in the artistic enterprise, what we try to do
is to achieve a seamlessness of fabric. When we speak of
these things that we make, we speak of a phenomenon in
which, shall we say, the distance, tension, or duality between form and meaning—or we can even say the physical, that is the texture or the material of the thing, and the
spiritual, or the significance of it—has been overridden,
overcome, or re-knit, if you will, or at least is in question.
In a perfect world, there is no division at all between the
experience itself and our standing over here looking at
the experience.

When we do that, we acknowledge a disjuncture, that the fabric has been torn and that our experience is not seamless. We know this psychologically. When you are listening to a Brandenburg concerto, absolutely respectfully, you are listening to it. The minute you think, "Wow. This is great. I am sitting here listening to the Brandenburg concerto", then you introduce any number of fissures into the fabric, because you've got yourself looking at yourself listening to the music, or how many other selves you can get onto the stage, and somewhere in there the business of the Brandenburg concerto has gone out the window. It simply becomes a component in a scotch-tape job. In a sense, art is not only a register or index or witness to our awareness of the tragedy of time, it is also a register or index or witness of our awareness of the fragmentation of the disjuncture, or the sense of fissure, in our experience, the non-seamlessness of our experience, the seamed nature of it.

The following is another piece of speculation, like my bit about the angels, but my hunch is that if we may speak at all about the Garden of Eden without going too far out on a limb, I do not think there was any art or liturgy there. I like art and I like Eden, but I do not think that there would have been any art there. Why not? Because there was an absolute perfect integrity between Adam and Eve's experience of life, so they did not need to get a handle on experience. They did not need to get in touch with their feelings. If our notions of eternity are at all on target, there was this perfect prism of their experience and nothing fugitive about it, nothing fleeting that led them to claw after the coattails of their experience, saying, "Wait, wait. Let me erect a monument." Of course, we do not know how long things went on. Then the fissure or disjuncture was introduced, and now you have a drama. Then is

when the story starts. I would venture to guess that you
cannot have a story in Eden as such, because in a state of
perfection, whatever it is that happens will not reveal itself
to narrative. You must have something bad happening
in order to get the story cranked up and going. So Eden, in
its state of perfection, is not the realm where you will find
art. By the same token, there is no liturgy.

What is the liturgy? The liturgy is our giving a shape
to our experience. It is inevitably our giving a shape to
our experience. There is no such thing as no liturgy. Some
people's liturgy involves nothing at all but sitting still, but
nonetheless we do give a shape to our experience. And if by
liturgy we mean that special observation of certain times of
significance at rhythmic intervals, in our context it would
mean worship. You do not need that in Eden, because the
entirety of life is of one fabric. It is nothing but the contin-
ual, continuous oblation of praise to God. Adam and Eve
did not set aside an hour at eleven o'clock on a Sunday
morning and say, "Right, we've got to get our act together
for the Lord", and then get back to the grind of the week.
Every Monday, Tuesday, or Wednesday, whatever their
days were, their eating, drinking, loving, sleeping, tending
the garden, was a nonstop, seamless oblation of praise to
God. There did not need to be a special part carved out
for worship. The liturgy itself, along with art, is an index
of our awareness of the fragmentation of our experience
and our attempt to return. That is what the liturgy is, like
the still point of a turning world. It is the clutter of the rest
of the week brought to a point of order and clarified, articulated, and given a shape.

So we find that art is an index of what we are. We do
not need to be enjoined to do it. It is in the nature of the
case physical. There is no such thing as a spiritual art. Even
drama, even the most abstract poetry, does not proceed on

abstraction. It proceeds via imagery. Even abstract paintings, abstract expressionism. Visit the Whitney Museum
in New York, and what do you see? You find some *thing*
there. Once I was on my way up to the second floor when
I saw a bunch of pieces of polystyrene foam. One of the
guards saw me looking at these piles of foam and said that
it was a sculpture by somebody like Robert Rauschen-
berg. He said there are a hundred pieces of polystyrene
foam scattered from the cellar to the attic, and this is just
one of the sculptures. All this by way of saying, you can
have art that thinks of itself as being an abstraction, yet
the irony is that the abstraction itself involves concretism.
I suppose it would be pressing things very far indeed if an
artist entered nothing at all in the exhibit. Yet his entry
is a thought, reflecting perhaps a theme of "greatness" or
something. Nobody is going to write a check for $300,000
for a thought of greatness. You must enter an object, even
if it's only a parking meter.

In any event, this is all by way of suggesting that we are
quintessentially physical creatures. This is how we shape
our experiences in the enterprise that we do call art. I am
speaking to an audience of religious or semi-religious or
would-be religious people who are at least familiar with
the Christian vision in one form or another. It is worth
reflecting that the central drama of our story, this tension
of which we are all aware between the physical and the
spiritual, the proximate and the ultimate, the seamed and
the unseamed, the temporal and the eternal, however you
wish to name it, was resolved in the event that we call
the Incarnation, the *Mysterium Tremendum*. The Incarnation itself was the apotheosis, when everything taken apart
came to a point, as Lewis says. The apotheosis is the whole
point of the drama of redemption, which is the salvage of
the ruins that we introduced in Eden. We are the ones

who ripped the fabric, saying, "This much of the business shall be ours." And at that point, we introduced secularism. Secularism says, "That which is hallowed and holy and belongs to God, I shall make a snatch at it, grabbing this much of it for myself."

At that point I am secularized. I have profaned something, and as Milton puts it, "Earth felt the wound", and nature groaned. That ruin with which we were left began to be re-knit in the drama of redemption. Of course, we are still en route to the final knitting-up of the whole thing, but we have the pledge of that re-knitting in the Incarnation itself. It is interesting that this drama of redemption, unlike so many of the religions that beckon us away from this world and where our bodies are thought of as a sort of a prison, and all forms of gnosticism and all forms of Platonism (and I love Plato! Any Christian probably agrees with Plato 93.75 percent of the time, but at some point we need him to move half a step farther), Manicheanism, spiritualism, and so on, eventually either denigrate or downplay or de-emphasize or absolutely loathe the flesh. They promise deliverance by weaning us from this prison, this trap, this mortal coil, and delivering us into a spiritual ether, one way or another.

Christianity is the polar extreme from that. The drama of our redemption was played out in the most unabashedly, unembarrassedly gross, carnal terms. The very first thing that happened after we ruined everything was blood, the pelts of animals. Straight off, God himself made them clothes with skins of animals. There is very little spiritual about that. And then you have this long, elaborate lineage of altars and blood and gold and linen and all of that down through the Old Testament, culminating in ... what? Gynecology and obstetrics.

The Annunciation. You thought that in the New Testament we were finally out of all the blood and guts, and now we are in the spiritual realm. And lo and behold, you are head over heels in gynecology and obstetrics at the Annunciation. Believe you me, this is more than just an ecstasy that the Blessed Virgin experienced. Whatever happened, happened in her womb. That is not amenable to us gnostics and logicians and Manicheans and Platonists and Buddhists and so on. Then you have the Visitation, the babe leaping in the womb. This is all embarrassing, very physical. Consider the Nativity and the whole sequence of events, which we remember in the Christian year. The Circumcision, terribly embarrassing. The Epiphany, the manifestation of Christ as savior. The Temple and those poor little turtledoves, slaughtered. Consider the Baptism. The Temptation of Christ. The Transfiguration. The Passion. The Burial. The Resurrection. The Ascension. That's a showstopper, isn't it? And you thought the Ascension was a spiritual event.

What happened? Our humanity was taken up into the mystery of the Trinity, the Godhead. Of course, language turns to nonsense at this point. Theological language falters. How do we talk about it? But there it is, the Ascension. If you and I had been consulted, we would have said, "Oh, for heaven's sake, leave the body in the grave, and let's please have something spiritual." But lo and behold, the body rose, and it is there in the mystery of the Holy Trinity. At the Annunciation, God came down on our earth in the body of our flesh and then for the rest of history left us bread and wine. Very embarrassing. What is our religion? It is the Incarnation. It is the drama of our redemption. Our vision, our religion, is Eucharistic, that is to say, the pledge of the mystery of that re-knitting.

What is the attempt of the artist? It is, somehow or other, to re-knit our experience, to find an objective correlative, a shape. To find something in this clay, this sequence of words, this music, this choreography, this building, whatever. To find something that will articulate and shape our experience, what is true, shall we say. To re-knit that torn fabric of our lives. Of course, for Christians it makes dazzling, overwhelming, and ravishing sense, because at the center of our theology, the center of our vision, we have the Eucharist, the place where that knitting-up is pledged to us. We see here the physical as the nexus, the coming together of earth and heaven. Again, it is an outrage to all Manicheanism and gnosticism and so on. I have participated in conferences on this campus where the question has been rightly raised and well considered as to why a certain kind of Christian teaching, a certain wing, has a very difficult time encouraging men and women in the artistic enterprise.

I think it is clear by now what the difficulty is. If you have a religion, a piety, a spirituality, a doctrine that is principally verbalist and abstract and propositionalist and categorical and expository and "spiritual"—if by spiritual you mean disembodied, which ain't what Saint Paul meant by it—then you will have effective difficulty in encouraging the artistic craftsmanship, not to say instincts, of the men and women who are the adherents of that religion, because their piety and their spirituality, on the one hand, is telling them, in order to get to the realm of truth, you must bid adieu to the physical world. You should be spiritual. Again, the word "spiritual" tends to be understood as disembodied, and, of course, that is a heresy. You know it, and I know it. That is a gnostic heresy to say that there is a duality in the universe between the spiritual, which is higher on the pecking order, and the material, which is lower. The spiritual is good, the material is at least gross if not bad, and that is a heresy. Christianity recognizes only one distinction in the universe, that is between the uncreated, a category of one, God, and the created.

Here again I am speculating, but my hunch is that Adam and Eve, however we want to understand the biblical narrative of the first man and woman who were in perfect harmony with themselves, God, their environment, and everything else, presumably experienced the whole creation as a seamless fabric, so they did not think of angels as existing in some other category. But they experienced the entire spectrum of the creation as one fabric. I myself doubt that Adam and Eve even had any self-consciousness. I think that self-consciousness must have come with the Fall, because that is a disjuncture, a fissure. If it is a me and a scrutinizing me, and a scrutinizing me scrutinizing the me who is doing the experiencing, then there is a disjuncture in my being and the integrity has been ruined. In any event, the artistic effort is the effort to find in physical or tangible or audible form some sort of shape or articulation or evocation that will answer to and exhibit our experience, upon which our experience can light and come to rest, if you want to put it that way.

And it is always physical. There is no such thing, of course, as a spiritual art. In our piety, our spirituality, our vision, our dogma, our teaching and so on, if we have pulled that rug from under our feet, if we have attempted to make a propositionalist scheme out of this drama of redemption, then we are facing difficulty.

We come back to the title, "Art as Incarnation". Art in one manner of speaking is the attempt on the part of the human imagination, our image-making faculty, to incarnate the abstractions of our experience. A religion that understands the division of Christianity, that understands the drama of redemption as the narrative, having been borne forward on this marvelous sequence of events, and the spiritualty that keeps that before our eyes, the Annunciation, the Nativity, the Circumcision, the Presentation, the Passion, and so on, is one in which you are going to find the artistic enterprise encouraged and fructifying.

I will finish with simply an observation, which is that it is interesting that when we are casting about for major figures of twentieth-century prose and poetry who happen to have been Christian and who have spoken to the twentieth-century condition, and you start listing the ones from the earlier years of this century, and you have T. S. Eliot and W. H. Auden and Graham Greene and Flannery O'Connor and Walker Percy and François Mauriac and others, all of them were incarnational, sacramentalist Christians. They were aware principally of the drama and physicality of redemption. The great focal, lodestar doctrine for them was the Incarnation, not these bone-crunching abstractions of—well, I will not name them. But they were incarnational.

My last sentence is the following. There is a rising order, which evinces the very thing I am talking about, the attempt to make A stand for B, to find a shape over in clay or song or dance or painting or narrative, to find some integrity there to make A answer to B, to serve or embody B. The rise in the pecking order would run this way. Down at the bottom we have ordinary similes. We use them all the time. A is like B. It's as smooth as glass. You evoke glass, yet an idea of smoothness. Or a different metaphor, "He's as smooth as oil." That's a whole different thing, isn't it? We use similes in our conversations. Let A help B, or let A gather up and articulate B. And then you have the whole world of symbol and sign. $X = Y$. That hexagonal red shape on the corner means stop, even if the word stop is not even written on it. The skull and crossbones mean, "Do not drink this." Let $X =$ whatever algebraic figure, and so on. The world of symbol and sign is rising on the scale. Of course, the whole thing is the world of metaphor. Then you have the serious artistic enterprise, genuine art, as opposed to me saying, "I feel like a rung-out dishrag." It is similar, yes, but I would hardly call it art.

In the artistic enterprise, you really do have our attempt to strain toward the knitting back together of form and meaning, scotch-taping A onto B not just as a useful show-and-tell device, but to demonstrate the seamlessness between A and B. You get that in art. Raise that one tier, and you get myth. One of the things of which you are aware about the mythic tale is that there is no meaning at all. The story is the meaning. There is nothing under the surface of a myth. Those are not symbols. There is absolute synonymity between the narrative and the meaning. You do not need to dig under the surface of a myth to pull out a meaning. In our pecking order, we are moving toward a greater and greater integrity of sign and symbol and art and myth and sacrament. There really is the coming together of the thing and the thing signified, if you credit the faith of the Church and John 6, and so on. Sacrament signifying Incarnation is at the top. Jesus is God and man. In the Incarnation we have that absolute integrity restored.

Mimesis and Incarnation

There has, perhaps, never been an epoch in which the hiatus between serious artistic activity and common taste has been wider. What appears in the galleries and in the journals of poetry is addressed frequently to the cognoscenti and leaves the public murmuring confusedly. Historically, this was not the case. Much of what we now call "great art" appeared in response to a direct commission from a patron or church or, in the case of epic poetry, was addressed to a listening audience of mostly uneducated people. The assumption was that everyone would understand what was being offered. There were not two worlds—the one of the artists and the few, and the other of the masses. Even into the eighteenth and nineteenth centuries, the novels and poetry that are now read only in graduate studies were written for anyone who cared to buy a book.

The cleavage between artist and public is so total now, however, that it is doubtful whether the name of a single serious painter or poet is familiar in at all the same sense as are the names of popular entertainers. This, of course, raises the question of blame: Has the public rejected the artist, or the artist the public?

This is a question that cannot be answered one way or the other, since both answers are right. Something can be said, however, about the present state of affairs. It is worth

Originally published in *Imagination and the Spirit: Essays in Literature and the Christian Faith presented to Clyde S. Kilby* (Grand Rapids: Eerdmans, 1971), 43–51. Reprinted with permission.

asking whence it arose and what sort of criticism is possible in the light of historic notions concerning the office of the artist and the nature of his world.

The public is understandably bewildered when it encounters soup tins, ropes, burlap, crumpled auto parts, plaster hamburgers, flags, and comics in the art museums and is told by the critics that it ought to be impressed and moved. The popular response is, often enough, disgust, fear, embarrassment, or blankness.

The rationale offered by its practitioners for much of current art may itself follow various lines of thought. There is the dogmatic nonhumanism of Ad Reinhardt, for example, who insisted on the entire independence of the artistic endeavor and disallowed most of the canons of nonrepresentational as well as representational art. The "op" artists employ their stripes, checkerboards, swirls of color, and dots with a rigor and exactitude second to none in the history of art, seeking not so much for images to be looked at as for forms that will arouse perceptual responses. The idea is to engage the viewer in an act that will, it is hoped, increase his awareness of his visual capacities and, hence, contribute to that great end of all high art, the heightening of consciousness.

Other artists, angrily or happily aware of the metamorphosis of American life into a vast travelogue of cola billboards, parking meters, ribbons of macadam, and gleaming formica-and-steel drive-ins, urge that, since this is the stuff of our existence, this is to be the stuff of the mimetic arts. Insofar as the Greek vision involved the glory of the human form, that is what one sees in the iconography of the epoch; insofar as the mediaeval involved annunciations and pietàs, that is what is figured; insofar as ours involves hamburgers, that is what we shall have. The artist is the seer who gives its own existence back to his age, transfigured for contemplation. Traditionally, the images in which he gives that existence back to the world are those that speak of the eternal, whether that be a religious eternity, as in the Christian vision, or a nonpersonalistic eternity of pure form, as in post-Enlightenment vision. Given the modern world, say these artists, we will give you your bibelots, which speak of nothing.

The "primary structuralists", whose work takes the shape of immense rhomboids, cubes, and hexahedrons, are seeking a nonillusive form. Since, in their view, the world is neither meaningful *nor* absurd ("It simply is", says Alain Robbe-Grillet),[1] the effort is to create solid, immediate objects that are nothing but what they are. They are "presences", it is urged, without meaning or referent.

It may help us see what is occurring in contemporary painting and sculpture if we inquire into the notions from which the mimetic activity of the last one hundred years derives.

Historically, it was felt that there is an onus of sublime affirmation laid upon high art. That is, that the office of the poet and artist is to "see life steadily and see it whole", in all of its beauty, ambiguity, and horror, and to find an imagery that not only figures that life truly, but takes the stuff of that life and transfigures it into forms that speak of ultimacy.

It is, perhaps, in the notion of sublimity that the discontinuity occurs between the art of earlier epochs and that which has arisen in the last century. Art traditionally proceeded on the assumption that there is an equation between Beauty and Truth and had for its aim the figuring of Beauty in images faithful to human experience. In the

[1] As quoted in "The Shape of Art for Some Time to Come: Primary Structures", *Life*, LXIII, iv (July 28, 1967): 44A.

nineteenth century, this aim was forsworn in the name of
Reality. There had been, in the wake of postmediaeval
methods of describing the world, a gradual dissolution of
confidence in myths and other ideas that were not verifi-
able according to the terms of the new methodology.[2] Sibyls, prophets, angels, priests—everyone who tried to bring
tidings from outside to the human situation—had been
discredited. The field for investigation and for imagination
was to be the one at hand. Since we see no titans, fauns,
heroes, devils, or archangels at play there, we must assume,
until they appear in our lenses, that there are none. Thus a
positivistic view, and thus the *Zeitgeist* that ensued.

Since we are to scrutinize our world dispassionately, we
will posit Reality in our own terms as our starting point and
leave the erstwhile notion of Beauty to fend for itself. If it
emerges from our experience, *tant mieux*; if not, *tant pis*.
We will not conjure it from a realm about which nobody
knows anything. The point was that the sublime is a notion
referring to nothing that we can verify in our terms and,
hence, is inappropriate as a referent for modern imagery.

The man who announced the emancipation of painting
from anachronistic notions of beauty and sublimity was
Gustave Courbet. Reality is to be the province of the artist
from here on, he declared. At about the same time, Whis-
tler announced his attempt to "divest the picture from any
outside sort of interest", in answer to Ruskin's charge that
he had "flung a pot of paint in the public's face".

Proceeding from Courbet, Edouard Manet focused
attention on the medium itself. In his view, the province of
the artist is paint and canvas, not what they "stand for". His

[2] See, in this connection, Walter J. Ong, S.J., *Ramus, Method, and the Decay of Dialogue* (Cambridge, Mass., 1958), and Owen Barfield, *Saving the Appearances* (London, 1957).

"Fifer" aroused dismay when it appeared, for it was clear that the artist had made no attempt to subject his paint to the demands of three-dimensional illusion: on the contrary, here was a brightly colored doll, in effect pasted flat onto the canvas. The focus was on the thing itself, not on the idea of a real little boy with a fife. Manet and those who followed him tried to get a scientifically exact record of the patterns of light that the retina registers, not the image we construct in our imagination in response to the phenomenon. They felt that artistic activity must become less and less servile to our figuration of the external world and more and more independent. The work of Renoir, Cézanne, Monet, Pissarro, Seurat, and Degas evinces this effort.

In the twentieth century, painting went in three directions from this beginning: toward Expressionism, toward Abstractionism, and toward Fantasy. Each exhibits its own special effort to discover significance in the world without reference to a discredited transcendence. Expressionism concerned itself with the emotional world, Abstractionism with questions of formal structure, and Fantasy with imagination, especially irregular imaginations and dreams.

The fathers of Expressionism were probably the "fauvists" (wild beasts), who aroused critical ire by appearing to do violence to human perception. Matisse, with his dancing curlicues, wanted to pursue the formal demands of design and color farther than had been done up to that point. Rouault saw vividly the corruption of the world and figured this in his "ugly" portraits, hinting nonetheless at a residue of nobility in the human face. Kokoschka, Kirchner, and Beckmann assailed the public eye with images of vacuity and damnation.

Picasso, Braque, Leger, and Mondrian became occupied with formal questions, abstracting from the apparent world suggestions of geometric structure. Picasso scandalized everybody with his "Les Demoiselles d'Avignon", which represents the methodical and violent breakup of classical notions of beauty. This sort of thing (known as Cubism) attempts to find an alternative to the external world by discovering a "building material" of angular chunks of voids and spaces (one cannot help but recall some of Cézanne's work here). Braque worked with scraps of this and that (wood, fabric, newsprint, tickets), calling attention to texture itself rather than to anything scenic perceived through the "window" of traditional painting.

Up to this point there was still a reference to the external world. Whether in terms of texture or form or image, the matrix from which the imagery arose was still perceptibly of that world, although it was sometimes in the form of disavowal. But Wassily Kandinsky made the disavowal final. He abandoned representation entirely and sought to present emotion directly on the canvas. He sought to invest pure form and color with a spiritual meaning quite apart from the familiar world of appearance, so that not only is it impossible to discover any imagery in his composition: it is a mistaken effort. There is none. Likewise, Piet Mondrian set about to apprehend "pure reality" in wholly nonrepresentational modes. He saw this reality to consist in an equilibrium achieved in terms of a balance of forms, and his blocks of primary color divided by heavy ruled lines are among the most familiar and pleasing objects of twentieth-century painting.

The third major stream in the painting of this century is that of Fantasy. The doctrine involved is that imagination is a more significant source for mimetic imagery than is the external world. It posits the psychoanalytic idea of a commonalty of subconscious images in all of us, although in its handling of these images it frequently becomes entirely private, so that the viewer may bring his own interpretation to the painting. In the dream visions of De Chirico, in the fairy-tale childhood memories of Chagall, and in

the "language of signs" of Klee, this sort of thing is visible.
It is visible in the Dadaism of Duchamp and others, who
declared that, as of the Great War, all value systems had
become otiose and who preached nonsense as the desideratum, and in the Surrealism of Dali and Miro, who sought
to explore "pure psychic automatism", that is, thought
free from the trammels of reason, morals, or aesthetics.

A drastic departure from even these iconoclastic activities
occurred in the work of Jackson Pollock, who announced
the centrality of the act of painting. He forswore the attempt
to figure anything at all on the canvas (dreams, pure form,
signs, nonsense), substituting for these traditional activities
an interest in the dynamics of the paint itself. It is not insult-
ing to him to say that he poured and dribbled and threw the
paint: that is precisely what he did. He moved, perhaps, as
far as it is possible to move from the view of the painter's
office as having anything to do with human existence.

We have already noted some of the post-Pollock activity, and it is possible to see in some of it a return to the
world of appearances, albeit a return that insists that things
are what they are, period.

The mimetic activity of the last century derives, then,
directly from doctrines that attended the intellectual
activity of the era. The doctrines entail, again, a final confidence in an analytic and descriptive methodology as the
sole approach to the world. There is a circular movement involved, in that the early decision to exclude from
inquiry all realms not scrutable by the methodology is
followed by the dogma that there are no such realms, since
the method does not perceive them. Corollary to this
is the view that it is not possible to discover any principle
of significance in appearances, in that there is nothing else
to be signaled.

There is an alternative view possible, of course. It is
the view, once universal, that the data of our world are

significant. The human consciousness has, from the beginning, figured its intimation of this in its mimetic activity. The method involved was synthetic and anagogical
rather than analytic and descriptive. The notion was that
one thing signals another, that there is a continuum of
significance from the lowest worm to the highest seraph,
that there is a form, an order, a harmony, a dance in which
all participate. It tended to feel, in contrast to our own
epoch, which urges that nothing means anything, that
everything means everything. It believed in the image
as a mode—perhaps *the* mode—of articulating what it
suspected. It is visible in the imagery of all times and all
places. And it uttered itself variously in the doctrines of
Aristotle, Caxton, Sidney, Shelley, Wordsworth, Arnold,
and Emerson—that the poet has upon him the high task
of perceiving the myriad hierarchic interchanges among
all things and of figuring that perception in noble images.
This notion has, often enough, attended the religious view
of the world.

In the Egyptian, Assyrian, Greek, and animistic worlds,
it was inseparable from religious vision: the imagery was
religious. The conjunction of aesthetic and religious vision
is, of course, most familiar to us in the West in mediaeval
and Renaissance—that is, in Christian—imagery.

The Christian vision affirms the significance of the
mimetic act. It does so because it sees here the human
echo of activity connate with the origins of things, and
because its own understanding of the world is one that
involves the notion of the Incarnate Word.

It sees the original creative energy as describable by
the term "Word". It understands this energy as tending
toward utterance, that is, toward the articulation of significance and, indeed, toward being, from nonsignificance
and nonbeing (cf. human language, which, far more than
serving merely as the mode by which we exchange ideas,

in effect calls our world into being for us by naming it). It is an articulation tending always toward concretion and identity, and not, as might be supposed, toward abstraction and anonymity. The energy utters itself in terms that we apprehend as soil and rock and fire and flesh. It uttered its form most nobly in man, and eventually in The Man—Immanuel. Which is to say that this Word, the Ground of all form and significance, the Referent for all phenomena and imagery, is such that its self-articulation tends finally toward Incarnation.

And the Incarnate, called Logos, embraced the limitations of this world and proclaimed authenticity and freedom and glory to us, not, as many prophets have done, via escape into the ether, but via participation in the actualities of human existence. The vision of glory declared here is one, not of dissolution and a denial of carnality, but, on the contrary, of a restoration of concretion and specificity and flesh in the unity and harmony for which it was made. The Christian agrees with Plato up to a point, but, unlike Plato, he suspects that the Ideal, far from being an abstraction, is harder and "knobblier" (C. S. Lewis) than anything we knock our shins on here. He sees this world, not as illusion, but as figure—that is, as the species under which we now apprehend Actuality. And, because he understands the Incarnate to be the finally authentic utterance of Actuality, he must affirm the validity of the world which that Incarnate affirmed.

The Incarnational view, then, would entail at least the following notions: it would affirm the immediate (because it believes in the Incarnation); it would affirm the transcendent (because it believes in the Logos); it would see the commonplace as the vehicle of ultimacy (n.b. the common manhood of the Incarnate and also his pedestrian *modus vivendi*); and it would insist on the public character of significance (again, because it believes in the Word).

A person who takes this view would have, then, various questions to ask concerning aesthetic theories and the imagery deriving from those theories. He would find himself, for a start, at a point midway between the two eternal human inclinations—the one that seeks Reality in an escape from this existence, and the other that disavows the transcendent in its effort to apprehend the actuality of this existence.

But in its final form, the tendency is gnostic and leads to a vision that becomes more and more ethereal and less and less congenial to any imagery at all and, hence, leaves the province of art altogether, since mimetic activity must presuppose a robust affirmation of the concrete if it is to have any matrix from which its images are to rise. (Hence the poor artistic yield of religions and cults that seek Actuality in purely spiritual terms: their categories reduce the possibility of imagery; the Reformation faith might ask itself some hard questions here.)

The view that, on the other hand, seeks Actuality in the stuff at hand has much to be said for it. Besides giving an impetus to scientific inquiry, it has given us the great vision of the Impressionists. However, at the point at which this view excludes the transcendent altogether, and seeks Actuality solely in the world investigated by the sciences—at that point its grasp upon even that world begins to slip. For it becomes increasingly difficult to posit the notion of significance and, hence, to draw images of power and sublimity from this matrix. Ironically, the quest for Actuality in these terms leads eventually either to a retreat from the recognizable into abstract and arcane forms (since the thing as-it-appears-to-us is nonsignificant) or to a myopic crawl into an inner universe of fantasy that yields images of greater and greater grotesquery and inanity. Often enough, the early stages of this quest yield compelling and powerful images. The work of Duchamp, Mondrian, and

Braque has surely opened our eyes to provinces of form and texture that we would have missed. And who can gainsay the power of the visions of horror in the work of Kirchner, Beckmann, and Grosz? Perhaps it took an anti-transcendentalist view to make this imagery possible. But, however compelling or intriguing or unsettling or shocking or amusing or engaging or diverting the imagery may be, it is difficult to find in it that troubling thing we call, vaguely, greatness, which seems to rise from the simultaneous awareness of limitation and sublimity and sees them both figured in the human situation. The mighty vision of a Michelangelo took the *donnée* (the human form) and transfigured (not twisted) it into forms that spoke of the eternal. Perhaps we need the twisting as an image of perdition; but perdition is of proximate interest only. Sublimity alone is final.

Again, the Incarnational view, with its celebration of the commonplace, would have to inquire into the worth of the bizarre and arcane as appropriate vehicles of authenticity. For it would suspect, unlike the more intoxicating view that freedom and fulfillment lie in the bacchic and the occult, that this freedom and fulfillment lie in the obvious and that participation in the given rhythms of existence (dawn and twilight, spring and fall, birth, marriage, work, eating and drinking) is the beginning of glory. Vermeer is the colossus towering above those who, on the one hand, seek increasingly peculiar images and those who, on the other, insist flatly on the nothingness but inevitability of what is at hand (hamburgers and rubber tires). In contrast to the former, Vermeer found luminescence and sublimity in a *room corner*; against the latter, he found *luminescence and sublimity* in a room corner.

Finally, the Incarnational view would suspect that the truly significant is public in its nature and that the private is of limited interest only. Because of the universal utterance of the Word, and because of the response to this in the great "*Benedicite, omnia opera Domini*", this view would look with suspicion on mimetic activity involving any esoteric doctrine or the tendency toward solipsism. Hence, while it is surely entirely permissible (and perhaps helpful to himself) for an artist to see his task to be the figuring of private visions and emotions directly on the canvas, the result is of minimal significance. High art is an eminently public thing, for, like the Word, it calls form from havoc and utters it in universal terms.

The criticism that this view would urge, then, against our own epoch is one that will raise again the questions that are not asked. It will urge no atavistic return to the manageable ages of supposed ignorance. Nor will it be nostalgic for some twelfth-century equilibrium of sensibility.

But it will ask whether the dogmas deriving from post-mediaeval methodology are quite axiomatic after all. It will ask whether the exclusion of the ghoulies and ghosties and longlegged beasties (and Apollo and the Virgin of Chartres and Immanuel) from categories of inquiry is not abortive. It will doubt whether the human imagination will ever be satisfied with the edict that declares that man comes of age to the extent that he disavows the notions celebrated in the imagery of other ages—candor, valor, caritas, beauty, glory. It will test with inquisitorial rigor the sensibility of an age whose imagery can speak truthfully only of banality and perdition and the immediate. And it will urge that only that mimesis rises beyond cleverness and topicality whose imagery figures the sublimity and fear in a handful of dust.

Arts and Religion:
They Need Not Clash

A son of the Reformation is quite at home in the Rijksmuseum in Amsterdam. He finds here a milieu to which his sensibilities are immediately congenial. In the paintings of Pieter de Hooch, Hobbema, the van Ruysdaels, van de Velde, and, of course, Rembrandt van Rijn, he finds a vision of the world that he can share with no difficulty at all. The celebration and immortalization of the bucolic, the tranquil, the humble, and the commonplace responds to the call that he hears in his own soul (and indeed, a call that all men must sense) for a vision of life that is immediate, lucid, and uncomplicated by the demands of sacramental transfiguration that the works of, say, del Sarto, Filippo Lippi, or Fra Bartolomeo make. The clean blue-and-white tile floors of Vermeer, the portraits of Van Dyck, Jan Steen, and Frans Hals, and Rembrandt's wonderful sketches of biblical scenes that look as though he drew them with a twig—here are things that evoke a world that he can understand and love.

But then he travels south into Bavaria and Austria and tumbles into a world of the baroque: a frantic scramble of gilded altars, painted statuary, frescoes, reliquaries, fonts, and baldachinos that he finds dizzying, if not altogether unsettling. He realizes that he has come upon a vision of God and the world that differs radically from his own, yet

Originally published in *Christianity Today*, January 21, 1966, 7–8. Reprinted with permission.

one that would call itself above all Christian. He can either decide that the whole thing is an unfortunate botch or pause to ask himself whether or not it is worth looking into.

And then he comes to Florence and Michelangelo. Here, surely, true religion has flown out the window, and Pan and Cybele and Bacchus have surged through the door. Here is a town, a Paradise, with its warm sunlit stucco set in the enchanting hills of Tuscany, cypress and olive trees and vineyards all about—a town that is crowded with painting and sculpture celebrating at once the celestial and the earthy. He eventually makes the disturbing discovery that the glory of the human form shines more brightly here than does the glory of Christ, the Virgin, and the Apostles. And he asks himself: Have we two antithetical worlds here, with no bridge between them? Is there, on the one hand, a "religious" world, represented by the churches, and, on the other, a world that is unapologetically pagan? Or is there a unity of vision here that sees no breakdown between the true worship of God and a profound sense of wonder at all the phenomena of life, that is not embarrassed over its joy in the human form?

The question that finally emerges, and with which these notes are concerned, is whether or not it is possible to have a view that has the proper priorities and hierarchies and yet is able to affirm with joy the Creation and say, "*Benedicite, omnia opera Domini.*"

Only if the answer to this question is yes can the discussion about evangelicalism and the creative arts go on. For if the answer is no, then we would do well to pack in and concentrate on our mission of discursive preaching. For it comes to this: the creation of great art presupposes a view that sees the stuff of *this* existence to be radically significant; indeed, that sees it (and not Paradise) to be the only matrix from which high art can rise.

To a non-religious person, this of course presents no problem. There is no other existence to which he can refer, and therefore any commentary must spring from and speak to this one. But to a person with a vigorously eschatological view of things—and I think we evangelicals fit in here—whose theology has taught him that the phenomena of this existence are meaningful only insofar as they find an ultimate point of reference in Paradise, such a view is sometimes difficult.

The water is often muddied in that, without ever having examined just why we look askance at the fine arts—or at least the appropriateness of a Christian's pursuing them—we argue that time is short and we must get on with the job of winning souls; or that painting, sculpture, and drama are mere embellishments to life and that people with a task of ultimacy laid upon them cannot truckle with this sort of thing; or that the world of the arts is so rancid with beatniks, libertines, homosexuals, and other frightening types that a Christian has no business getting embroiled.

But the philosophical problem is prior to all these. And there *is* a problem. We must decide whether or not the patent transitoriness of this existence and the heavy urgency of being spokesmen for what we understand to be the Word from God cancel the fine arts as a field for excursion. Put more simply, it is the question that has hundreds of students in evangelical institutions gnashing their teeth: May I—*can* I—before God, explore passionately my obvious artistic or poetic or dramatic talent without any immediately utilitarian motives? Or shall I find areas where my talents can be used "for the Lord"?

There is the rub. "For the Lord." Our understanding of this has been a utilitarian one. To us it means one thing: souls. But how shall we test the work of Dante, Milton, Bach, Rembrandt, Dr. Johnson, G. M. Hopkins, T. S. Eliot, and a thousand others by this? These men were all Christian. Obviously it cannot be done. (One does not think of Dr. Johnson as a soul-winner. Boswell does not have much to say about his witness in the coffeehouses of the city.) So that either we must find warrant for art that is not subject to this test, or these things must retire as candidates for our attention.

This is, let us be candid, a partisan article. I am sure my position is no secret. I do not feel the utilitarian test to be valid. I believe that the radical affirmation of human experience crucial to art is one that can—nay, that must—be made by the Christian. We must have the courage to shape our anguish and our joy into beautiful forms—into poetry, into pictures, into ballet. We must celebrate beauty—all kinds of beauty—on instruments of ten strings, and with a chisel. We must paint the tawdry, the spurious, and the hideous as it is: Shall we leave this to Toulouse-Lautrec, Rouault, and Kokoschka? We must try, with all that is in us, to affirm our conviction that form, and not havoc, lies at the bottom of things—and shall we leave this quest to Mondrian, Giacometti, and Larry Rivers?

Of the utilitarian test, I can only say that evangelism is one thing, art another. It is unfair to apply the canons of either to the other. We must have an end to pitting them against each other. They are no more at odds than apples and wool are.

It would be a mistake to suppose, however, that we can begin a concerted effort to produce "evangelical art". Committees, movements, retreats, and courses have never, in the history of the world, produced art. It can come from one source alone: the soul of the artist. Here is the other side of the question, the personal and non-philosophical side, the side that is not subject to our views pro or con. What of the appearance in our midst of an artist? None of us can make himself an artist. But, anguish of anguish, if one of us, or one of our sons, discovers that he has been assaulted by strange inclinations and that he must create or die, what shall our religion say to this?

I believe that we can call a loud bravo. I believe this because I believe in three great doctrines: the Creation, the Incarnation, and the Resurrection—three acts whereby God attests to the profound legitimacy of the human, the flesh (I do not use "the flesh", as Saint Paul uses it frequently, to mean a *spirit* that is anti-God). I do not see it to be our calling to cancel the earthly in the name of the eternal. This is not what the Church has understood her task to be. The Athanasian Creed speaks of the Incarnation as "not [the] conversion of the Godhead into flesh, but [the] taking of the Manhood into God." It seems to me that there must be a seizing of human experience, with all of its beauty, ambiguity, and tragedy, and a transfiguration of it into forms that speak of the eternal.

And, given that elusive thing called genius, an artist is someone who has been assaulted by these three things: beauty, ambiguity, and tragedy. He cannot fend off this assault any more than he can slough off his own being. And so he is forced to come to terms with it by creation. Michelangelo, Mozart, Tiziano, Gide—what do they all have in common? I believe it is the attempt to exorcise the daemons of human experience; to shape into *form* the chaos of beauty, ambiguity, and tragedy that they sense. It might have been possible with all of them to have brought about quiescence in purely religious terms, but who will insist that the whole lifelong agony of creation was not God's way of bringing them to himself?

Beauty, then. What, exactly, is a human being to do when his awareness of beauty becomes unmanageable? We applaud the results when we have the perspective of

a few hundred years and can see the sublimity of Michelangelo's creations. But was the course he took one that
would have suited us at the time? How would we have
dealt with his intoxication with the nude male form?
Would we have tried to huddle him into safer, more
obviously utilitarian pursuits? Would we have encouraged
his frenzied dedication to his art—this art that has given
us the David, an image of a sublimity and perfection and
power and sensuousness that can only wrench from us
tears of awe and joy. Who has ever said more eloquently
than this statue does, "What a piece of work is a man"?
And how is it possible, in a dissertation on the glory of
the Creator, to say one-half of what this thing says? Then
one goes from the Accademia, where the David stands,
to the Sagrestia Nuova di San Loranzo, where there are
nine marble figures by Michelangelo. Who can gainsay
the serenity, the overpowering beauty, of these things?
Shall we whittle down a man's struggle with beauty in the
name of religion?

For it is just that: a struggle. Alas for the man for whom
the vision of beauty, in whatever form it approaches him
(for Michelangelo, it was the human body; for Wordsworth, it was the Lake District; for Mozart, it was music),
becomes, no longer a reverie to be indulged at will in syb-
aritic melancholy, but a searing agony that ravages him
daily, hourly, in images too sweet to bear. How shall our
religion speak to this sort of thing?

Perhaps here is one difference between the artist and the
rest of us. The artist is above all *vulnerable*. He finds himself
wounded with stabbing visions of some aching and elusive
joy, some burning fever of desire; and he knows that in
order to be true to his own being, he must *invite* the shafts
and ask where in God's name they come from, while the
rest of us must offset and quell these lance-like imaginings

with practical considerations in order to make our way in the world and keep our sanity. It would, of course, be havoc if we were all artists; but let us be sure that we have not excluded them from our world.

Secondly, the artist is assaulted with the consciousness of ambiguity. One does not have to look far to find it. What shall we say, for instance, of the dreadful breakdown between aspiration and fulfillment that every human being experiences? or again, of radical limitation imposed on half the human race—blindness, insanity, poverty, injustice, paralysis? or of the awful hiatus between appearance and what we suspect to be reality? or of the jostling coexistence in human life of overpowering sexual desire and moral stricture? All of these things are answerable by theology; but when we have answered them, they still make us cry out in anguish, and it is with this anguish that the artist wrestles. He must begin by being haunted, perplexed, astonished, and tormented by life. He must insist on asking the questions, loudly and shrilly, that plague all men and that most of us try to meet by evasion, platitudes, and neuroses.

Thirdly, the artist senses the tragic nature of life. Shakespeare (in *Hamlet*), Pope (in the "Essay on Man"), and all artists have sensed the position of man, which *is* tragic: we are caught—strung—between the animal and the angelic, and we set one against the other to our destruction. Various forms of the hedonistic principle would have us assert the animal to the obliteration of the angelic, and various forms of religious asceticism would have us do the opposite. Both fail of God's idea for man. We are not angels, but we have their consciousness of the divine and find, alas, our feet in the mud. Animals are free to be wholly animal without guilt; we sometimes want passionately to be wholly animal but are not free to be so. Sometimes (though not often) we want to be angelic and find that we cannot if we will (cf. Saint Paul).

The artist senses as ultimate the tragedy of decay. Father Hopkins, a Christian, said it as well as anyone:

> ... *no, nothing can be done*
> *To keep at bay*
> *Age and age's evils, hoar hair,*
> *Ruck and wrinkle, drooping, dying, death's worst,*
>   *winding sheets, tombs and worms and*
>   *tumbling to decay;*
> *So be beginning, be beginning to despair ...*

It bothered Keats, too:

> *The weariness, the fever, and the fret*
>   *Here, where men sit and hear each other groan;*
> *Where palsy shakes a few, sad, last gray hairs,*
>   *Where youth grows pale, and spectre-thin, and*
>   *dies;*
> *Where but to think is to be full of sorrow*
>   *And leaden-eyed despairs ...*

One contemplates the marbles of Michelangelo and realizes that here is the highest that we can achieve in immortalizing strength and youth and beauty. The stone is not subject to decay (relatively speaking). And so the stone David outlives the beautiful model, whoever he was; and the figures in the plastered frescoes outlive by centuries their flesh-and-blood originals. And yet, even here there is an ironic twist, for the mere flick of a vandal's chisel would demolish instantly one of the most sublime things ever— the ceiling of the Sistine Chapel in Rome.

A great scholar and historian of the Reformation, J. H. Merle d'Aubigné, has this comment:

Protestantism has often been reproached as their [the arts'] enemy, and many Protestants willingly accept this reproach.... Let Roman Catholicism pride itself in being more favourable to the arts than Protestantism; be it so; paganism was still more favourable, and Protestantism places its glory elsewhere. There are some religions in which the esthetic tendencies of man hold a more important place than his moral nature. Christianity is distinct from these religions, inasmuch as the moral element is its essence. The Christian sentiment is manifested not by the productions of the fine arts, but by the works of a Christian life ... so that if the papacy is above all an esthetical religion ... Protestantism is above all a moral religion.... After a man has studied history or visited Italy, he expects nothing beneficial to humanity from this art. [*History of the Reformation*, p. 376.]

This is a view widely espoused. It is an unhappy one for an evangelical who finds in himself not only a great love for Florentine painting and sculpture but also a passionate conviction that there is something radically legitimate about the plastic immortalization of human beauty and the effort to shape visibly the chaotic phenomena of life; and who feels that there need be no tension between a vigorous evangelical orthodoxy and an assertion of the significance of the arts.

C. S. Lewis and Purgatory:
An Anecdote

I cannot pretend to belong to the circle of C. S. Lewis' friends and acquaintances. But I did meet him one time. It came about in this way. When I was in the Army in the late 1950s, I was stationed at Fort Benning, Georgia, as a chaplain's assistant (this did not mean that one was religious: it meant that one knew how to type). There was no war going on at that time, and thus the Army had to occupy itself with whatever it is that an Army occupies itself with in peace time. For myself, it meant that the bulk of my week's work of cleaning the chapel, taking care of the altar, doing the chaplain's secretarial work, and so forth, was finished by about eleven o'clock on Monday morning. Hence I had a great deal of time to read.

Being a chaplain's assistant was especially nice, since it meant that one had an office to oneself in a building of which one was the sole occupant for many hours during the week. The chaplain tended to be out "with the troops" on the firing range, and someone was needed to mind the store, so to speak. Most clerk-typists had to do their work in big, open office spaces with twenty or more desks, which meant that the air was full, all day long, of smoke (the Surgeon General had not weighed in yet) and of profanity. I spent my days in blissful solitude and silence. I read a great many books. I read Luther's big work on

Originally published in *The Chesterton Review, Special C. S. Lewis Issue,* August/November 1991: 389–91.

Galatians, J.H. Merle d'Aubigné's enormous history of the Reformation, William Law's *A Serious Call to a Devout and Holy Life*, Philip Doddridge's *The Rise and Progress of Religion in the Soul*, Richard Baxter's *The Saints' Everlasting Rest*, and that sort of book. People sent me things to read, and a friend sent me a hitherto unheard-of work called *The Hobbit*, by one J.R.R. Tolkien.

I found myself overwhelmed, and in my excitement I fired off a letter to C.S. Lewis, addressed, I suppose, simply to Magdalen College, Oxford, England. I'm not sure just why I wrote to Lewis rather than to Tolkien: perhaps it was that I felt better acquainted with Lewis, since I had been reading his books for some time, and Tolkien was a totally unknown figure. In any event, I wrote to Lewis. Everyone who ever wrote to Lewis had the gratifying experience of getting a letter back from him, in his very small, neat handwriting. He answered my letter, and said:

> Oh, but believe me, you are still only paddling in the glorious sea of Tolkien. Go on from *The Hobbit* at once to *The Lord of the Rings*; three volumes and nearly as long as the Bible and not a word too long (except for the first chapter which is a botch—don't be put off by it). *The Hobbit* is merely a fragment of his myth, detached, and adapted for children, and losing much by the adaptation. *The Lord of the Rings* is the Real stuff. Thanks for all the nice things you say about my own little efforts.

Two or three years later, while I was living in England teaching school, I visited a friend of mine who was studying law at Queen's College, Oxford. Lewis kindly invited me out to his house at Headington and instructed me which bus to take and how to find my way to the lane that led to *The Kilns*. He answered the door himself: in fact, during the hour I spent there, I did not see anyone else.

I suppose Len and Molly Miller must have been backstage somewhere, and Paxford, and perhaps Warnie: but I didn't see them.

Lewis was all that one expected and hoped for: booming, bell-like voice, twinkling eyes, rubicund face, baggy tweeds, jovial small-talk, and all. We sat in a small sitting room in overstuffed chairs by a gas fire. I can't remember whether or not it was burning. I asked him many questions, and, among other things, about Purgatory. "There might be such a place", he said. His point, which readers of his work will already know, was that the work of grace in us is to bring us to the measure of the stature of the fullness of Christ (to borrow from Saint Paul via the Authorized Version), or, to put it another way, to perfect us all in Charity. This work probably isn't finished when physical death overtakes us. Hence, God says, in effect, "He which hath begun a good work in you will perform it until the day of Jesus Christ." The work doesn't halt at death. Nor are we given a sudden ticket that exempts us from the rest of the lessons, so to speak. The work goes on. In one of his poems, Lewis uses the phrase, "aeonian poverty in Lenten lands". This picture of things does not at all stand over against the notion of justification by grace through faith, as many Protestants fear it might. Nor is it unscriptural. All we know about the state into which we enter at death, before the *Parousia* and the Resurrection, is that we are "with Christ". Certainly we are with Christ as our schooling in Charity proceeds, Lewis would urge. And since we are outside of time, there need be no punctilio about how long the business takes: Abel, the first man to die, won't have been dead any "longer" than the man who dies sixty seconds before the Last Trump.

In this purgatorial state of affairs, we are not, in Lewis' understanding of things, "earning" our way into heaven (another fear that many people have about the notion of Purgatory). Rather, we are proceeding on through the very same work of grace that had been begun in us in our walk through the world below, namely, the perfecting of Charity in us. Our whole experience of grace in this world is that, far from waving instant wands and granting us various virtues on the spot, grace always says to us, in effect,

> Ah: you are asking for Patience? Fine. Here are a thousand lessons in that school, starting with a garrulous roommate, and going on through the necessity of driving in Boston traffic, to waiting in lines at the post office while a slow-witted clerk copes with an even slower customer, and so on and so on.

Anyone who has read *The Great Divorce*, not to mention Dante, will know the picture. Lewis, as an obedient Anglican, believed what the Church Catholic teaches, namely, that we are justified by faith. Luther did not invent that doctrine. It is indeed all grace. But grace leads us through the steps, as it were. It isn't magic. While we talked, Lewis smoked cigarette after cigarette. I didn't get to see him fiddle with his famous pipes. Not wanting to monopolize his afternoon, I left after about forty-five minutes or so. He died six months later.

The Light of Eventide

Senescence: That is not a word that springs to one's lips in this epoch of Senior Citizens, Golden Agers, and other plucky euphemisms. If one has any tag-ends of information left over from grammar-school days in the 1940s, one might remember the Latin *senex*. The trouble is, it means *old man*. I myself arrived in this questionable category some years ago.

The topic is one that may be hurriedly swept under the rug, of course. Or it may be smothered under gay garlands of cosmetics, spas, cruises, bonhomie, exercise classes (I swim), party hats, and so forth. The stark actuality of the business is not one that especially pleases our own era.

Certainly senescence offers "the dear, dead days beyond recall" to our musings. I can remember my mother speaking of memories from "years ago". To my small-boy imagination, this evoked Noah's Flood or the Hanging Gardens of Babylon. "The olden days" always seemed to have been halcyon days, suffused with a golden light that had been discontinued, by God I supposed, just before I was born, never to be mustered up again.

With a certain amount of sheer time for reminiscence now, one trots out all sorts of items. Five-cent Cokes. No cars on the roads (the Depression and the War—*the* War). Gas for eighteen cents a gallon. One telephone in the house, with a lady on the other end asking, "Number,

Originally published in *Touchstone*, March 2007. Reprinted with permission.

please?" Hiking in the White Mountains with no other hikers anywhere to be seen.

The nineteenth century almost capsized in great warm marshes of sentiment(alism) about this inevitable decline: "Darling, I am growing old ... Silver threads among the gold" or "All the world am sad and dreary / Everywhere I roam / Still longin' for the old plantation / And for the old folks at home."

Charles Dana Gibson, the vastly fashionable pen-and-ink artist of the 1890s, drew one picture, guaranteed to make you choke up, of a dear old couple on a sofa in front of a low fire, her head on his shoulder, with Cupid behind them trying unavailingly to keep the Grim Reaper, scythe, black hood, and all, from pushing the door open. Not a picture to be found in any AARP publication in our own blithe era.

The Past, then, floods things, at least if one wants it to. I am sure there are brisk souls who never look back.

But then there is The Present. T. S. Eliot speaks of "A time for the evening under lamplight / (The evening with the photograph album)." There is also, for some of my friends, golf, fishing, shooting, foxhunting, and backgammon. I myself like to walk along "the stern and rockbound coast" near our house.

But when diversions and distractions have done what they can do, then what? Do I want to arrive at the Throne having sought only pastimes? How ought one to live these days richly?

I am always flagged down by the custom, centuries old, in various Mediterranean countries, of the women, upon reaching a certain age, dressing in black—dresses, stockings, Cuban-heeled Oxfords, and, often, babushkas. This seems to me to suggest a realistic outlook and an acceptance of the particular dignity that age brings with it. I have heard that there is also an element of mourning in it, which itself is very far from being unhealthy. (Loud shouts of horror from all pop-book and TV experts on living affirmatively.)

The main thing, of course, is to receive these days from God, embrace them, give thanks for them, and offer them back to him for his glory and in behalf of all the others in this mortal life who are old. One may thereby find grace in whatever limitations this state of life brings with it.

I myself am not an expert in this connection, but I do, however, have a small notebook in which I jot fragments that come to me as I say my prayers and mull things over. On one page, I have the heading "Detachment", a word one comes upon in the writings of the saints. I seem to have broken up the list into three headings, scarcely my own invention, of "The World", "The Flesh", and "The Devil".

When it comes to The World, I can only speak as a man. Men more than women, I suspect, have a form of vanity that attaches them in a particular way to the world. Scripture and Tradition hold up the Blessed Virgin as in some sense the archetype of the mystery of Femininity, always granting that she is also the very type of us all in her attitude to the Divine Will.

Women seem to know in their bones and marrow something about the truth of the matter that men try to find by charging about conquering kingdoms, sailing the seas, running companies, writing philosophy, symphonies, books, articles, and so forth. Women are perfectly able to pursue such accomplishments, but taking the whole of myth and history into consideration, they do not seem to have been quite so hag-ridden on this point as men are.

Under "The World", then, I have listed the following: the affairs of life—not scuttlebutt here; simply the business of life; enterprises of great pith and moment; one's own "importance"; society; diversions; travel; influence; acclaim; variety of experience; prestige, even service, forsooth. It is almost impossible for a man to detach his soul from such concerns.

Under "The Flesh", I have the usual: fantasies; pleasures (food, wine, etc.); and amenities.

"The Devil"? Need one dilate here? Unhappily, I do have some specifics that I suppose I may attribute to our Enemy, but that I all too eagerly harbor: vindictiveness; vengefulness; petulance; irascibility; arrogance; fatuity; venality; cravenness; pusillanimity; parsimony of soul; pique; fretfulness; officiousness; acedia (sloth); envy; and an unhappy host of other items.

But my topic is old age and detachment. Manifestly, our lifelong struggle is to fight against anything in such lists that is sinful.

But most of the items under "The World" are neutral in themselves, becoming the occasions for sin only when we grasp after them. But in old age, most of those things draw away from us. There are, of course, some happy men whose eminence grows and grows the older they get. For most of us, any eminence we may ever have supposed we enjoyed calms itself down.

Which brings me to another page in my notebook. I seem to have written down the following sequence: "Set your affection on things above.... Now we see through a glass darkly.... This slight momentary affliction.... Cast thy burden upon the Lord...." And so forth. The effort at work here was merely that of trying to gain a sharpening in focus, from our world to the World to Come, as the Creed puts it.

It is an appropriate set of considerations during the days when my allotted time is dwindling. I myself have passed my threescore years and ten. I am aware that the time even of infants is dwindling: but things take on starker colors when you are old.

Old age may of course bring with it a certain increase in dignity and venerability, if I act my age and am not foolishly trying to appear forever young. And there are luxuries and privileges that hitherto eluded one, most notably time. If one still has one's spouse, this part of life is rich in ways hardly dreamed of during the years of hurly-burly. There is also, for some, the maturity and marriage of one's children and, hence, the joy of grandchildren. Reading Beatrix Potter to small tots is one of my life's crowning pleasures.

But there are other visitants to one's old age. Ignominy, for one thing: to find oneself shuffling along hospital corridors in a johnny, going from X-ray to MRI to blood work to physical therapy has a way of calling into question what is commonly recommended to us as self-esteem. T. S. Eliot notes the fear, in old age, of "belonging to others"—to nurses, for example, and therapists and technicians and orderlies and the transport people, not to mention doctors. I scarcely need to descant on the details here.

Then there is, often, solitude or silence. I myself am fortunate, so far, in having a very great lady as my wife, and she is in good health and spirits as I write. What more can a man ask? But still, there are small periods of reflection in one's study.

One's mind reverts on rare occasions to the days crowded with students, assistants, audiences, friends, and all the boards, committees, symposia, and travel that bundled one along in the academic world. A man could live forever in that bustle. But things do quiet down. To what do my reveries run? Repining will hardly do: It is one of the most effective ways of banishing the virtue of hope. But then, what did one hope?

The psalmists and saints keep telling us to seek the Face of God or to desire the courts of the Lord. Eliot, again, speaks of the people who are "distracted from distraction by distraction". It could be that while I am "old and full of years", as the Old Testament was pleased to call it, I am being given the chance, long held at bay by responsibilities or distractions, to think on the Four Last Things now and again, along with the pleasures reserved for old age.

I made another list in this connection, at which readers may be pardoned for letting a sigh escape. What do I do these days? It's all very dim, from one point of view. Morning ablutions; breakfast; morning prayer; Mass; tea with my wife; email; *Lectio Divina*; the Rosary; walk; reading; evening prayer. Et cetera. Quite dim.

But I cannot pretend that I do not enjoy this sort of schedule. Readers are not to suppose, however, that this aggressively Catholic program sets me among the higher echelons of souls. One takes on all of that by way of some gesture toward "holy living and holy dying", as Jeremy Taylor will have it.

It is not that one takes up the hair shirt or the lash. God be thanked for family and friends and food and wine and hilarity.

One last list, scarcely my own. The twilight of one's life, surely, ought to illumine one's path toward the attitudes of which the saints speak: resignation; recollection; renunciation; detachment; silence; waiting; patience; withdrawal; simplicity; stillness; contentedness.

Some of these attitudes are exacted from us willynilly, in these latter years. The trick here is to learn to embrace such necessities with some effort toward gratitude. I speak as one who sees the syllabus, but has barely matriculated.

So. Shall I fend off the silence with unremitting hours of television? It seems to work for some people. Or will

I chafe against the requirement of patience by—well, by chafing? Shall I forfeit the great treasure offered by detachment by snatching at the *ignis fatuus* of pleasures that belong to the years that are now past?

It is to be most sedulously urged here that all of this exists in the region of aspiration for me, not of achievement. I lay down my quill here to return to the business.

The Burden of God

A year or two ago I had to spend a night with friends in the
Cotswolds in England, not far from the ancient town of
Cirencester. The house where we stayed was an old one:
some late additions had been made during the reign of
Elizabeth I, but otherwise it was fourteenth century. It
was not a castle, just an old farmhouse set in a tiny green
pocket of a valley that looked as though it had been laid
out by Peter Rabbit or perhaps a Hobbit. Those little lanes
and hedgerows and rounded green fields, and the soft,
textured, yellowish-grey stone of the cottages and manor
houses—these stirred up in our imagination lovely pictures of an epoch, long gone, of tranquility and repose,
when life moved at a pace other than pell-mell, and people
lived in some sort of courteous harmony with their world.
We were greeted in the old cobbled courtyard by the lady
and brought into the kitchen, where we had to stoop to
avoid the herbs hanging from the great wooden rafters.
She offered us heavy goblets of cowslip wine that she
had made from flowers gathered on the place. For supper
she gave us good thick soup from wooden bowls, brown
bread, and butter. That night we slept under feather beds,
and we woke in the morning to look out through leaded
casement windows set in three-foot-thick stone walls at
the meadows still white with the early mist.

Originally published in *Christianity Today*, April 28, 1972, 5–9. Reprinted
with permission.

The ambiguity I am aiming at here is perfectly clear: we have all had some experience or other that raised in our imagination this ambiguity, or at least this odd discrepancy in things—the discrepancy between what looks good and simple and human (the old days), and what we've arrived at by means of that movement we are pleased to call "progress". The word implies, of course, a going *ahead*, and that implies "to better things" (you don't go forward to worse things). In any case, we progress from century to century, or from decade to decade, and things get faster and straighter and cleaner; but every once in a while something (an overnight stay in a Cotswold farmhouse, a picture, a poem, a scene, a memory)—something will jog us a bit, and we feel like saying "Hey. Wait. Stop the music. Now what is it, exactly, that we're doing?"

You may by this time have said to yourself that this article is turning out to be a back-to-Eden plea, the sort of thing you might expect from Wordsworth or D. H. Lawrence, or some romantic; and that that's always an appealing invitation, but not one, really, that promises anything very helpful to us now.

Well, it's not a call back to Eden, except in one way, which I'll get to in a minute. But why *can't* we go back to Eden—to simplicity and innocence and purity and spontaneity? Surely Western civilization, and especially American, we are told, has managed to sell its soul for a mess of computers and pollution, if not pottage. Can't we take up arms—flowers or placards or Molotov cocktails—against this horror? Can't we begin, via bells and beads and bare feet, to enact and celebrate that Edenic simplicity and innocence and perhaps change the face of society?

We are told we can, and some millions of people under twenty-five believe in the possibility of this vision. I emphasize the word "possibility", since I do not suppose

there *is* a human being, from Hitler on up, whose reveries
do not take him to some such Eden of tranquility. Everyone loves the vision. Nobody likes the imagery of *1984* or
of *Brave New World*—those hells of metallic efficiency and
automation and control. So the quarrel, I suppose, would
not be between visions: everybody wants Eden. The quarrel is between those who think that Eden is forever lost to
our history because of one implacable fact (some people
call it the Fall, and all mythology has some such notion),
and those who think that by deciding to do things differently we can somehow restore Eden. I suppose there is
a third group (and this is where the prophets of the day
would put the military-industrial-labor complex, the big
construction and real-estate speculators, and the money
men and the politicians) who, though they may share the
dream of Eden in their private dreams, find themselves so
caught up in the avalanche of civilization that they hardly
ever give a passing nod to the idea of stopping to find out
what we're up to.

I am not among those who think that a shift in style of
life, a new imagery of earthiness and innocence, or a new
generation of creatures somehow untainted with the pox
that infected the rest of the race for the rest of history—I
say I am not among those who think that these things
promise a real, historical shift and that we may look for a
greening of America if only we will listen to what "these
kids" say.

I suspect that that is not the way things are. I suspect that
an authentic response to the horrors of our epoch—the size
of cities and the cost of living and the population explosion and the shrill crescendo of non-negotiable demands
by one group and another and the ecological crisis and the
war—includes neither the effort to fly to Eden nor armed
revolution.

I believe this because I believe that there is more than mere horror in our epoch. There is a bitter irony at the root of it all. A bitter irony. And it is this, that not only our obviously gross inclinations but also our best efforts contribute to the chaos. Somehow, ironically, by the way we have set about fulfilling the mandate given to us at the beginning of civilization—the mandate to subdue the earth and have dominion over it—we have ended up creating a hell. It wasn't by embarking upon something obviously grotesque that we ended up with a grotesquery. That horror came about, somehow, as a by-product of our way of doing what we were *supposed* to do.

For what is the human job on this planet? We, of all earthly creatures, do have a job. Lions and clams and elm trees seem to have been given the happy task of being gloriously themselves. I used to sit watching a tiny Yorkshire terrier that we had while we lived in New York City, and it struck me one day as I watched him drowsing on a cushion of the sofa in the morning sunlight that he was doing the will of God. He was being a Yorkie and doing what Yorkies are supposed to do. His day involved playing, eating, sleeping, and generally carrying about and embodying that particular form of perfection and glory that we can see only in Yorkshire terriers. That was his job in life.

We men are supposed to do something, and a good share of that something is to have dominion over this planet. But it seems that, in the process of claiming that dominion of setting about doing what we were supposed to do, we somehow botched it. The irony appears when you look, not at the clearly bad things we've done, but at what accompanies the *good* things we've done. We seem to have succeeded in making the good items add up to a bad total.

For example, if you come across a tool or a method that allows you to do a job in half the time it has always taken you, you will, of course, start using it. Not to do so would be stupid. You have been dragging loads on sledges for years, and suddenly the man in the next cave comes up with a new device that eliminates two-thirds of the work. You waste no time in making one of these items yourself, and thereupon your town has advanced way beyond the town on the other side of the crag: you have wheels. Work gets done faster, and life is better. This is a good thing.

The only difficulty is that if you leap across a few thousand years and a few thousand such discoveries and inventions, you find your great-great-great-grandchildren trying to find somewhere on the planet where they can leave behind their wheels and everything that wheels have made possible. Whatever it was you made possible for them, it somehow didn't bring about the repose and joy you thought you'd gained. By making every single individual task easier (planting, reaping, cooking, traveling, communicating), you somehow, ironically, made the whole picture more terrifying. You raised visions of a whole earth cemented over, its rivers vomiting sludge and trash into a choked sea, its air opaque with smoke and gas, its mountain ranges gutted and its wells leeched dry, its fish drowned in oil slicks and its trees poisoned and wilting, and its neurotic citizens sitting in thousand-mile traffic jams.

Five years ago we would have had the luxury of chuckling at this description of things. Now we don't, since we see ourselves hurrying headlong toward that state of affairs. We will number, they tell us, eight billion souls in a few more decades. It frightens us, so we begin to take measures to counteract it; but we end up with more frightening pictures than ever.

What, for instance, do we do about the population explosion—which is itself the direct product, let's face it, of our legitimate effort to fulfill our human task of claiming dominion over the planet? We have assailed disease after disease, thus drastically reducing the infant mortality rate and raising life expectancy. Each one of those achievements is wonderful: certainly Jonas Salk wasn't doing wrong when he developed his vaccine. (My son is alive now because the hospital knew how to destroy the thing that a few years ago would have destroyed him.) The sum total of those good achievements amounts to a terror, however—an increase of our numbers that promises a pushing, heaving struggle for elbow room on this globe that will make the worst wars in history look like pat-a-cake.

So now we turn to *that* problem with our knowledge, skill, and good intentions, and we get a cover story in *Time* magazine, treating as sober realities what Aldous Huxley and George Orwell fancied not too long ago as futuristic nightmares!—the calculated, determinative, test-tube manipulation of human existence from conception to death (and beyond: they're thinking of freezing us instead of burying or burning us now, so that we can be resuscitated when they find out what it is that makes us die and get a vaccine for *that*; religious people have had a way of thinking that that particular vaccine won't show up in laboratories—it comes from the veins of God).

Well, it was all very enchanting. Enchanting, we say: Why enchanting? That has to do with magic, but the good woman there was neither a fairy nor a witch. The only brew she stirred was that good soup and some thick oatmeal she gave us for breakfast—all covered with heavy cream, of course. What, then, was the spell that seemed to be at work there?

Surely it was something like the spells you get in old tales: we were somehow spirited away from our ordinary world into another world—one that appeared to be free from the plagues that curse our own world and that took us back somewhere—to some remote past where things were "better".

Now I know this is fanciful. I know perfectly well that I could have been seized with appendicitis that night and have had to be rushed to a hospital, at the risk of a smash-up on the road, and that the faster the car, the straighter the road, and the more gleaming the hospital, the happier I would have been.

But we can't have it both ways. We can't have wooden bowls and quiet, winding lanes and the creak of wagon wheels, and at the same time speed, sterility, and efficiency. Our world has to be one or the other, it seems. We've got to have things either old and simple and quaint (and hence inconvenient) or new and complicated and metallic (and hence horrifying). All the plastic and stainless steel and concrete has been added, surely, to make life better, easier, and more human.

Wherever we look, we see the irony: that the good and necessary fruits of our labors—our God-commanded labors, if you like—are somehow botched and tainted with doom and that what we call progress may be hurrying us into a howling nightmare. Do we really, in the long view, want to split atoms? We get not only Hiroshima but atomic waste to cope with. Do we really, in the long view, want another six lanes of concrete along the Schuylkill or the Hudson? Do we really want to get to Paris in forty-five minutes, sonic boom and all? Do we really want every single hillside and meadow in Westchester County bulldozed into used-car lots, trailer parks, and McDonald's stands (I happen to like McDonald's hamburgers)?

Our efforts at power, speed, and convenience seem to go askew somewhere. Even our efforts to look inside ourselves seem touched with rottenness. Has the rise of behavioral sciences contributed to the equanimity of the race? Has the supposed knowledge of the deeps inside ourselves made us more or less frightened? Were the citizens of twelfth-century London more or less able to cope than their children of twentieth-century Philadelphia?

This is all very bleak. Shall we, then, opt out of it all in sheer terror or disgust? No. No reflective person, and certainly no one who takes the Judeo-Christian view seriously, can take quite that attitude about history and human existence. There is more to be said than "alas". But I am not about to offer either the onward-and-upward view that sees the City of God just beyond the next round of legislation and reform or the cop-out view that says, "Well, since there's no hope, we can pretend human history and existence are unreal."

There is an old notion, however, about the origin of this tragic irony in things, and a view that grasps the human situation in that light and proceeds from there, rejecting, on the one hand, the utopian nonsense that holds center stage at the moment and, on the other, the defeatist cop-out to which well-intentioned religious minds sometimes fly.

It goes something like this (and this is where we must go back to Eden and look at what happened in that old account): In that lovely Paradise, we (let us read "we" for "Adam") rashly shouldered a burden we ought never to have picked up. It was a burden too heavy for human backs to bear. It was the burden of the god. It was called the knowledge of good and evil.

Presumably the knowledge particularly appropriate for our species in the design of things is a knowledge of good. I do not, alas, understand the state of innocence, so I cannot try to explain just what our outlook and our relationship with our world was like in that state of affairs. But whatever it was, we imagine that there was a lovely harmony between man and the earth. We were certainly free—that's one thing. It was, of course, a freedom that is terribly difficult for the twentieth-century mind to grasp, since it did not mean "self-determination", or "lib", or an absence of rules. It involved responsibility and submission to certain strictures. There was a hierarchy of being, and our particular place was here, with such and such a kind of knowledge appropriate to this level of things. (There were seraphim, with another kind of knowledge, and archangels, and so on, and they did not have and were not supposed to have exactly what we had. They were not men.)

In any case, we thought differently and reached out for a foothold higher up. Surely, if there is a fuller kind of knowledge, we deserve to experience it, we thought. We can handle it.

Alas. This inclination is what the old poets used to call *hubris*, and it is what sent all the tragic heroes crashing down. It was the effort to muscle one's way up the scale to what looks like a freer, more privileged, more powerful place. Presumably it would be hubris for a clam to want to be a Great Dane, a lizard to be an eagle, or Macbeth to be king. And for a man to want to be a god. You get what goes along with that higher station, and it turns out to be more than you can control. It doesn't work. The clam finds that Great Dane-ness is too much—it runs away with him. The result is chaos.

This ancient account, it seems to me, suggests that, for whatever reasons, the kind of knowledge we reached out for in Eden was too much for us. It was like Great Dane-ness for a clam. It was appropriate for higher orders of being than we are, and it ran away with us.

We do not know what the history of civilization would have looked like if that primeval tragedy had not occurred. But we do know what it looks like now that the tragedy *has* occurred.

It is perhaps one way of understanding what that heady and interdicted "knowledge of good and evil" was, and one way of understanding our own resulting situation, if we say that at that point we shouldered the burden of a knowledge too keen for ourselves—a knowledge that could probe so far into things and open up such vistas of discovery for us that we, not being gods and hence lacking both the wisdom and the authority to *control* it all (remember the clam and the Great Dane), found ourselves whirled and dragged along by our knowledge rather than controlling it. And that is a great evil. It opened up possibilities of power and ecstasy, and it is the scramble for power and ecstasy that has engendered all cupidity and cruelty and hatred.

So once again we seem to have come to a point where we might well say, "Right. Fie on history. Fie on human existence", and where we are left either with despair or with some gnostic cop-out.

But (to borrow from a well-known contemporary thinker) we must not immanentize the eschaton.

The prevailing political and philosophical manifestation of that error is to be seen in the ineffable liberal (and third-world) inclination to insist, in spite of all, that we can, given a teeny bit more patience and pulling together, immanentize that lovely classless, pluralistic, amiable eschaton. There is also an antiphonal variation of the same error to which the conservative (and certainly the religious) mind finds itself inclining, if only in its reveries. It is the wish to immanentize the eschaton by rejecting the validity of human history and existence and by *merely* looking for Apocalypse. Repeat "merely", since it is part and parcel of the view that takes the imagery of Eden and the Fall seriously to take the imagery of Apocalypse seriously. But we do not have the luxury of turning in our keys and sitting about clucking and tut-tutting about how awful everything is. There is more to do than that. We must live and participate in our own epoch.

But any orthodox Christian is, I should think, in an ambiguous position vis-à-vis his own epoch. On the one hand, he probably harbors deep skepticism about the ultimate efficacy of human efforts to solve human problems (and hence cannot but hear most of what goes on in public dialogue as nonsense); but on the other, because his faith is a historical faith, anchored in real events and processes in history, and above all because the God he affirms is a God who appeared in our history and in our flesh, he cannot, no matter how bleak and chaotic things seem to be, deny the validity of history. And, since history is made up of human events and enterprises, it is assumed that one will find his vocation in some relation to those events and enterprises.

His race—and hence he himself—has taken up the burden of the god. There is no redoing that. Nostalgia for a lost perfection, anger at the poor job we have made of history—these attitudes are hardly biblical. Redemption itself—that whole great glorious scheme whereby all things *are* made new—was unfolded in our history and will culminate our history. Because of that unfolding, in the Law, the Prophets, the Incarnation, and the Apocalypse, a Christian sees history as invested with literally infinite significance.

He accepts, then, the burden of the god; but he does not pretend it is other than a burden.

Notes upon Hearing Mozart's Bassoon Concerto

How shall we speak of Mozart? We are always struck by his sprightly lyricism, of course, which offers us immeasurable delight but at the same time brings tears to our eyes—the tears that arrive when we find ourselves hailed with pure beauty. Grandeur, hilarity, bliss, poignancy, joy—what words suffice?

I was listening to Mozart the other day, which I do on most days. Upon hearing this particular concerto, I found myself contemplating an oddity. On the one hand, there is joy for us all. But on the other, if you think about it, the whole thing proceeds upon the most unrelieved slavery. For a start, Mozart himself *must* "obey" the rigorous pattern imposed upon his genius the moment the work begins to take shape in his imagination. He is very far from being free to "express himself". That will be the farthest thing from his mind, since "himself" is nothing at all to the purpose here. And we, his audience, are not a group met to "share". We want to hear the concerto. Once his quill had started across the staff lines on the paper, he found himself less and less free to follow mere whim. The thing itself supersedes all. (How any artist's genius collaborates with the materials—marble, gesso, pigment, words, notes—and with the pattern that is taking shape opens up questions that seem intractable.) And then we have the conductor—the

Originally published in *Crisis*, November 1, 2006. Reprinted with permission.

maestro. But again, he is bound to obey the score, no matter what sort of prima donna he may suppose himself to be. He must obey a *sostenuto* here and a *vivace* there if that is what Mozart has indicated.

Things only get worse when we come to the orchestra. Here is the concertmaster, a man bringing to his task weary decades of toil ("I *can't* get that interval"), renunciation ("No, I can't swim this afternoon; I have to practice"), and fidelity ("Pay attention, boy! Can't you *see* that e-flat?"). He, if anyone, merits some freedom, surely? Not to mention all the other musicians: Questions of each one's own dignity and achievements, or of whatever "issues" he may lumber around with, are utterly taboo on this stage. But surely this is an outrage? Don't they know who I *am?* they all might shout. Wouldn't they like me to share my *identity* with them?

No. No, no, no. It seems brutal. What can be said to ameliorate this serene interdict that seems to ignore the musicians themselves? Very little, actually, at least on this level. It is to point out the obvious, of course, to remark that all good musicians, from Mozart to the drummer, scarcely think of the problem, having long since been drawn into the higher enterprise of the music and away from the attitude that insists on itself as the cynosure. As long as it is a question of *me*, then that is all we will get— not, really, what we came for. It is, eventually, hell— where ennui, bickering, anguish, jealousy, hatred, and futility preside.

The paradox is that when one has been drawn into an enterprise so great that he is no longer the whole point, there arises for him, and for the audience, a joy unimaginable so long as he insists that it is he who finally matters.

But there is more. Oddly, this clamorous self is transfigured at the far end of the wearisome years of obedience to the demands of catgut and horsehair, or reed, or mouth-piece, or score. So long as he supposed that the whole enterprise was principally a matter of discovering some elusive "identity", then very little music would have appeared, and no joy for any of us. But when that *me* is sacrificed in the interest of *something else*, then we get Vladimir Ashkenazy and Dennis Brain and Jean-Pierre Rampal and Itzhak Perlman.

The saints seem to speak of something like this.

On the Trajectory of the Ascension

Christians, affirming as they do that the Bible is the Word of God, will naturally look into this book with a set of expectations that they do not bring to any other literature, no matter how exalted, noble, or elevated that literature is. To be sure, Sophocles and Dante are "inspired", if by that we mean that every gift, including poetic genius, is from above and is given to men by the Father of Lights. A keen mind, a lithe body, a glorious soprano voice, a quick ability with sums, a green thumb, a special efficiency in housework—these, surely, are all gifts to us men from heaven.

But the Scriptures of the Old and New Testaments are unique, somehow, on the Christian view. Historic orthodoxy has ordinarily had it that they *are* the Word of God. Efforts to lessen the difficulties that this affirmation raises for our imaginations have been persistent and inventive. The Scriptures "contain" the Word of God, or they "become" it, or they "witness to" it. All these ways of phrasing it are fair enough, as far as they go, of course, and they are attempts to grasp more realistically the dynamic nature of God's Word to us men than formularies of, say, dictation, could do, with their efforts to safeguard the uniquely divine character of the Bible.

The trouble with any theory of mere dictation as a description of the dynamics of biblical inspiration is, for most

Originally published in *Christianity Today*, March 15, 1974. Reprinted with permission.

Christians, evangelical and otherwise, that it does violence to our perception of how God appears to work in all other situations. He seems to operate, that is, paradoxically—*via* the humanity of his human agents. The great patriarchal and prophetic and apostolic figures in Scripture, who were singled out to obey and enact and exhibit in their lives the special activity of God, were far from being ciphers. Abraham was no nonentity. Jacob, surely, was no wallflower. Moses was no pawn. And so forth, with David and Ezekiel and John the Baptist and Paul, to say nothing of the post-biblical figures who loom in Church history: Athanasius and John Chrysostom and Augustine and Francis and Luther and Knox and General William Booth.

The point about this survey of characters is that they, and a host of others like them (no—unlike them), with all their oddities and inclinations and limitations—cultural, temperamental, physical, and intellectual—with all their *humanness*, in a word, have functioned somehow, in the annals of the people of God down through history, as bearers of the Word to us. In their experience, or by their preaching or writing, or whatever it has been, they have disclosed God to us in one way or another. In all of them, we could see *God* at work; but that work did not ride upon the flattening out of the human figures via whom it went forward.

We can never, of course, quite work out the paradox. The work is all of God, all of grace, we say; and that will be the song of the redeemed at the final consummation of things, when we are given to see the whole sweep of the work of God. It is, in fact, all of God. But the other pole of the paradox is that it was, indeed, *that* man who did *that* work. It was his obedience that responded to the call of God; it was his arm that wielded the sword, or his feet that walked from Ur to Canaan, or his mind that constructed the sermons, or his voice that sang. And the work had that particular flavor and hue because of that man. Savonarola, Zwingli, Calvin, Menno Simon—the work looked like that because the man was like that. Perhaps there is a clue here.

Perhaps it can be said that at every point where the eternal touches the temporal, or where the divine touches the human, or the ultimate the proximate—however we want to phrase it—perhaps at that point we have a mystery that can never *quite* be unscrambled by human efforts at explanation. So that we can never, for example, "explain" the Protestant Reformation by looking into Luther's personality, with all of its oddities; any more than we can, on the other hand, talk as though it were all a purely divine action of the Holy Ghost in the Church, engineered from above, with no reference to the kind of mind and emotions Luther had.

Or again, we can never get very far with questions that ask how much of a man's salvation is to be attributed to anything *he* did, and how much to God's activity. Neither of the two extreme explanations will do at all; but exactly where the nexus of the divine and the human is to be found, no one can say. Or again, when we speak of our own responses to Scripture, say, in the process of sanctification: How much of it are we to see as a matter of sheer obedience to Scripture, and how much of it does God bring about in us?

The question itself becomes paralyzing and, hence, nonsense. It cannot be a quantitative matter. It cannot be a matter of sorting two separate things out from each other. It is a paradox—the paradox you get every time the eternal touches the temporal.

Perhaps it is this way with the Scriptures themselves. They are, most assuredly, what anyone can see them to be: an odd collection, made over hundreds of years, of various sorts of writings—such as poetry, parable, history, epistle—by an astonishing assortment of hands, and got together eventually by who knows what procedure. Textual studies and archaeology, and so forth, can uncover this and that about them. But these pursuits can never quite establish the divine nature of these writings, any more than gynecology can quite yield the mystery of the Incarnation to us, or geometry can plot the trajectory of the Ascension. The very phrase makes us wince with the awareness that we have somehow, suddenly, got into an absurdity. "*That's* not what we're talking about when we say we believe Jesus ascended into heaven. It's nothing any *lens* can scrutinize." "Oh, well, then, you don't really believe it was anything real. Just a sort of spiritual metaphor?" "No, no! Christians do, in fact, believe that the man Jesus of Nazareth really did 'ascend into heaven', to quote their Creed. But that event brought us to the edge of the divine mysteries themselves, like the Incarnation, or even the Creation: What *is* the relationship between the eternal and the temporal? We affirm the mysteries and the reality of what the mysteries proclaim."

Perhaps the Scriptures exist on that same frontier, so that, just as we do not hesitate to describe the Incarnate Word as a provincial Jewish boy brought up under the instruction of Joseph the Carpenter, and thereby affirm a great mystery, so we do not hesitate to describe the written Word as a peculiar collection of all sorts of literature got together in a very odd way, and thereby affirm a similar mystery. Perhaps the paradox of the one gives us a clue to the paradox of the other.

Manners and Holiness

My wife and I have a friend, a lady—and "lady" is the right word here—who is what earlier centuries, especially in England, would have called "highborn". I suppose the term "blue-blood" might apply. There is an air about her that has occasioned several piquant conversations between my wife and me.

This "air", be it said hastily, is at a polar extreme from what one might run into in this connection on Broadway or in cheap novels and journalism and popular imagination. Quite the contrary. Our friend arrives at the front door in a great breeze of good cheer. She is happy to see you and finds everything you say to her over lunch to be nothing but interesting and encouraging. She quite genuinely wants to know about you and your children, what you all are doing these days, and how everyone is getting on. You realize afterward that not once did she seize the chance to turn the conversation to herself and her own family and concerns. Oh, to be sure, she will cheerfully fill you in (not at any great length) if you ask her about herself. But then you get, "But tell me about your two grandsons. I must hear about them."

We have known this lady for perhaps thirty years and have been with her in all sorts of situations. Her forthcoming and cheerful approach to life seems to be unflagging. She is wholly interested in what someone has to say at a cocktail party, for example. You never hear from her any

Originally published in *Crisis*, July 1, 2006. Reprinted with permission.

of the usual fatuities that prevail in these situations. Her random daily contacts with the grocer, say, or with the gardener or the gas station man evince the same thing. But there is nothing frivolous or merely "social" about any of it. Life has brought her some great sorrows, and even though she would never volunteer a syllable touching on any of them, you find a true and sympathetic understanding of anyone else's troubles.

She is always perfectly dressed. Saint Francis de Sales would be happy with her response to his counsel to the women to whom he gave spiritual direction:

> As to the material and style of our clothing, decency should be considered in reference to the various circumstances of time, age, rank, company, and occasion.... It is a sort of contempt of those you associate with to frequent their company in unbecoming attire. At the same time avoid all affectation and vanity, all extremes and frivolity. As far as possible keep always to the side of simplicity and modesty, for this is undoubtedly beauty's greatest ornament. (*Introduction to the Devout Life*)

The question here that I raise while my wife and I have our morning tea: Where is the line between mere manners and sanctity? One struggles along in the Christian life, fencing forever with irritability and petulance and parsimony of spirit and pique and so forth. The lessons in the school of charity in this connection are far from easy. Really, one needs the word "warfare" here rather than "lessons", it seems. Do the manners that seem to derive from a background of gentility, grace, and self-effacement exempt fortunate people like our friend from the Holy Ghost's salvific chastening?

Our friend wouldn't think so. She happens to be a Christian now, and no one knows, of course, what goes on in her prayers and in her soul. But we knew her before her conversion, and she seemed just as wonderful back then.

Well, we mortals look on the outward appearance. God alone knows our hearts. The question, however, still intrigues me.

T. S. Eliot

In a letter to a friend of his, T. S. Eliot once said, "You cannot conceive of truth at all, the word has no meaning, except by conceiving of it as something permanent."

That is not an observation likely to attract much enthusiasm in our own epoch. The general notion abroad now is that we come at the truth of things and ourselves by incessantly innovating and that, insofar as an idea is well worn, it is probably false; nay, that truth itself is a "dynamic" affair, growing, modifying, changing, as we continually recast the molds in which we propose to receive it.

The commonplace "We now know", with its variants "Science has proved" and "Research has shown", is brought to bear with all the weight and solemnity that modernity can amass on question after question. For example, it was all very well and good for the ancients to suppose that the gods had something to do with the universe we live in, but of course We Now Know that this was all whistling in the dark. Science has proved.... Or, similarly, it was a very fine thing for those same ancients to speak of God with a royal vocabulary, but We Now Know that all that imagery of God's majesty was culturally determined and has nothing to do with anything beyond the borders of tribal imagination. Or again, it was one thing for these people to circumscribe human relations by confining sexual congress inside holy bonds, but We Now

Originally published in *Christianity Today*, January 3, 1975, 12–14. Reprinted with permission.

Know that that sprang from a superstitious and adolescent understanding of human relationships, and, having come of age ourselves, we can define our own (new) relationships, choosing on an *ad hoc* basis what appeals to us and jettisoning the outworn proscriptions.

And so forth. In politics, behavior, ethics, art, and the sciences, the desideratum is the "breakthrough". Frontiers are there to be *crossed*; bonds are there to be snapped; taboos are there to be overleaped. If the angels won't rush in, get them out of the way.

The Christian imagination is perplexed by this sort of thing, in that it does suspect that in the end, there *are* "permanent things" (Eliot's phrase), and that there *are* mysteries on whose hither side the angels do well to falter, and that taboo may well be the recognition of a real interdict. But, on the other hand, the Christian is obliged not only to grant but to welcome thousands of the "breakthroughs" accomplished by that very curiosity and derring-do which has so damaged the supposed permanent things. Which breakthroughs shall we welcome? Copernicus? Galileo? Magellan? Of course. Darwin? Freud? Germaine Greer? Well, ah . . .

It is not, then, a question of change versus no change. We live in "merry middle earth" (C.S. Lewis' phrase) and can't ever get things *quite* fixed. We do have to be tinkering. It is the question of how we are to know, and, knowing, to preserve, the really permanent things. Which things, if any, are off limits? We destroyed the flat-earth concept: May we destroy the male/female distinction? We scotched the geocentric theory: May we scotch the marriage theory? We got rid of the gods: May we get rid of the children-obey-your-parents notion?

It is not easy to find the border beyond which it is unlawful to venture. And the whole matter is queered for us nowadays by everyman's terror lest he be found to be "reactionary". Not to be briskly in the van of contemporaneity is to be a eunuch.

It is to our uncertainty and anxiety in the face of ambiguities like this that the voice of the prophet speaks. At least part of the function of the prophet has been to recall the people to the permanent things and to articulate freshly for them what those things are in order that they may be grasped firmly once again.

If there are prophetic figures in our own century, one of them is surely T. S. Eliot. Most of us run into his work only in an English class (if at all), and then it is only "Prufrock" and "The Waste Land". Perhaps we see a production of *Murder in the Cathedral* once during our lifetime.

But this will not do. At the crunch in which we find ourselves in history, with morals in tatters, public sensibility in hot pursuit of the bizarre, the grotesque, and the brutal, and the imagination of decent people everywhere stunned and hesitant, it is not overstating the case to say that a great deal of what needs to be said right now has been said for us in our own time by this man.

It is an ancient exercise, and a salutary one, for people to recall their ancestors' wisdom. Our own Scriptures are full of exhortations to do so: and the Greeks, and all mediaeval and Renaissance men, knew the value of harking back to "auctoritee", that is, to wisdom uttered by men long dead (which wisdom, contrary to our own suppositions, was held to have *gathered* weight by its very antiquity).

T. S. Eliot has been dead only a decade, but already his words seem oracular in their clairvoyant relevance to our situation. Indeed, this oracular quality about his pronouncements irritated his critics even while he was still alive. Of the many studies of Eliot that have appeared, none that I know of deals so massively with Eliot's whole vision, particularly with respect to the alarming issues of public imagination and morals in our epoch, as Russell

Kirk's *Eliot and His Age*, published at the start of our decade (Random House, 1971). We might not do wrong to pull it off the shelf, here in the middle, as it were, and see what we can see.

Eliot, Kirk says, "labored to renew the wardrobe of a moral imagination", by which he means, using Burke's definition, "that power of ethical perception which strides beyond the barriers of private experience and events of the moment". It aspires to apprehend "right order in the soul and right order in the commonwealth". Eliot felt, like Burke, " 'that *we* have made no discoveries, and we think that no discoveries are to be made, in morality....' " At least part of his achievement was to reinvigorate for us "those perennial moral insights which are the sources of human normality, and which make possible order and justice and freedom".

Now this is nonsense to the doctrinaire modern, who is committed to innovation, creativity, and experiment on all fronts, moral and psychological as well as educational and scientific. The notion of there being some fixed order that presides over the changes and chances of time and fashion and that judges these ephemera is abhorrent to the central doctrine of Modernism, namely, the doctrine of "progress", understood as self-validating innovation.

Eliot, sometimes almost alone, it seemed, stood over against the avalanche of Modernism. He believed in the "older certitudes" and in "the painfully acquired wisdom of the species". He wrote in 1948 that "we are destroying our ancient edifices 'to make ready the ground upon which the barbarian nomads of the future will encamp in their mechanised caravans.' "

In his early poetry and comment, written before he became a Christian, Eliot articulated for us the ennui, impotence, debility, solitude, and senescence of modern man, with images that hail us with the horror of hell itself. We all know poor Prufrock, with his trousers rolled and his hesitation over the challenge of eating a peach. And "the Waste Land" with its dismaying barrooms and "the young man carbuncular" and its "empty chapel, only the wind's home," and so forth. This poem in particular enraged the modernists. Kirk puts it this way:

> "Eliot," they say, "is snobbishly contrasting the alleged glory and dignity of the Past with what he takes for the degradation of the democratic and industrialized Present. This is historically false and ought to be repudiated by all Advanced Thinkers" (p. 81).

Not so, says Kirk:

> The Present, Eliot knew, is only a thin film upon the deep well of the Past.... The ideological cult of Modernism is philosophically ridiculous, for the modernity of 1971, say, is very different from the modernity of 1921. One cannot order his soul, or participate in a public order, merely by applauding the will-o'-the-wisp Present (p. 82).

In this connection, Eliot proclaimed himself a "classicist" (as well as a royalist and an Anglo-Catholic, not one of which claims was particularly welcome to his contemporaries). He meant that he lived within Tradition, and that, as Kirk has it, "he stood for right reason, as opposed to obsession with alleged originality, personality, and creativity; for the permanent things, as opposed to the lust for novelty; for normality, as opposed to abnormality" (p. 146).

Moreover, Eliot distrusted what we might call the intellectual democracy of liberalism. He said this about liberalism:

> "[It] tends to release energy rather than accumulate it, to relax, rather than to fortify ... by licensing the opinions of the most foolish, by substituting instruction for education,

by encouraging cleverness rather than wisdom, the upstart rather than the qualified, by fostering a notion of *getting on* to which the alternative is a hopeless apathy. Liberalism can prepare the way for that which is its own negation: the artificial, mechanised or brutalised control which is a desperate remedy for its chaos" (p. 277).

As is frequently (always?) the case with the prophetic imagination, Eliot's political and social concerns sprang from his prior vision of an order that defined and judged our life, one that we ignored or flouted, in our morals and politics and imagination, to our own damnation. In Eliot's case, of course, that order was the biblical accounting of the universe, received and passed on in the Magisterium of the Church. He attributed the disorder and havoc that especially mark our epoch to our having cut the moorings of tradition and dogma that held us to our true center. On point after point, his analysis of the modern situation derives directly from a particular Christian assumption.

For instance, Eliot saw our groping about in aesthetics, political activism, social engineering, and tepid benevolence for answers to the staggering problems of society, and our utter impotence to come to any understanding much less solution, as an index of our loss of the sense of Original Sin:

> If you do away with this struggle, and maintain that by tolerance, benevolence, inoffensiveness, and a redistribution or increase of purchasing power, combined with a devotion, on the part of an elite, to Art, the world will be as good as anyone could require, then you must expect human beings to become more and more vaporous (p. 213).

Again, Eliot might astound us by tracing the fascination with evil and abnormality, in modern fiction, drama, and painting, to a denial of the Incarnation. Kirk says: "If one denies the divine Incarnation, Eliot believed, one must affirm a different though inferior power. The diabolical enters into literature, and into society, when we grow fascinated with 'the *unregenerate* personality' " (p. 215).

Or again, Eliot saw the paradox of the modern effort to liberalize and democratize the human order coexisting with an apparently incorrigible drift toward totalitarianism on the Left as well as the Right, and he suspected that you get this paradox when you try to build a social edifice on any foundation other than religious truth. Kirk quotes Eliot:

> "No scheme for a change of society can be made to appear immediately palatable, except by falsehood . . . until society has become so desperate that it will accept any change." The alternative to a totalist order . . . is a social order founded upon religious truth. "That prospect involves, at least, discipline, inconvenience, and discomfort; but here as hereafter the alternative to hell is purgatory" (p. 417).

Eliot set the utopianism of modern liberal ideology over against the transcendence of Christian revelation. Kirk speaks of Eliot's opposition to "the pseudo-religion of ideology—which inverts the religious symbols of transcendence, promising here and now, upon earth and tomorrow, the perfection of our nature that religion promises through salvation of the soul" (p. 171). The Social Gospel was, for Eliot, "the Great Commandment with its first clause excised".

In his drama as well as in his poetry and his criticism, Eliot tried to introduce once more into contemporary sensibility at least the acknowledgment of the permanent, and of the transcendent that judges us. If he could only, somehow, pluck modern men by the elbow and remind them of this much, perhaps the ground would be that much broken to receive the full message, eventually, of what it is (or Who, really) that judges us. Kirk says, "If he could not redeem the stage from Bernard Shaw, at least he might remind the public that there persist older views of the human condition than the Shavian" (p. 403).

But Eliot never supposed that what he had to say would win the day:

> "We fight for lost causes because we know that our defeat and dismay may be the preface to our successors' victory, though that victory itself will be temporary; we fight rather to keep something alive than in the expectation that anything will triumph" (p. 418).

A desperate frame of mind? Some call it that. But Eliot knew history, tradition, and Christian dogma too well to be able to look with anything more than a tentative and proximate hope on even the very best efforts of society toward amelioration. And he also saw that it is seldom indeed that those efforts can be called "best".

Any Christian, in any century, finds himself in a highly ambiguous relation to his society, knowing as he does that he must applaud and assist in any genuine effort to bring justice and mercy to bear on public life, but knowing at the same time that Christian imagination can never hold out any but the bleakest expectations for these efforts. Somehow we build Babel and not Jerusalem every time. The clarity and keenness of Eliot's criticism of our epoch, if it will not save us (as he knew it would not save him), may at least define and articulate the nature of our (Christians', that is) confrontation with that epoch and, in so doing, may at least save us from mere muddle, which brings it fear. And, for those of us who cannot tackle the entire corpus of Eliot's writing itself, Russell Kirk has done a rare and encouraging service.

Witness for the Faith: What Catholics Can Learn from Billy Graham

The name of Billy Graham is virtually synonymous in the minds of most people with the word evangelization. Here is a man—a Protestant, to be sure—who circles the globe, decade after decade. Literally millions upon millions of men and women, in every continent now, have heard the Christian message as Graham casts it, namely, Jesus Christ is the Son of God, His death on the Cross was the sacrifice for the sins of the world, and His rising from the dead the victory over sin and death. Come to Him—believe in Him—commit yourself in total obedience to Him—accept Him as your Savior—and you will have eternal life. You will be a Christian.

I can think of three responses to Billy Graham that might be put forward by Catholics. On the one hand, we might find many who would be reluctant to endorse him at all since, on their view, his is an attenuated message. He says nothing of the Church, nothing of the sacraments, and nothing of baptism. The stress is all on the individual's conscious acceptance of Jesus Christ. In other words, *sola fides*. These Catholics would nevertheless applaud the clarity and courtesy and vigor with which Graham speaks.

A second Catholic view might be that this sort of boiling-down of the Gospel is inappropriate to our epoch. These people might wish to stress the enormous ambiguity

Originally published in *Crisis*, April 1, 1991. Used with permission.

of modern life and ask just what it is, after all, that constitutes religious conversion, and, further, to raise the question as to whether, in fact, Christians have any warrant
to insist that theirs alone is the salvific word. Shouldn't
we leave Protestants, Jews, Muslims, Buddhists, and the
nonreligious to pursue their own lives according to their
lights? Surely we cannot, at this late date, still be insisting,
like Saint Peter, that "there is no other name under heaven,
given among men, whereby ye must be saved." And furthermore, isn't Graham's stress on heaven grotesque in
an epoch like ours, with its gigantic problems of poverty,
racism, oppression, and injustice in a thousand forms? To
whistle people away to Paradise when they scarcely have
rags to cover their nakedness—isn't this cynicism?

Third, some Catholics might say simply, "Right on!"
After all, he *is* preaching what the Apostles preached,
and anyone who thus converts to genuine faith in Christ
may certainly be shepherded further along by the Catholic Church. I was interested recently to see on television the Roman Catholic primate of Hungary on the
platform at an immense Billy Graham meeting in a sta-
dium near Budapest: surely here was a loud message to
Hungarians—"The Catholic Church, far from distancing
herself from this preaching of the Gospel, is here in open
support of the enterprise."

As you know, Billy Graham appears at the hither end of
a lineage that reaches back through Billy Sunday to D. L.
Moody, Charles G. Finney, and thence to John Wesley
and beyond. A question arises here: Is this kind of evangelism a strictly Reformation phenomenon? Is it a vitiated
Gospel? What, exactly, was the message that, say, Martin of Tours preached among the Gauls? Or Augustine to
Ethelbert and his Kentish subjects in A.D. 597? What did
Cyril and Methodius preach on the banks of the Danube?

Or Saint Philip among the Ethiopians, or Thomas on the banks of the Ganges?

Here is where, frankly, I find myself stumped. I spend hours and hours turning over this question of Catholic evangelization, for this reason: my own nurture was among the evangelicals, and I know two things about them. First, they love the Gospel in all of its thrilling clarity; and second, their conversions are genuine. Of course, any of us can trot out flash-in-the-pan statistics—someone we knew who "went forward" at an evangelistic rally and eventually threw in the sponge on the faith. But too many of us know too many people—and the statistics here may be multiplied literally by millions worldwide—who have done a 180-degree turn in their commitment to Christ, as He was being preached, say, by Billy Graham, and whose lives have been completely changed from that hour. Their own way of phrasing it would be something like this: "I went from darkness to light." Or, "I was born again" (and remember, that phrase was not invented by Jimmy Carter: you can find it in the third chapter of Saint John's Gospel). Or, "My life was completely changed from that day." We all know people like this.

These converts can by no means be located in a handy socioeconomic group or any Appalachian locale. There are poor and rich, white and black, Western and Asian, Oxford graduates and peasants—everyone, cutting across all possible groupings. And what shall we say of the tidings that we hear now from places like Brazil and the Philippines? This was turf that was safely Catholic for four hundred years. But now we find hundreds of thousands of converts to evangelicalism from Catholicism. We may lament a merely cultural or nominal Catholicism in Latin America, for example, but that only highlights the news: masses of people accepting Christ as their Savior, as far as they themselves will tell you, for the first time in their lives.

Former Catholics

Which brings me to a phenomenon much closer to home than Brazil or the Philippines. It is local news. For fifteen years I was on the faculty at Gordon College, an evangelical liberal arts college not far from Boston. Because the students knew of my "high-church" proclivities, those with ecclesiological questions used to find their way to my office. It is the stark, unvarnished truth that many years ago I found that I had lost count of the students who arrived in my office with the following: "I was a Catholic until I was sixteen, then I met Jesus Christ." Or, "I was a Catholic until I was eighteen, then I became a Christian."

I, like you, wanted to paw their arm with, "Well, wait a minute: wouldn't it be more accurate to say that you were eighteen when your faith, which had been nominal until then, sprang up into new vigor and articulateness?" I did not, of course, say this very often, since I knew their stories well enough and knew that they would insist that they really had not been Christians in any but the remotest and feeblest sense of the word until some encounter with Young Life or Campus Crusade or some local Baptist youth group.

There is some energetic communication and evangelization going on around us, and we would be whistling in the dark if we told ourselves that it is all ephemeral or merely cultic. We cannot lump the evangelicals together with groups like the Jehovah's Witnesses, the Mormons, or the Reverend Sun Myung Moon's outfit, since the evangelicals are as briskly Nicene, Chalcedonian, and

Constantinopolitan as the Catholics. Their critique of the cults would be identical with the Catholic critique: you people have added new and unwarranted notions to the apostolic faith.

I spend a great deal of time asking myself just exactly what view I am to take of these ardent brethren of mine. The ecclesiological question matters to me: obviously I would never have bothered to splash across the Tiber if I had felt that it didn't. So it bothers me that they aren't Catholic. One somewhat whimsical notion has flicked across the screen of my imagination from time to time, and I wonder, actually, whether there might not be something to it. It is that, just as the Lord said that he was able to raise up children to Abraham from the stones on the ground, so perhaps what we have in this energetic, intelligent, highly bibliocentric and robust sector of Christendom (evangelicalism, that is) is a phenomenon like that: men and women of faith raised up quite outside of the apostolic lineage, if by that we mean the sacerdotal and episcopal and petrine succession that we believe to be of the *esse* of the Church. Whatever the nuances of our ultimate position on this, it is a phenomenon that no Catholic who proposes to talk seriously about communication and evangelization can quite ignore in our own day.

One question, it seems to me, that follows upon any consideration of the enormous success of Billy Graham and the evangelicals when it comes to attracting all ages and all sorts of people all over the world to the Gospel, is this: Is evangelization *in that sense* an activity that the Catholic Church considers to be appropriate at all? There is no Catholic figure analogous to any of the mass evangelists who have sprung from the Reformation. In our own time, Bishop Sheen was probably the closest analogue. In the early centuries of the Church, of course, something like mass

evangelism certainly took place with the preaching of figures like Martin of Tours or Augustine of Kent, when
whole kingdoms converted. Do we, when we speak of
evangelization, visualize some electrifying Catholic figure
analogous to Billy Graham?

How, exactly, *do* we visualize Catholic evangelism?
What is it, precisely, that we have to say to people, whether
"people" means teenagers whose world is MTV; or Latin
American workers and peasants; or fast-lane, disaffected
Catholic yuppies in Italy bombing along the Autostrada
in their Lamborghinis; or our own parishioners, perhaps,
who if you asked them what is meant by "the gospel"
might mumble awkwardly about trying to be decent.

I have found myself, over the last twenty years or so, in
my musings on this question of evangelism (I was thinking
about it before I became a Catholic), wondering just what
to make of a certain kind of phenomenon that, if it is not
precisely germane to our topic here, at least presents us
with intriguing data. I am speaking of various individuals,
or groups, who have changed the face of the globe by their
"evangel", if we may use this word in some odd contexts.
I would go so far as to say that they have changed history.
Let me give you four examples of what I am talking about.

In the 1950s, when all was still calm, we began to
become aware of a furious young man called Stokeley
Carmichael. He had a message—an angry, uncompromis-
ing, strident message. He was not interested in civilized
"dialogue" or in sweet reason, still less in patience and
prudence. He wanted a whole race of people out from
under oppression, and he was not going to waste time in
committees. I can remember being outraged by his rhetoric and wanting to muffle him. Well, forty years later, we
have, if not quite the world that Carmichael called for, at
least a Himalayan shift in consciousness. Who speaks of

"colored people" now, or even "Negroes"? Carmichael did not bring this about by himself, heaven knows, but he was an early, and a fiery, apostle, and the white world was obliged to listen to him. He got us by the jugular, so to speak. He had an evangel, and he communicated it, and we heard it, by golly.

My second example is Kate Millett (or you can fill in Germaine Greer or Gloria Steinem here if you want). Here was a lady, or rather a *woman* (we choose our words gingerly in this post-Millett era) who dropped a thermonuclear bomb in our laps, and she and her fellow apostles changed history. The English language walks on eggshells now, and all executives and academic deans who do hiring, and all legislators who must speak in public, and anyone who must write a business letter or a brochure, moves along with red lights winking and beeps beeping all around him. Him. There you have it. I said "him", referring to any and all of the above categories of people, and by using that pronoun, I have betrayed myself as one who is not in touch with history. Kate Millett brought something big to pass in the history of human consciousness. She had an evangel, and she communicated it, and we heard it, by golly.

Another example: when I was living in England in 1961, there were four boys with guitars whose hair just touched their ears. Within a very few years these boys, with their hair getting longer and longer, and their clothes funkier and funkier, and their music farther and farther out—these boys had changed the look of the entire globe with a thoroughness to be envied by Alexander of Macedon, Tamurlaine, or Vasco da Gama. There is no street in any city on this planet, and certainly no classroom in any school or university, and scarcely a household, where we cannot see the effects on dress, demeanor, sensibility, imagination, manners, speech, and aspiration wrought by this tiny sodality of boys. They had an evangel, and they communicated it, and we heard it, by golly.

And my fourth example: I was a teenager in the 1940s before I ever even heard the word "homosexual". Many centuries had cloaked the category under the hushed and horror-stricken rubric of "the sin against nature". Dante had the men guilty of sodomy wandering about over burning sand with flakes of fire falling around them. Then when I lived in New York, I discovered that there was something called "the gay world", but it was a hermetically sealed world, with its own positively Byzantine complexities of manners, speech, protocol, and humor. "Straight" people did not know the vocabulary—words like camp and drag and queen and butch and even the word *gay* itself. But all of that changed. It was decided that the time had come. The straight world would jolly well sit up and take notice. Not only that: the straight world would change its entire way of thinking—about sex, about family life, about identity, and about morals. A crusade was launched. They had an evangel, and they communicated it, and we heard it, by golly.

My point, I think, is clear enough by this time. I have adduced four examples of people who broke upon modern consciousness and who did not rest until radical and universal change had taken place. They did not apologize. They did not fawn. They asked and gave no quarter. They never asked us how we felt. They did not bother to find out if we resonated to what they were saying. They never rapped with us and nodded and affirmed us and said, "What we hear you saying is...." They obliged us to hear what they were saying. They did not ask us where we were coming from. They did not try to build bridges. They trumpeted their gospel *at* us. They were, ebulliently, furiously, joyously, unabashedly, even gloriously, themselves, and we danced to their tune before the tango was over.

I can think of one other example here. I am acutely aware of all of the questions raised by my adding this name. I am speaking, of course, of Jesus Christ. He said his piece. It hurt. It scandalized. It infuriated. It outraged. It challenged. But it also promised solace to anyone who labored and was heavy-laden and who would, as he put it, come to him.

Making a Difference

We might object to this juxtaposition of Jesus Christ with Stokeley Carmichael, Kate Millett, the Beatles, and the gay caucus. As with any such analogy, there is only a narrowly limited similarity, in this case, the sense in which all of these people have tweaked humanity by the nose and made it pay attention. I leave to a different forum the question as to which of my examples may have been in any sense salvific, and which calamitous, for the human race.

And I would have to lodge here a demurral of my own that, I should think, any Christian would find himself reaching for, namely, that the gospel, unlike these four "gospels", has always gone forward, not in anger and stridence and harshness, but in weakness and fear and humility, to use Saint Paul's description of his own apostolate. There is a sense in which a Christian, unlike the people I have listed above, must always accept defeat if his hearers won't hear. He may cry out in the streets, be a *vox clamantis in deserto*, appeal to men's intelligence on the Areopagus, speak boldly to Herod the Tetrarch or Caesar, walk a

Via Dolorosa to defeat, or be thrown to the lions. There is no guarantee that he will sweep all before him.

But surely the message to us, what with one thing and another in our own decade—the widespread slumping away of loyalty to the *Magisterium* on the part of the Catholic laity, and the plummet in vocations, and the sheer decibel-level and speed and razzle-dazzle of the messages drowning out the Christian gospel, and the melancholy efforts at shoring up catechesis in our parishes by curricula that will undertake anything in heaven and earth *except* to hail kids abruptly with Christ Jesus the Savior—surely the message to us is, at least: Whatever else you are doing, tell your children, tell your parishioners, tell the yuppies and the paupers and the dying and the disfranchised and the complacent and the perplexed—tell them that God so loved the world that he gave his only-begotten Son that whosoever believeth in him should not perish but have everlasting life.

John Stott: A Catholic Reflection

During the autumn of 2011, there died in England a man whose death aroused worldwide attention. It also occasioned affectionate musings in my own mind.

His name was John Stott. Like the whole evangelical Protestant world—and even, apparently, the English public and the secular media—I knew, and mourned, that a giant had gone from the rest of us who were still left here in this mortal coil. The following remarks do not qualify as biographical in any sense. That has all been done. I cannot offer much in the way of dates and events in his life, even though I knew him for over sixty years. In any case, I need not do so. His life and achievements have been canvassed, scrutinized, and hailed by the media.

He visited in our household when I was a boy. But I know—or perhaps I should say remember—nothing, for example, of his parents, or of the religious flavor of the Stott household, or even of the particulars of his own coming to faith.

He was, perhaps, the godliest man I have ever known, along with my own father. He emerged into a certain public view in the 1940s, I seem to recall, when he began to give talks, often in evangelical university circles. His own world had been the somewhat exalted world of the English public school and Cambridge University. It was the appearance of his early book, *Basic Christianity*, that

Originally published in *Books & Culture*, March/April 2012. Reprinted with permission.

expanded, almost globally, his reputation, again principally in the evangelical Protestant domain. He eventually gained a virtually apostolic eminence, certainly by
no ambition of his own. There seemed to be no remotest tincture of vanity anywhere in his entire being. Like
Enoch, he walked with God. Like Moses, he was meek.
Like Abraham, he was the friend of God. Like Samuel, he
was among those who called on God's name.

Over the years, he and I met and talked now and again.
He was, for one thing, a birdwatcher like my father, and
since I had grown up regaled with prothonotary warblers,
semipalmated plovers, winter wrens, hermit thrushes, and
white-throated sparrows, John and I had much to talk
about in that vein before we embarked, inevitably, on
matters of the faith. He very much admired my father,
who was not only a gentleman of the (very) old school
like Stott himself, but who, much to John's delight, could
both identify the birds and imitate their songs with such
perfection that they would come flitting into the branches
over his head. I remember John once saying that one of
his own keenest hopes was to see the fairy wren some day.
I think he did eventually find one—in Southeast Asia or
somewhere in that part of the map.

As time went on, my own religious itinerary drew me
from my own free-church evangelical moorings to Anglicanism and, thence, to the ancient Catholic Church.
This, of course, might easily have introduced an obstacle
between John and me, since he was, on the surface of
things anyway, a "low-church" Anglican, meaning that
the English Protestant Reformers would have been the
men to whom he looked when it came to matters ecclesiological and, I think, spiritual nurture. I had once asked
him, since I trusted him wholly and looked to him for wisdom, if he could give me the rationale for the Church of

England, thinking he might be able to offer me a substantial ecclesiology in this connection. He said that the Anglican liturgy offered a dignified ordering for public prayer. This appeared, at the time, to be the whole of the point he wished to make. As the decades went on, I gathered that his global ministry in a wide array of ardent Christian groupings had opened his sympathies to such a wide extent that his Anglicanism became less and less important a category in his Christian outlook. Certainly he ceased wearing the clerical collar very early on.

Once when he and I were having lunch together, the topic of the Eucharist arose (I suspect at my own behest). I was still Anglican at the time, but my reading in Church history, and most especially in the Church Fathers, was drawing me inexorably toward the ancient point of view in the matter. The witness of the Fathers, including those who had been pupils of the Apostles themselves, had confronted me with a difficulty. Obviously it was we, that is, the Reformed tradition, who had set on one side the ancient teaching here. Those early witnesses, to a man, held the Eucharist to be, in a mystery, what Saint John's language in chapter 6 of his Gospel would seem to suggest. One finds no notion of symbolic language in this connection in the first-century Church, or in the centuries that followed. (In the ninth century, Paschasius Radbertus and, following him, Ratramnus and Berengar of Tours, and then in due course Ulrich Zwingli, taught that the bread and wine are just that: bread and wine, which view later became the accepted Eucharistic doctrine for Protestantism and *a fortiori* evangelicalism.) Ignatius of Antioch (A.D. 36–107), Justin Martyr (100–165), Irenaeus, Cyprian, Athanasius, Basil, Gregory of Nyssa, Hilary, Ambrose, and Augustine all understood, and taught, that the elements prayed over at the Eucharist do, in fact, become, in a mystery, the Body and Blood of Christ. (Obviously, no chemical analysis of these elements will yield anything other than wheat and grapes, just as no examination of the foetus in Mary's womb will discover anything other than a human child.)

The point aroused titanic controversy in Christendom in the sixteenth century, as we all know. But the scene at lunch with John discloses something of the grace that marked this noble and godly man. At no point did the conversation become "difficult". Everyone who knew John will already know this.

What I had in mind as I sought his understanding in the matter was that Ignatius of Antioch, for example, apparently the pupil of the Apostle John himself, puts things this way: "Mark ye those who hold strange doctrines touching the grace of Jesus which came to us, how they are contrary to the mind of God.... They allow not that the Eucharist is the flesh of our Saviour Jesus Christ which flesh suffered for our sins...." Or Justin Martyr (second century): "We do not receive these as common bread.... [T]he food which has been eucharized by the word of prayer from him is the flesh and blood of the Incarnate Jesus." Augustine, much later, says, "That Bread which you see on the altar, having been sanctified by the word of God, is the Body of Christ. That chalice, or rather, what is in that chalice, having been sanctified by the word of God, is the Blood of Christ."

Being young, I was curious as to why John followed those later gentlemen in the matter of the Eucharist, rather than the testimony of the early Fathers. He did not argue with me. I think that would have seemed churlish to him. He simply remarked quietly, "We do not see it that way", and we turned to other topics.

As time has gone on, I as a Roman Catholic would, of course, hold an entire stock of views that might scandalize the evangelical world of which John Stott might be thought of as the very icon. But "scandalize" is not a word that would crop up in any consideration of this man, formed as he was by true gentility but, more than that, formed as he was by Grace. There was nothing but Charity in his responses to people because, of course, there was nothing left in his soul but that Charity, the greatest of all gifts on Saint Paul's view.

What views? The nature of the Church and the apostolical succession of the episcopacy as the Apostles and Fathers shaped it in accord with what they understood to be scriptural; the Mass; the Marian mystery, set altogether on one side by evangelicalism; the Communion of the Saints, drawing as it does on Christ's death and Resurrection which, by overthrowing the tyranny of death, brings those on pilgrimage here on earth into one living intercessory body with our High Priest and with those who are now before the Throne; and the whole understanding of faith which frequently obstructs fellowship between Catholic and Reformed believers.

I, as a Catholic man, and as a friend of John Stott at whose feet I sit in so many matters, naturally find myself ferreting away at the sort of questions that follow upon the above matters. *How can this noble, gigantic, and holy man demur on so many matters that would seem to have the imprimatur of the ancient Fathers?*

That would be a shrill and scrappy way of putting the question. But one cannot quite put it that way. In the presence of manifest holiness, one finds oneself hesitant. John Stott scrutinizes me, not I him.

Clearly the riddle touches on the mystery of the Church. In the West, it was divided, apparently irreparably, in the sixteenth century. A remorseless and juridical logic would insist upon a verdict that would expose one side or the other as *wrong*: "If so and so is the case—this doctrine or that one—then any demurral constitutes heresy." Any Catholic and any Protestant is, on that level, bound to see things that way, no matter how valiantly he struggles in his inner man with Charity. In a different essay, and with a lesser man than John Stott, I might be tempted to wax energetic. Instead, I leave the matter as the mere account of my friendship with that man of God.

Clyde S. Kilby

During the autumn of my first year at Wheaton College, my best and oldest friend began to harry me with news of an Intro to Lit course he was taking. "Tom, you must sign up for a course with this man Kilby. He is a philosopher! He is a great man! It's unbelievable!" and so forth.

Because I respected my friend's judgment, I did so. I signed in to a course in the Romantic poets—Wordsworth & co.

Very soon I felt like the Queen of Sheba upon visiting Solomon: the half had not been told me.

Here was this man (who took a wicked [I suspect] delight in billing himself as a Mississippi cracker and talked as though he were in a flat-bottomed rowboat with some local, fishing in a bayou), retailing what one very soon came to recognize as luminous and blissful Truth. We were all agog. The boy sitting next to me whispered to me at one point, "I think I'm going to break out in boils"— boils of rapture, it may be said.

And the thing about it all was that Kilby was clearly passionately in love with the vision of things that he so unobtrusively offered for our delectation. It was not unusual to find him stumped—groping for words, not because he was inarticulate, or because his vocabulary was inadequate, but because he himself was ravished by the vista opened up by Wordsworth or Keats.

Previously unpublished essay. Published by permission of the Marion E. Wade Center, Wheaton College, Illinois.

After this I signed up for every course that Kilby taught. And, over the next three years, I found myself with increasing frequency at the second-floor flat where he lived with his wife, who herself we soon recognized to be the very icon of the good woman. They were childless, but heaven knows how many of us are still walking about owing our very souls to these two. You would ring the doorbell and push open the door downstairs, and presently came exclamations of pure delight from above, as though nothing in the world could have pleased them more than a visit from this acolyte. As you went up the stairs (if it was evening), you could hear the strains of a Mozart horn concerto, and here they would be, laughing and chortling with welcome, at the top of the stairs. Beautiful little polychrome porcelain figures (they had a name that I forget) dotted the shelves among the books in the living room, and very often a telltale aroma of lovely pastries came in from the kitchen.

There was nothing highbrow about their demeanor (although I would argue that they both were, despite themselves, true highbrows). They were "salt of the earth". Hour after hour we listened to BBC tapes of Winnie the Pooh and *The Wind in the Willows*. He also had some recordings, from the 1920s, of two old cronies in hilarious dialogue, which recordings would now be banned by a world gone politically correct.

I once dedicated a book to Kilby, with the inscription, "For Dr. Kilby, who took my arm and said, 'Look.'" I cannot say it better than that now. He threw open the shutters at the "magic casement, opening on the foam / Of perilous seas, in faery lands forlorn." He pointed to the things that had troubled the very marrow in one's bones, but for which one had never had the vocabulary to summon into visibility.

When the Narnia books came out, and then when we all stumbled upon Tolkien and Charles Williams, his ecstasy knew no bounds. He was a pied piper leading us all, not into the dark mountainside, but out onto vistas of Joy—and one must capitalize that.

And with all of this, he and his wife were your archetypal "simple Christians", by which I mean the sort of person Our Lord meant when he said "Except ye be converted and become as little children...." I think he suffered the pains of the damned over some of the high jinks that marked the rather hectic religion abroad at Wheaton in those days: but in his years of retirement, he found solace in the ancient liturgy of the Church, which was balm to his soul, I know.

I am happy to pay—however inadequately—some minuscule fraction of my incalculable debt to this man. I often wonder if the souls in Paradise are vouchsafed any glimpse of the harvest that accrues to their work here on earth. I hope so.

In Middle Earth: J. R. R. Tolkien

One hundred and ten years ago, J. R. R. Tolkien was born, a unique figure in twentieth-century literature. On the occasion of the release of the first film taken from The Lord of the Rings, *we offer here an interview with the American professor Thomas Howard, a great scholar of Tolkien's work. "A Catholic masterpiece", "analogy with life", the struggle between good and evil ...*

Thomas Howard taught English literature for twenty-five years at St John's Seminary in Brighton, Massachusetts, until 1998. A convert from Evangelical Protestantism, Howard is the author of numerous works, including the book *Evangelical Is Not Enough*. He was a friend of C. S. Lewis and an expert on the work of Charles Williams, both of whom, along with Tolkien, were members of The Inklings. Howard recently taught a course on *The Lord of the Rings* at the International Theological Institute in Gaming, Austria.

Above all, does it make sense to speak of *The Lord of the Rings* as a "Catholic masterpiece"? Or, after the attempts made by the right and the left to co-opt the work, does one not run the danger of "baptizing" what is principally a (most beautiful) story?

Originally published in *Traces*, edited by Michael Waldstein and Fabrizio Begossi, February 2002. Used by permission.

Both on the surface of things, and at a profound level, we are entitled to speak of *The Lord of the Rings* as a "Catholic masterpiece". Our first warrant is Tolkien himself, who said that he could not have written the saga if he were not a Catholic. He also identified various elements of the narrative as specifically analogous to Catholic categories (in a conversation with Clyde Kilby, he remarked that he thought Gandalf was probably an angel). At the deepest level, of course, we find that the entire fabric of Middle Earth is 100 percent recognizable to any serious Catholic. Goodness and evil, for example, are identical in both Middle Earth and in our world as it is understood by the Church. Evil is parasitical and has no function other than to destroy the good solidity and beauty that mark the creation. Gollum would be a case in point: he used to be a hobbit-like creature, but evil has reduced him to a hissing, snarling, scorched shard of any good "hobbit-ness". Likewise with the landscape of Mordor: evil has blasted all fruitful and beautiful features, and we are left with ash heaps and slime.

"Vicarious" suffering is also, of course, central to the saga, as it is for Catholicism: the Company of the Ring endure what they endure for the sake of the salvation of the world, so to speak. This bespeaks what is central to our own story, namely, Our Lord's suffering, and that of the saints, on behalf of fallen humanity. One caveat: Tolkien disliked allegory most sedulously (he thought Lewis' Narnia was too allegorical), so there is, in fact, the danger of "baptizing" the whole thing too eagerly. Frodo is not Christ, nor is Aragorn (the unknown, but legitimate, returning king). Galadriel is not an allegory for Our Lady, pure and lovely though she may be. But, at the end of the day, we may, with Tolkien's approval, speak of the saga as a Catholic masterpiece. A postscript to this might be the observation that no Protestant could conceivably have written this saga, since it is profoundly "sacramental". That is, redemption is achieved wholly via physical means—cf. the Incarnation, Golgotha, the Resurrection, and the Ascension—and the tale is sprinkled with "sacramentals", such as lembas, athelas, Galadriel's phial of light, mithril, etc.

More than the communication of a hidden message, the main value of the book seems to be that of being a great allegory of life. As C. S. Lewis said, "no other world is so obviously objective" as that created by Tolkien: men are men in a truer way, friends more friends than we often experience in daily life. In sum: reality in transparence. How is it possible that a fantasy-world brings us close to the nature of things?

Again, the word *allegory* would make Tolkien unhappy. *Analogy* would please him more. Characters and places and objects in his saga are not symbols, or allegories, of anything at all. They are what they are, for a start. But it may also be said that they are "cases in point" of this or that, which we recognize from our Primary World over here. Again, Gollum is not a symbol of a soul swiftly en route to final damnation: he is a case in point, recognizable from our world, of what evil in fact does to a creature. The only difference between the two worlds is that, in Middle Earth, we get to see the difference, whereas in our story one may "smile and smile, and be a villain" (*Othello*). The sense in which such a "fantasy" world, paradoxically, brings us closer to the real nature of things in our own world (whereas to a superficial observer such fantasy might seem the most unabashed escapism) is that this sort of narrative gives us distance and perspective. It takes us by surprise. Our guard is down. I once asked Lewis why the Passion of Aslan (cf. *The Narnian Chronicles*) moved me more than the Crucifixion story, when I knew perfectly well that Aslan is "only" a fantasy. Lewis replied that when I read the Gospel, all my "religious" expectations are up and quivering ("I *ought* to feel a certain response, namely, gratitude and perhaps grief"), whereas I am taken unawares by the Passion of Aslan and hence may find myself overwhelmed. Likewise, we find, to our surprise, that the very rocks, water, forests, and hamlets of Middle Earth quicken our capacity to "see" rocks, water, and so forth, in our own world. How many of us have said, in the course of a mountain walk, "Why—this is almost good enough to be Middle Earth!"

Gandalf, the wizard, is surely one of the most fascinating figures created by Tolkien, besides being certainly the most powerful among those that fight for the good in Middle Earth. At root, he seems to be a divinity that has assumed the limits of the human form. In the first part of the trilogy he dies (fighting with a demonic being from the bowels of the earth) in order to rise again purified. Why does Gandalf spend his energies above all in order that everybody commits himself freely in the fight against evil?

Gandalf spends his titanic energies in this selfless way because that is "how things are", so to speak. That is, one of the mysteries at the heart of things (in our world; in Middle Earth) is that the Good must be chosen, not imposed. It seems to be a property of the Good—this freedom. Coercion cannot bring anyone, be he man or elf, to goodness. Gandalf knows this. Hence, he can only do so much. He cannot wave his wand and make the Ring go away or make Saruman good again. He is a servant of the Good, not its owner. It might also be pointed out here, with reference to the phrasing of the question, that we cannot say that Gandalf "dies". He "descends to the lower parts of the earth", certainly, in his fight with the Balrog. And in his account of this later on, he touches sketchily on the experience entailed—cf. The Harrowing of Hell in our story. But Tolkien stops short of telling us that Gandalf dies.

Frodo has received the Ring, and so it is his task to provide for its destruction. Gandalf, who would be certainly more qualified, never seeks to replace him, but exhorts him to bring his task to conclusion, likewise the others in "the Fellowship of the Ring". In the last stage of the ascent to the Crack of Doom, Frodo is no longer able to go on, and Sam, who cannot bear the "burden" in his place even for a few feet, takes his friend on his back. Friendship and task: Is there a connection between them? And then there is the tender friendship that binds the hobbits together. What is friendship in *The Lord of the Rings*?

Surely friendship in *The Lord of the Rings* would be akin to what Lewis discusses under the category "phileo" in *The Four Loves*. It is one of the manifestations of love. There could be no friendship among orcs or the Dark Riders. Sauron loathes his minions. But Goodness depends, as it were, on this disinterested bond between Frodo and Sam, or among all the members of the Fellowship, since it is a property of true felicity (deriving from Goodness) that we "bear one another's burdens and so fulfill the law of"— Christ, in our story—the Good, in Middle Earth. There is a twofold appropriateness, surely, to Frodo's being obliged to be the Ringbearer: 1) it will fool Sauron, who would sneer at the very notion of halflings undertaking such a daunting task; 2) God has chosen the weak things of this world to confound the strong (and we may translate this into Tolkien-esque terms with very little trouble). Gandalf's very power would be the danger point if he were the Ringbearer—as he and Galadriel and Elrond all recognize about themselves. Hobbits are not, by nature, much interested in power, so there is an aspect of their nature that "cooperates with" grace—or whatever we would like to call grace in the saga.

One of the most significant omissions Peter Jackson made in the film is cutting out Tom Bombadil entirely. What does *The Lord of the Rings* lose with this primeval man, without original sin, and his surprising relation to nature?

The film misses a very great deal in omitting Tom Bombadil. But on the other hand, he would, I think, elude all the resources of cinema if the greatest genius of a director undertook to show us Tom. The cinematic result would be a sad travesty of the sheer joy, freedom, and merriment of Tom.

There are qualities that will yield themselves only to certain forms (certain emotions can be caught only when the soprano hits the high A-moll; certain aspects of the ineffable are to be descried in the arches of Chartres and in no other modality; certain properties of sorrow find their unique epiphany in the *Pietà*). Cinema would fail—perhaps any conceivable visual mode would fail—to bespeak Tom Bombadil. What is lost to the film, of course, is precisely Tom's glorious and merry innocence. He shares some qualities with the unfallen Adam, for example, he is the "master" of the Old Forest, not its owner. Tolkien judged that his tale needed this icon of sheer, unsullied goodness to stand in stark contrast to all the evil abroad in the land. Good as are Gandalf, Elrond, Galadriel, and Treebeard, not to mention the hobbits, in Bombadil we have a particular epiphany of sheer goodness.

Boromir, Saruman, and Gollum are some examples of characters of various measure being corrupted by the Ring. Its power seems to act upon a predisposition present in all, including Frodo, perverting a desire that is at root positive. What is the temptation of the Ring?

The Ring, for Middle Earth, must be in some aspects analogous to the "fruit" in Eden. That is, its promise is to make you wise and powerful—to raise you above your particular station (the Middle Ages would have called it your "estate") and make you a god. The good that may lie at the root of this vulnerability would be the sense that any intelligent creature—hobbit, elf, or man—would have of the dignity that attaches to his being. The trouble is that this sense very quickly turns to "ambition" in the old sense of one's wishing to insinuate himself illegitimately up the hierarchical ladder, hence evincing a state of discontent with the state appointed to him. "Better to reign in hell than serve in heaven", says Milton's Satan; and thus say Sauron, Saruman, and even Gollum, although his imagination seems to fall pitiably short of anything so lofty as dominion. He just wants his "precious". If Adam wants to be a god, he misses tragically the majesty that attaches to "man"—and presumably if an archangel is eaten up with the ambition to be a domination or a princedom, he is in trouble. An archangel, or a hobbit, or one of the Valar, carries out its glorious destiny by being just that, just as a golden retriever carries about in his being the unique excellence that attaches to golden retrievers and not to eagles.

In the novel, the divine element never participates in the action, and references to it are obscure for those who have not read *The Silmarillion*. Besides, the characters do not have religious attitudes. And yet the wisest among them resist condemning anyone without appeal, because before the end everyone "has a part to recite". The world seems to be ordered according to a plan. What is there, beyond the sea, in the West, and what importance does it have?

The apparent absence of any supreme being ordering things for the Good naturally puzzles many readers of the Trilogy. "God" never intervenes. The characters seem to be left to their own powers and do the best they can against Evil. This is a piece of genius on Tolkien's part. In lesser fairy tales, there is usually some talisman that will do the trick. In Middle Earth, there is not. This is because Tolkien's tale is located on an infinitely higher and more serious level than your Rapunzels and Rumplestiltzkins.

Those tales are fetching, but Tolkien's tale is as serious as our own story. And one of the baffling aspects of our story is "the silence of God". The Ring Company (like the saints in our story) have to muddle along, doing the best they can with their resources, without the luxury of some ready hocus-pocus that will dissolve Dark Riders or send orcs packing. Our story, often, seems to us mortals to be like this. Where is God? And Tolkien's characters are not "religious". No one says his prayers (there is one instance where Faramir and company pause before they eat, but this is, I think, as close as we get to prayer, unless the cry "O Elbereth! Gilthoniel!" may be thus understood). Readers may think the following observation somewhat capricious, but, as a latecomer to Catholicism myself, I recognize in this inarticulateness as to "faith" on the part of the characters a very Catholic quality. Catholics don't chat about the faith ordinarily. Protestants, especially evangelical Protestants, are stumped by this muteness. Catholics must not be believers, they think, if they can't croak out at least some "testimony" to their faith. But Tolkien, as a cradle Catholic, would not, nay, could not, have his characters forever nattering about God, any more than he (Tolkien himself) could have any part of a testimony meeting. The fugitive references to the West, and the spectacle of the elves "passing, passing, passing" to the West, tincture the whole narrative with the tincture of glory. Not here, not here, the word seems to be, is your ultimate home. Beautiful and appealing as the Shire, Rivendell, or Lothlorien may be, even they are not the final locale of felicity. All must go West. Here again, Tolkien has made the very fabric of his story virtually indistinguishable from the fabric of ours and, hence, has gained a seriousness otherwise impossible.

What role has Tolkien played in twentieth-century European literature, particularly in Catholic literature?

Tolkien has played a role in twentieth-century European literature—indeed, world literature—that has infuriated the critics. He has simply ignored the entire tradition of fiction that has been sovereign since the eighteenth century, that is, the tradition of "realism" and the psychological novel. He has reached back to the most ancient and noble mode of narrative, namely, the Epic. Cartesian man has no categories with which to cope with this sort of thing, other than to patronize it as "primitive" or "frivolous". For a Catholic, Tolkien's work comes like a freshet of clear glacier water into a noisome and stinking fen, bringing with it all the glories that vanished with the advent of modernity—such glories as majesty, solemnity, ineffability, awe, purity, sanctity, heroism, and glory itself. Descartes and Hume would have a difficult time accounting for glory via the vocabulary they chose for themselves, and their unhappy descendants have no remote notion of what has been lost. Tolkien may have re-introduced the pauper-children of modernity to Glory.

A Note on the Isenheim Altarpiece

Most of us will have seen, if only in reproductions, Matthias Grunewald's terrible (I say that circumspectly) painting of the crucifixion that is commonly known now as the *Isenheim Altarpiece*. It is as much as one can do to look at it at all. Benedict XVI calls it "perhaps the most moving painting of the crucifixion to be found in all Christendom" and goes on to speak of Our Lord, "who, by his suffering, had become one with all the suffering of history".

The following is a line of thought that could very quickly sink into bathos. Nevertheless, it does follow from what the Church believes about the mystery of that suffering: that no suffering was excluded from his suffering, even the suffering of animals.

I have brisk Christian friends who stiffen when this sort of thing is mooted, their idea being that sentimentalism will very soon swamp all efforts to carry the topic forward with any clarity. Certainly we all have some sympathy with such misgivings, since animals, and most notably their sufferings, do call forth affections that can, indeed, swamp us all. I speak as one who drops shameless tears as we bury our dogs and cats and can scarcely visit zoos, worrying about the bars. On the other hand, I do not beleaguer the people who wear fur coats or march in behalf of snail darters and sloths.

But what about the suffering of animals in connection with the suffering of Christ? Does it not threaten to trivialize this great mystery if we veer off into this byway?

Originally published in *Crisis*, June 1, 2007. Reprinted with permission.

I do not think so, and I think the Church might agree. We are admittedly in the region of speculation, and hence at least two rules preside over any discussion here: First, we cannot wax dogmatic; and second, we cannot linger or allow our considerations to distract us for very long from the one thing that must occupy us above all else, namely, charity.

Having acknowledged this, what can we say? For one thing, we know that "the whole creation groans and travails" because of our sin. The sun hid its face, and the rocks split at Golgotha. Milton was surely onto something when he said that "earth felt the wound" in Eden when we mortals sinned. The very time went out of joint, to bring Hamlet into it. It is most certainly not the animals' fault that they suffer.

Once in a film I saw a dying hippopotamus, with drying froth at her mouth, stagger across endless baked clay in a drought. No water. Or, at a zoo, a golden eagle sitting, alert, looking sharply about, in an outdoor cage just wide enough for her body. No wingspread at all. Or, in my own neighborhood, in the house of some people I know, a Dalmatian whom they disliked, chained in a cellar, unfed, in the dark. I tried to intervene and got my fingers burned.

Does the most marble-hearted of us suppose, for one instant, that the God who made these noble creatures will say to a single one of them at the Last Day, "Oh. Yes. That was a pity, to be sure. But that was just your bad luck. It had nothing to do with Redemption." (I know: There's no resurrection for animals. No. Certainly not. Certainly not ...) I am on tricky (and very nonmagisterial) ground here, and I will not contest the point with anyone. I can only appeal to what we do know of God, not to what we don't know.

Ecce, Agnus Dei qui tollis peccata mundi. What vast toll of suffering did he take on with that? Are we sure what he did not take on? Saint Paul says that the whole creation groans, waiting for the redemption. It is worth pondering. The next time you hear the Kyrie at the hands of Victoria, Tallis, Palestrina, Bach, Mozart, or Gorecki, as you pray it for yourself and for us all, you might say one prayer for the animals. It won't hurt.

(1) Modern Drama:
Its Religious Sources

There has never been a very happy concordat between Protestant forms of religion and the theatre, and it is not hard to see why.

The Reformation, with its variants in Puritanism and Pietism, insisted on purity of heart and on a weaning of the believer away from this world with all of its spectacle and dazzle. Thus Protestantism has at the center of its imagination the preaching of the Word. Its emphasis is on the unseen realm as the locale of the Reality that we encounter and celebrate in religion. It is the Bible, the worship of the heart, and the fellowship in the believing community that are held to be important; and it does not take much outward *show* (goes the argument) to keep these things alive. Preaching, praying, singing, witnessing: these are eminently "Protestant" activities.

The theatre, on the other hand, has not (let's face it) ordinarily been a seedbed of such virtues as purity of heart, simplicity, or faith. The world of the theatre has, in virtually every society, been a world marked by tumult, indulgence, opulence, and cynicism. The powder and lace cuffs and scandal, the snuffboxes and fans and badinage, the silvery laughter and boudoirs and concupiscence that we attach in our imaginations to the late seventeenth- and eighteenth-century theatre in London and Paris—it's not

Originally published in *Eternity*, July 1975, 38. Reprinted with permission.

all a fiction. It really was like that, and people of God did not ordinarily frequent those stalls and drawing rooms.

So that Protestants, looking at drama, have got to peer over some high barriers. But it is especially interesting for Christians to note the phenomenon of mediaeval drama, for it was *in the Church* that drama was revived after centuries of silence. (At first glance, mediaeval drama may appear to be a hopelessly dusty and crabbed topic. But give it a second chance!)

Those barriers to drama are not so high for the Catholic eye—not because Catholicism (and the Church in the Middle Ages, the mediaeval Church, *was* Catholic) has never taught or celebrated the moral chaos that sooner or later attaches to the theatre world, but rather because the Catholic religion has at the center of its imagination an assumption that is also at work in drama. That assumption is the principle of *enactment*.

The principle manifests itself in this way: in the liturgy, that is to say, the Mass, the entire Gospel is enacted in word and movement and ceremony, each time the celebration occurs. The liturgy is an act, not an "experience". It is held to be the act whereby the believing community marks, celebrates, and participates in the whole drama of salvation, and all the events attending that drama are enacted by the various rites and ceremonies.

From the Introit, with the procession approaching the altar chanting a hymn of approach to God, and the Kyrie, when the congregation sings "Lord, have mercy upon us", right through to the Sanctus ("Holy, Holy, Holy") and the Benedictus ("Blessed is he that cometh in the Name of the Lord"—sung immediately before the bread is consecrated), and then the Communion itself: it is all a great enactment of what Christians believe. The idea is that, during this enactment, time is, as it were, suspended, so that what happened "back there" in history is made immediately present to the imagination of the faithful.

The whole ritual is carried forward by means of music (chant, canticle, and hymn), movement (procession, genuflecting, kneeling, standing), word (the reading and the preaching of the Scriptures), color (the rich vestments, each garment of which is itself symbolic of some aspect of the gospel story), and smell (incense). The idea at work is that the Gospel is something that addresses more than our thinking minds. Because we are more than thinking creatures, we need to be hailed with more than exhortation and preaching. *All* of our being—our bodies, with all of their faculties—need to be brought into play. Hence the music and movement and incense, and so forth. Protestants, of course, affirm this principle up to a point: they sometimes kneel in prayer or bow their heads, and these are simply bodily gestures acknowledging unseen realities.

So: the principle of enactment. It was from this principle that drama arose, quite naturally, in the mediaeval Church.

(2) Church and Drama—
"Off and Running"

In last month's article, the liturgical background for the rise of drama in the mediaeval Church was sketched in. The idea was that, for people already accustomed, in the liturgy, to the principle of *enactment* (the liturgy is, in fact, an enactment of the Gospel), there is nothing odd or unnatural about the use of drama in worship.

But besides the obvious liturgical matrix from which drama arose in the mediaeval Church, there was also a lively tradition of preaching that may be thought of as a *forerunner of the drama*.

Since very few people were literate until the sixteenth century and afterward, religious instruction depended mainly on what the clergy told the people. Hence preaching was an enormously important activity in the Middle Ages. But because of the illiteracy and ignorance of much of the local parish clergy, religious instruction became more and more meagre over the centuries, until the two mendicant orders of friars, the Franciscans and the Dominicans, arose in the thirteenth century. They took on the burden of preaching, the way various extra-parochial groups nowadays, such as InterVarsity and Young Life, help in the nurture of the faithful.

In any case, preaching in the Middle Ages became a vigorous and vivid activity. Preachers would get carried

Originally published in *Eternity*, August 1975, 35–36. Reprinted with permission.

away telling the biblical stories, virtually carrying on one-man shows in the pulpit. And not only in the pulpit, but on *scaffaldi*, set up in the open air where they could attract the attention of the busy market crowds and passersby, they offered their homiletic wares.

But the first actual "drama", if we discount the mime and histrionics of the enthusiastic friars and pastors, was a little "trope", or embellishment, in the Easter liturgy, called the *Quem quaeritis* ("Whom seek ye?"). It was a four-line exchange giving the dialogue at the empty tomb between the Marys and the angels.

Sometime in the ninth century, this dialogue was prefaced to the Introit for the Mass of Easter, representing a small departure from the prescribed text for the Mass. Then the trope became attached to the office of Matins, which is the first service of the canonical "hours", and precedes Mass. Here the liberty was taken of adding a bit of acting by having two members of the choir (they were monks) appear in white robes at one side of the altar representing angels, and two or three in black, representing the women, appear at the other side.

It was, as we can well fancy, a most dramatic moment in the cloister at dawn on Easter morning. Here is part of the instruction for the trope, taken from the *Regularis Concordia* (an appendix to the monastic rule of Saint Benedict) drawn up by Saint Ethelwold, Bishop of Winchester in the tenth century:

> While the third lesson is being sung, let four of the brethren vest themselves, one of whom, vested in an alb, is to enter as if to participate in the service. But let him unnoticed go to the place of the sepulchre, and there sit quietly holding a palm in his hand. While the third responsory is being celebrated, let the remaining three follow, and

be vested in copes, and bear in their hands thuribles with incense, and advancing tentatively as though uncertainly seeking for something, let them come before the place of the sepulchre. [Quoted in V. F. Hopper and G. B. Lahey, eds., *Mediaeval Mysteries, Moralities, and Interludes.*]

The instructions go on to direct the whole exchange, concluding when the Prior, "sharing in their jubilation at the triumph of our King, who in conquering death rose again, begins the hymn *Te Deum Laudamus*. After this has begun, let all the bells be rung together."

Bit by bit, the scene was lengthened and elaborated, with the dialogue growing longer and longer, with more characters appearing—Peter and John racing to the sepulchre, for example. Then, naturally enough, a similar sort of thing was introduced at Christmas, with shepherds coming to adore the Child; then the Magi, with all the opulence of costume and retinue that they suggest, then Herod, and the Slaughter of the Innocents—and the Church was off and running with drama!

(3) Drama in the Marketplaces

In the last column, we looked at the beginnings of mediaeval drama in certain additions to the liturgy, mainly the scene at the empty tomb on Easter, with the angels and the women being represented by choir members on each side of the altar; then the elaboration of this to include other scriptural episodes such as the visit of the shepherds, the Magi, Herod, et cetera.

No one knows exactly how the transition came about from these liturgical "tropes" to the much more elaborate forms of drama that later became popular in the fourteenth century. But the fact is that, by the middle of the fourteenth century, there was an elaborate kind of drama afoot in England, quite different from what we moderns think of as theatre, but drama nonetheless.

The plays, developing somehow from the originally simple tableaux included in the liturgy, eventually landed outside the churches, either in the churchyard, in the streets and meadows, or in the marketplace. They took the form of "cycles", that is, sequences of short scenes representing the history of redemption, from the Fall of Lucifer, through the Creation, the Fall, Abel, Noah, Abraham, Balaam (!), and the Prophets, to the Nativity, the Passion, Crucifixion, Resurrection, Ascension, and Last Judgment. In other words, all the great doctrines were enacted for the people to see.

Originally published in *Eternity*, September 1975, 49–50. Reprinted with permission.

The responsibility for these plays seems to have passed from the clergy to the laity somewhere in there, and the trade guilds are the groups who presented the various scenes. There is a (to us) slightly humorous assigning of certain scenes to certain guilds: the shipwrights did Noah; the bakers, the Last Supper; the vintners, the miracle at Cana; the goldsmiths, the Magi; the butchers, the Crucifixion, and so forth.

The pageants (for they were really this, rather than full-fledged drama) were presented in one of two ways. If a fixed location, such as the churchyard or the cathedral green, were chosen, there would be a stage of sorts, with props, and the sequence would be performed much as we see a play today on a given stage. The other method was a movable process. Here there would be a number of locations designated throughout the city, and wagons with stages built on them would lumber along from location to location.

So, for instance, wagon 1, say, with the fall of Lucifer, would begin at location 1. Then, when the skit had been performed, it would move along to location 2, and wagon 2 would then move into location 1, and so forth. This way a person could stay in the same spot and witness the entire drama of salvation, episode by episode, as the procession moved through the city.

It is generally supposed that this outdoor performance of the cycles was somehow connected early with the Feast of Corpus Christi. This is the feast commemorating the institution of the Holy Eucharist, and it is celebrated on the Thursday after Trinity Sunday. (Maundy Thursday would be the obvious time to mark the feast, since that is the day of the Last Supper; but it was held that the celebration would divert attention from the mysteries of the Passion itself, so the feast was moved to the first possible

Thursday after Easter). The feast became widespread in England early in the fourteenth century and was marked by tremendous processions of the Blessed Sacrament through the city streets. Many scholars believe that the cycles were attached to this procession.

We can well imagine the festivity and fun that attended these occasions. The day was a holiday, of course, with all the excitement that goes along with that. And there was the liturgical procession through the streets, with banners and incense and vestments and chant. And then the tradesmen's wagons rumbling up with God and the devil and all the host of heaven aboard.

Naturally and inevitably, a certain amount of humor came to mark the pageants: pots and pans were rattled and kettles smoked to represent hell; the devils were there with cloven hoofs, tails, horns, and all, acting like asses (mediaeval theology held that evil is, ultimately, inane); God was there, valetudinarian and august in white beard; Adam and Eve in tight-fitting white leather to suggest nudity; Noah doing his best to corral his shrewish wife; and so forth.

The whole spectacle is an astonishing and delightful one to us who labor along in a century that knows no such commonalty of belief as would be required in a society to make this sort of celebration possible. In our time, would-be Christian dramatists and Christian critics worry at the question of how to give dramatic shape to the Christian vision in a secular age. T. S. Eliot and a few others have managed it, in a way. If one is enthusiastic about the notion of Christian drama, the fourteenth century will look positively golden.

(4) The End of the Play—
Heaven or Hell

Historians of the drama in England often speak of three types of drama that arose in the latter Middle Ages: the mystery plays, which were the cycles of biblical episodes we spoke of last month; the miracle plays, which concerned saints' lives; and the morality plays, which had for their characters allegorical figures such as Everyman, Death, Good Deeds, and so forth, and presented situations dramatizing moral choices familiar to Christians.

To a modern observer, the plays seem nakedly didactic, and this is a point against them from our point of view. For reasons that we might do well to look into, we become skittish if we think an author or a playwright is preaching at us. Insofar as there is any "message" at all in a book or a play or a film, we don't want to hear about it in straight lines from the characters' mouths. It must be diffused throughout the whole warp and woof of the fabric of the drama.

But not so for the Middle Ages. The mystery, miracle, and morality plays of the fourteenth and fifteenth centuries were not the slightest bit reticent about articulating plain old dogma and showing this dogma unmistakably at work in the outcome of men's choices. Salvation and damnation were very much in the cards, and you ended up in

Originally published in *Eternity*, October 1975, 62, 66, 83. Reprinted with permission.

either one state or the other, period. (One of the indexes of how far we have moved from this brave frame of mind, surely, is our reluctance to speak very forcibly, certainly in attempts at fiction and drama, of the categories of salvation and damnation, or heaven and hell. C. S. Lewis and Charles Williams have done it vividly enough via mythic fantastic modes; and perhaps Flannery O'Connor has done it in her fiction.)

In any case, the plays were unabashedly didactic. Unlike the theatre of the modern world, from the Restoration of the seventeenth century on forward, mediaeval theatre (it was not "Theatre", of course) applauded virtue and deplored sin. It did this by using Bible stories.

One of the best known, perhaps, of the mystery plays is *Abraham and Isaac*. A modern viewer would be struck by its fidelity to the biblical story. In the past decade, we have had *Jesus Christ Superstar* and *Godspell* and, before that, *J.B.* In each of these, the dramatist has felt free to make the characters over, one might say, into modern men. But in the play *Abraham and Isaac*, the simplicity of the narrative in Genesis is preserved.

Furthermore, since Christians in the Middle Ages, like their evangelical descendants, took a highly typological view of the Old Testament, seeing in every episode some sort of foreshadowing and type of Christ, the dramatist was confined by the typology involved, beyond the mere Genesis story. That is, since Abraham is a type of the obedient servant and a type of the willing victim Christ, there can be no question of working up any dramatic fireworks by having either of them rage against the decree of heaven. Their obedience would present problems for a modern, or perhaps even an Elizabethan, dramatist, since it is hard to come up with the necessary "complication" to the plot, and the corollary dramatic zip if you have passive characters.

But this play brings it off, simply and beautifully, by dramatizing the anguish of the father and the simple fortitude and pathos of the son. An interesting tension is set up finally between Isaac's desire to have the thing hurried up (and hence over with) and Abraham's agony in bringing himself actually to plunge the knife in. The lines are simple: "Now truly, father, all this tarrying, It doth my heart but harm: I pray you, father, make an ending." "Come up, sweet son, unto my arms. I must bind thy hands in two. Although thou be never so mild."

At the end of the play, we have a bit of exhortation and homily that would sit ill with many a modern audience. A doctor ("an austere scholar, dressed in cleric's robes") enters, and we conclude thus:

> Lo, sovereigns and sirs, now have we
>   showed
>   this solemn story to great and small.
> It is good learning to learned and
>   ignorant,
> And the wisest of us all,
>   without any searching.
> For this story showeth
> how we should keep, to our power,
>   God's commandments without
>   grudging....
> Now Jesus, that wore the crown of thorn,
>   bring us to heaven's bliss.

(5) Godly Consensus: Drama's Lost Era

Perhaps the two best-known plays in English, before we come to the great Elizabethans and Shakespeare, are *The Second Shepherd's Play* and *Everyman*. The first is a mystery play (that is, a biblical episode), and the second a morality play (about allegorical figures).

The Second Shepherd's Play is often taken as showing definite marks of the secularization of the drama. The three shepherds who figure in it can very easily be seen as types of downtrodden laborers of northern England. "We are so crippled, For-taxed and crushed, We are made hand-tamed, With these gentlery men", complains the first shepherd.

Critics often remark on the "realism" at work in the play—a quality that is supposed to be the special province of the modern (secularized) theatre. Again, the three shepherds may be taken to represent the three ages of man: old age, middle age, and youth, with all the social and psychological implications that this suggests.

The story has most certainly been elaborated well beyond any strictly biblical narrative. The three shepherds, after bewailing their cold lot out in the winter weather, are joined by a village rake named Mak who, when they fall asleep, steals one of their sheep and hurries with it back to his hut.

He and his wife, Gyll, put the sheep in swaddling clothes in a cradle, and when the shepherds come looking for it

Originally published in *Eternity*, November 1975, 54–55. Reprinted with permission.

and eventually find it, they claim it is their own true child, misshapen by an evil spell cast on it at birth by an elf. The shepherds respond with predictable disgust and return to their fold with the sheep. Whereupon the Angel appears, announces the Nativity of the divine Child, and the shepherds hasten to the manger and adore.

The humor and suspense built up in the play are highly diverting. The three shepherds are ruddy, leather-jerkined country clouts, and Mak is a first-rate comic villain. Will they find the sheep in the cradle? What will Mak and Gyll say at the discovery of their crime?

Not the least of the comic elements for anyone with any historical consciousness is the way these (pre-Christ) shepherds swear with complicated mediaeval Latin Christian oaths: "*Manus tuas commendo, Poncio Pilato*", says Mak in Latin outrageously garbled both grammatically and theologically. "Christ's cross me speed, And Saint Nicholas!" says the third shepherd, shivering in the wind and rain. Further, when they come to the cradle of the Holy Child himself, they adore him with theological insight that did not develop in the Church until after the Apostles.

With *The Second Shepherd's Play* and its ilk, English drama was well on its way toward its later achievements in character and situation.

The morality play *Everyman* is as straightforward as *Pilgrim's Progress*. None of your dramatic subtleties and oblique angles here. We begin straight off with a messenger who tells us in plain enough words that we are about to see "a moral play—*The Summoning of Everyman* called it is, That of our lives and ending shows How transitory we be all day." God is next on stage, and he says, "I perceive here in my majesty, How that all creatures be to me unkind, Living without dread in worldly prosperity ... Drowned in sin, they know me not for their God."

God summons Death to go to Everyman, who is something of a fop, and hail him to his final journey. Everyman ("visibly shaken") wants to know what God wants.
A reckoning, says Death. Everyman ("defensively and a
trifle beseechingly") asks for time to collect his wits. Death
is adamant. Everyman ("stunned by the impact of sudden
realization, his manner now conciliatory and ingratiating")
says, "O Death, thou comest when I had thee least in mind
... a thousand pound shalt thou have, And defer this matter till another day."

The play follows Everyman's progress toward his end, as
he is forsaken, one after the other, by the gifts of Fortune
(goods, kindred, friends) and the gifts of Nature (Beauty,
Strength, Discretion, and Five-Wits). Only Good Deeds
stays with him to the end, whither Everyman is conducted
by Knowledge, who utters the words made familiar to
us by the motto of the Everyman series of books: "Everyman, I will go with thee, and be thy guide, In thy most
need to go by thy side."

Knowledge conducts Everyman to the house of Salvation, where he encounters Confession and Penance and the
Holy Sacrament. In the end, the Angel appears and says,
"Come, excellent elect spouse to Jesu: Hereabove thou
shalt go ...", and a learned doctor in clerical robes speaks
the epilogue to the audience:

> And he that hath his account whole and sound, High in
> heaven he shall be crowned; Unto which place God bring
> us all thither That we may live body and soul together.
> Thereto help the Trinity, Amen, say ye, for saint charity.

This sort of drama seems quaint to us, five hundred
years later—to us with our subtleties and our celebrated
sophistication, and our sensibilities refined to the point

where drama has for its subject virtually nothing at all. It is, of course, not possible to rerun the Middle Ages and recapture that high and palmy time of widespread Christian consensus. And nothing is to be gained by our sinking into nostalgia for this lost era. But perhaps, by having looked briefly at these early English dramas, we will have a sharper view of where we and our own drama stand in the whole picture.

(6) Shakespeare—We've Botched It

Without any debate at all, we can say that the greatest period of English language drama is the sixteenth century—the time of the great Elizabethan tragedies. And, of course, the figure who bestrides this period like a colossus is Shakespeare.

After the beginnings of English drama that we saw in the Middle Ages, with its liturgical connections and its unabashedly Christian subject matter, we find that drama follows the course of general Western sensibility into the so-called Renaissance. Here, we are often told, Western man turned away from God and focused on man, and this breaking free from faith and superstition is responsible for the enormous efflorescence of learning and art that we associate in our minds with the Renaissance.

But this is an oversimplified, not to say a false, picture. The Renaissance was as religious as the Middle Ages. Orthodox Christianity had not yet been widely called into question. All the artists and dramatists and philosophers and humanists accepted the ancient faith as a matter of course. ("Humanism", which is a big word in the Renaissance, did not then have its present philosophical connotation; it referred simply to the revival of the study of Latin and Greek letters.)

It is hard to piece together the exact combination of historical, social, linguistic, and intellectual factors that

Originally published in *Eternity*, December 1975, 55–56. Reprinted with permission.

combined to "produce" the Golden Age of English drama in the latter years of the sixteenth century, during the reign of Queen Elizabeth, but one thing is certain: it is not to be attributed to some general shaking loose from Christian faith.

But of course, whereas we are head over heels in Christian sentiments in mediaeval drama, we have to rake hard in Elizabethan drama, and in Shakespearean drama in particular, to find specifically "Christian" sentiments. There are, to be sure, dozens of passing references to accepted Christian orthodoxy in Shakespeare, perhaps the most specific being uttered by poor Isabella as she begs the frosty Angelo to spare her brother, guilty though he may be:

> Alas, alas!
> Why, all the souls that were forfeit
>   once,
> And He that might the vantage best
>   have took
> Found out the remedy. How would
>   you be
> If He, which is the top of judgment,
>   should
> But judge you as you are? . . .
> (*Measure for Measure*)

But to hunt for specifically Christian "texts" in Shakespeare is to fiddle. Much more important for our understanding of the whole curve of English drama (and, indeed, of Western sensibility as a whole) is what we might call the moral world that is evinced in Shakespeare's plays. Shakespeare at his best writes tragedy, and tragedy is proximate. The Big Story is Comedy, not in the superficial sense of arousing amusement on our part, but in the much more radical sense of affirming victory and joy at the end. Dante did not name his huge work a "Comedy" for nothing. But Shakespeare, in his greatest period of dramatic activity, wrote tragedies.

This was not because he thought that the whole show was a grim one, grinding down to meaninglessness (which we will see when we come to twentieth-century drama). Rather, he was dramatizing the thing that all great poets and dramatists had always seen, namely, that somehow we manage to botch it, that this botch is somehow our own fault, that the price we pay is somehow just, and that there is, in the contemplation of the fall of a great man, something chastening for our spirits.

We are accustomed in our own day to drama (including cinema) about murder and incest and pillage and chaos. Shakespeare, we see, affirmed a moral order in which evil is thrown into stark relief and is revealed for the destructive thing that it is. In our own, we see evil evoked as typical of the general mayhem that is seen to characterize our existence. In the fall of a Hamlet, a Lear, an Othello, or a Macbeth, we see gigantic falls. There is no "fall" for modern man, since what is wrong with us is not, on our view, our fault. Shakespeare would quarrel with us.

(7) Drama's Barren Era of Frivolity

In the general sweep of English drama, one usually skips from Shakespeare and his contemporaries (late sixteenth and early seventeenth centuries) to the so-called "Restoration" drama, which was popular on the London stage at the time of the return of the Stuart kings to the throne in 1660, following the eleven years of Cromwell's Puritan Commonwealth.

As one might expect, given a scenario like that, popular drama took on a cavalier, not to say a bawdy, tone. Everyone was weary with officially imposed righteousness, and it was back to velvets, laces, plumes, boudoirs, and coquetry with a vengeance. Drama tended toward satire, sentimentalism, and the mock-heroic. The names that loom in the drama of this period are not ordinarily seen to be quite on a par with Shakespeare: Villiers, Wycherley, Etherege, Otway, Congreve, Rowe, and others.

But it is a period of English drama worth glancing at, if only briefly. Satire ran high. It is interesting to note the situations in history that nourish satire. It seems to arise, as often as not, at that stage of a civilization when the tone of public discourse and morality is heavily flavored with the preoccupations of a cultivated, leisured, privileged, and therefore bored, set. The art of conversation is brought to a polished brilliance, and a vague coarseness seems to spice

Originally published in *Eternity*, January 1976, 48–49. Reprinted with permission.

everything. Genuine seriousness becomes more and more difficult to maintain because of a fevered self-consciousness in the air, so that efforts at seriousness either slump over into sentimentalism, on the one hand, or are given up altogether in satire and mock-heroics, on the other.

There are two ways that a moral imagination may see the sort of satiric drama that flourishes at a time like this. On the one hand, one may say that satire and drawing-room farce are good for society, in that they hold up to our gaze our own foibles, and, by enabling us to laugh at ourselves, they perform a praiseworthy service. By focusing on the trivial, they put the trivial in some sort of perspective for us, thereby delivering us from the tyranny of the trivial.

Not so, says the other viewpoint. Theatre that reflects and echoes the foibles of its age does not, in fact, have this effect. On the contrary, it *feeds* those foibles. Satire is, ironically, counterproductive: the more we hold up to ourselves, the more fatuous we become. So that if you have a society already given to a sort of drawing-room/boudoir mentality, with playfulness and frivolous talk and general mockery being the order of the day, then this very mentality will gobble up your satirical brickbats and grow fat on them.

This latter description of the situation would appear to be the closer of the two viewpoints to the truth. The latter seventeenth century, during which time the featherweight form of drama known as "Restoration" flourished, is not one of the periods in English history known for its sobriety and rectitude, nor for the worth of its literary output. Indeed, a vigorously religious viewpoint would see English society declining rapidly during this time, to be turned back to its senses, not by the dramatists, but by the preaching in the next century of Wesley and Whitefield.

This might appear to be giving short shrift to this period of English drama. And to pinch off the whole discussion by saying that it was only Wesley and Whitefield who saved the country is hardly a satisfactory way for a literary commentator to end his piece. But if we are thinking of the history and development of English drama in its relationship to particularly Christian concerns, then we will have to say that this period is a barren one. After we have mentioned the office of satire and touched upon the general flavor of the time, there is not much more to say that is to the point.

(8) Modern Drama:
Discovered Solitude

If we skip the nineteenth century entirely in this brief canvass of the development of English drama, it is not because
there were no plays written then. It is, rather, that the
nineteenth century did not see any really significant devel-
opments in theatre. One does not think of Victorian drama
as one of the pinnacles of achievement in theatre: indeed,
if you have ever studied nineteenth-century English literature, the chances are that you read no drama at all. The
great novelists (Thackeray, Jane Austen, Dickens, George
Eliot, and Hardy) and poets (Tennyson and Browning)
and critics (Arnold, Carlyle, etc.) dominated the period.

But twentieth-century drama is another matter. The
stage has been, in our own epoch, right in the vanguard of
the forces shaping public sensibility, along with painting,
sculpture, fiction, and poetry. If history manages to stay
afloat for another hundred years or so, the historians of
the future will certainly look back at our century as one
of the most ebullient (if not one of the greatest) periods in
the arts, including the stage.

The point is, during the latter half of the nineteenth
century, it became finally and publicly clear that what had
been happening in the West during the previous two or
three centuries (the whole shift from a theological to a

Originally published in *Eternity*, February 1976, 44–46. Reprinted with
permission.

secular understanding of the universe) was pretty devastating. All of a sudden it comes through to us that we are alone in the universe and that the gods *are not* watching our story, much less watching *over* it. We go to our coffins alone. Existence, then, is mad.

We are all familiar with this. The books of Francis Schaeffer have helped to popularize in evangelical Christendom an awareness of the shape of modern intellectual and moral history. Almost the entire corpus of art, literature, and drama in the last hundred years bears witness to our newly discovered solitude.

No affirmations can be made. The old sureties have evaporated. Hence we get painting retreating farther and farther from the world of solid external actuality, fiction fleeing deeper and deeper into purely formal or psychological concerns (James, Woolf, Lawrence, Joyce), and poetry speaking with a more and more allusive and mysteriously prophetic voice (Pound and Eliot). And drama driving pell-mell into the theatre of the absurd.

The big names in theatre—Arthur Miller, Tennessee Williams, Samuel Beckett, Harold Pinter, Eugene Ionesco, Edward Albee (and we can't even touch here on the enormous world of film, which must somehow be taken into account in any record of dramatic activity: what shall we say of the great European filmmakers—Fellini, Antonioni, Bunuel, Robbe-Grillet, Renoir, Bergman, Truffaut, and the rest?)—all these names are virtually synonymous with the probe into the void.

If you have encountered serious theatre in the last twenty years or more, the chances are that you have been assailed with images of deterioration (*A Streetcar Named Desire*), impotence (*Death of a Salesman*), havoc (*Rhinoceros*), hate (*Who's Afraid of Virginia Woolf*), meaninglessness (*The Bald Soprano*), inanity (*Waiting for Godot*), and so forth—hardly a lineup of noble and heroic images such as those with which Greek and Elizabethan tragedy hailed us.

The irony of our modern situation is that, having gotten rid of the gods in our effort to "come of age", we find that we have gotten rid of man as well. We are making our exit; not with a bang, as Lear did, but with a whimper. For the Christian, it all makes enormous sense, of course. It all attests to what we believe to be true. The modern dramatists are telling the truth about the modern secular dilemma.

But the question is, where does society go now?

On Evil in Art

On the recommendation of a friend, I went to see the current film *The Devils*. It is about an outbreak of supposed demon possession in a convent in Loudun, France, in the seventeenth century. Before the depicted situation gets sorted out, everyone has been embroiled in political intrigue, carnal chaos, emotional havoc, inquisition, cruelty, and the most bizarre forms of voluptuous decadence imaginable.

The makers of this film chose to handle their subject matter as vividly as they could. The opening scene whisks one straight into a perfumed moral bog, with Louis XIV participating in a dionysian frolic in front of a bored and elegant Mazarin. From then until he leaves the theatre, the viewer is up to his neck in blood, incense, silk, tinsel, grapes, powder, wine, and flesh. Why speak of this to readers of a Christian journal? Isn't this sort of thing as well ignored? Isn't it simply more of what is to be expected from Babylon?

The answer to the latter two questions is, I should think, yes. So the first remains. The answer to that one is that the film exhibits rather vividly a matter that is worth our attention. It is a matter we encounter in one form and another again and again in our own epoch. It has to do with the *zeitgeist*, and with public imagination, and with

Originally published in *Christianity Today*, December 1971. Reprinted with permission.

the discussion and portrayal of moral issues, and, eventually, with the whole aesthetic question.

Perhaps what I am referring to ought to be cast as a question: Does there come a point at which the artistic portrayal of evil crosses a certain line and itself begins to participate in the very evil it is portraying?

All the red flags are up and aflutter as soon as anyone embarks on a line of thought like this. Censorship! Tyranny! The index! Didacticism! Inquisition! Prudery! Victoria! Mrs. Grundy! But perhaps if we back off a bit and look at what is entailed, it will not appear so outrageous.

We would have to back all the way off to the question of what art *is* if we were really to get the discussion on a firm footing, but what with Aristotle and the Renaissance Florentines and Elizabethans and Goethe and Shelley and a thousand others, we would never get to the matter at hand. It may be enough here to say that art, whatever else it does, represents the effort of the human imagination to get hold of its experience of life by giving some concrete *shape* to it all. That shape may appear in stone or syntax or oils or melody, but the whole enterprise of poetry and sculpture and drama (and hence cinema) does bespeak that effort.

Parenthetically, the question of entertainment might arise here. Isn't all this appeal to heady aesthetic doctrine likely to dignify and elevate something that isn't half so weighty? What about mere enjoyment? What about the books that have been written and the plays that have been produced simply to divert people for a couple of hours? Let's not read Armageddon in every playroom scuffle, or the Beatific Vision in wallpaper.

It is not easy to find the border between "art" and "entertainment", if indeed there is one. By its very nature, art aims at furnishing pleasure, and we are entertained by pleasure. But the word *entertainment* with its suggestion of diversion and lightness doesn't serve very well when we speak of Dante or Vermeer, say, since the pleasure we get from what these artists have done seems to partake rather of sublimity than of mere diversion. Perhaps entertainment is a subdivision of pleasure—or a low rung on the ladder whose top reaches to Paradise.

It is a fact, of course, that a great deal of what we call "great art" came into being for rather utilitarian reasons—a rich man's commission, a new cantata for next Sunday, a play for the Globe Theatre; and on that level it is hard to untangle the occasional from the sublime. What happens is that an occasional piece may turn out to be sublime because the man who made it is a genius. His sonnet about the Piedmont massacre or the death of the Countess, unabashedly occasional, somehow participates in the sublime because he has a great and noble imagination. On the other hand, we can get planning committees together and decide to have a breathtaking spectacle and hire all the necessary professionals and work out all the logistics and blow all the trumpets—and succeed only in bringing forth appalling bathos (viz. Radio City Music Hall Christmas and Easter productions, or the cinematic biblical extravaganzas that started with *The Ten Commandments*).

Let us say, then, that authentic art emerges from a noble imagination whatever the occasion is that has asked for it. And, further, that if a noble imagination is at work, authentic art appears, whether the subject matter happens to be "high" or "low". It is not very difficult, on the one hand, to see how great feats of courage, skill, or strength (as in Beowulf, Achilles, Hercules) can give rise to noble treatment. By the same token, the longings, perplexities, or doubts that beset the human mind have been fruitful sources of high utterance (for Shelley, Browning, and

Wordsworth, for example). Or the soul's experience of God often furnishes the matter for genuine poetry (Donne, Herbert, Eliot). These are easy enough to cite in connection with a theory of good art.

But what about evil—real evil—as subject matter? How do we work this in? Dante, for instance, writes about hell, which is as low as you can get. And he writes explicitly and at great length. Here are all the damned, pictured vividly, with discussions of what it was that landed them there and of what their particular torment is. There are explicit notations of sin—lechery, gluttony, wrath, avarice, sloth, and so on.

Or take Shakespeare. What, after all, is *Macbeth* about? Foul murder. We watch Lady Macbeth turning herself into a monster. Or what about Chaucer? One of his most mature poems, the *Troilus and Criseyde*, is about illicit love. Then there is one of the most towering figures in all of English poetry—Milton's Satan.

It will be obvious here that a distinction needs to be made between "good and evil", on the one hand, and "high and low", on the other. Clearly, great evil can furnish "high" subject matter (as in Dante and Milton). The *Inferno* and Satan are "low" only on some cosmic hierarchical accounting. They are "high" in the sense that they embody the biggest issues conceivable by the human imagination.

Similarly, really "low" stuff can afford the matter for genuine art. Take Fielding, with his tumble of hilarious but scurrilous situations in eighteenth-century England, or Evelyn Waugh's brilliantly funny novels about upper-class decadence in early twentieth-century England (or, for that matter, Faulkner's wholly serious handling of American decadence).

What seems to emerge from this line of observation is that it is entirely the *treatment* that decides the worth (and hence the goodness or badness) of a piece of art. There can be good art about bad things, and bad art about good things (a discussion of this last would embarrass us all, alas).

Which brings us back to the question about *The Devils*. It is, to use the favorite word of blurbs and critics now, "frank". Isn't that a point in its favor? It treats demonism (or bogus demonism—that is never really decided), and all the carnality and terror and horror that follow in its wake, colorfully and explicitly. What's wrong with this? Can't we be bold? Can't we call a spade a spade? Haven't we done well to shake off our nineteenth-century humbug and timorousness (and by this time, we all know we can be talking about only one possible topic—sex)?

No. We have not done well. In its frenetic disavowal of sexual reticence, the twentieth century has torn the veil and blundered into the Holy of Holies, as it were—and you can't do that with impunity. It is in the nature of the case that the Ark be secluded: you can't use it for a saw-horse. It is in the nature of the case that the shewbread be reserved—David didn't eat it for lunch every day. And by the same token, it is in the nature of the case that human sexuality be shrouded. It is not a public matter. (Some-one will bring up the *Canticles* here: that is a great poem of carnal love; perhaps it is not a *public* poem?) Not only is nothing gained by the louder, shriller, more frequent and explicit discussion and portrayal of sexuality, but there is every reason to suppose that something is being lost—something good, along with the humbug and prudery.

And this is not necessarily to take a huggermugger or sanctimonious view of sexuality. Anyone who misses the fun—even the funny—in sex is missing part of it. But, like a tiresome three-year-old's pun, the humor cloys when it is insisted upon too loud and long. But sex isn't really the center of the matter. The guilt of *The Devils* (and of a hundred novels, plays, revues, and films one could trot out) is broader than that. It is that it fails to preserve *distance*. It not only points to the stew. It stirs it. It jumps in.

To isolate and articulate the difference between Dante's handling of hell and this film's handling of Loudun is difficult. Perhaps it has to do with a leer. If anything is leering from Dante's pit, it is leering at the poet as well as the reader, whereas you get the uneasy feeling in *The Devils* that not only Louis XIV leers at you from the screen but the filmmaker as well.

We cannot say, of course, that *all* filmmakers (and novelists and poets) whose work fails because of this failure of distance are leering. That would be to pass a dangerous judgment on a great many people. Perhaps there is a prior fault in the era that the artists, because they live and work in the era, can escape only with difficulty. The fault would have something to do with the erosion in the modern world of such categories as absolute truth, glory, and the holy, and thence of such responses as awe, humility, and reticence.

Finally, one has the unhappy feeling that in a great deal of contemporary art, literature, and cinema, inadequate imaginations are attempting very high summits. Scriptwriters, directors, producers, agents, and the rest, whose interest must be, above all, commercial, are addressing themselves quite blithely to imponderables that would give pause to the most sublime imaginations of history. The result is a proliferation of peepshows in Vanity Fair.

Sacramental Imagination

Tolkien claimed that all of his work was massively influenced—nay, determined—by his Catholicism. Questions crowd in straightaway:

"I've read the trilogy and *The Silmarillion* ten times, and I never saw anything Catholic in it." Or, "How can he say that? The characters have to get along in their quest without a bit of 'divine' help."

True, the hobbits and the men of Aragorn's ilk don't seem to have any "god" to invoke, though there are some talisman-like cries for help from above—most notably "O Elbereth! Gilthoniel!" But unless one has read *The Silmarillion*, one has only the sketchiest notions of the immense theological backdrop to the trilogy's "fragment" (see p. 28).

The saga of The Ring most certainly draws upon Norse and Icelandic saga for its ethos and not, *apparently*, on Catholic categories. Tolkien, like his friend Lewis, was intoxicated by "northernness". When they came upon the Nordic tales, each found himself pierced with the dart of *sehnsucht*.

This is a sweet desire; an insupportable nostalgia for— for what? It is an inconsolable yearning that finds itself not only not satisfied, but intensified, by any small taste of beauty available to us mortals. Dante's Beatrice, the Alps at sunset, T. S. Eliot's "moment in the draughty church at smokefall"—such glimpses serve only to drive the knife deeper into the wound.

Originally appeared in *Christianity Today*, April 2003. Reprinted with permission.

Midgard, or "middle earth", was the name given to our world in Nordic saga. And the world of which Tolkien writes *is* our world, only the events occur in a "time" not locatable in our calendars. The Age of Men is about to come forth in Tolkien's trilogy. Titanic events mark the waning of the elder world. The elves and their kind are "passing, passing", throughout the whole drama and finally disappear through a gray screen of rain just before the final scene, when we return to the meat-and-potatoes world of Mr. Samwise Gamgee, his wife, Rosie, and their baby, Elanor.

All of this seems distant from Catholicism, unless we wish to suppose Tolkien's religion was a mere fancy that found a lodging in the immense mystery of the Church of Rome. Certainly many people suppose that conversion to Catholicism entails a large dollop of romanticism.

But first, Tolkien never converted to Catholicism: he was born into it. And second, no convert *to* Catholicism finds anything like the Pre-Raphaelite magic that he might, in his non-Catholic days, have fancied lay in the region across the Tiber River.

Tolkien's Catholicism was, if anything, at a polar extreme from the romantic or the nostalgic. It was utterly and unsentimentally matter-of-fact. We would never have found Tolkien rhapsodizing about the Faith. He got himself to Mass regularly, and he said his prayers, and he counted on the Sacraments and banked on the Magisterium of the Church as the authoritative teacher of Sacred Scripture—and that was that.

Tolkien's Catholicism was as intractable and given as the stones of the old buildings at Merton College. Odd as it may seem, there isn't much to say about Tolkien's faith unless one wants to embark on a log of Catholic dogma. He simply bought the whole package. And that is archetypically "Catholic". His "faith" was of one, seamless fabric with his body, his teaching, his daily routine, his writing, and his family.

So. What about this flinty Catholicism of Tolkien's and its effect on his work?

First, Catholics are profoundly narrative. Where Protestants gravitate toward the immense abstractions of sovereignty, election, depravity, atonement, and grace, Catholics characteristically come to rest on events: Creation; Annunciation; Gestation; Parturition; the Agony in the Garden; the Passion, Resurrection, and Ascension. The Mass is an enactment, as opposed to the Protestant service, with its center of gravity in the sermon.

Second, Catholicism is sacramentalist. The point where the Divine touches our humanity is a physical one. Creation; pelts for Adam and Eve; the Ark; the Tabernacle; the Womb of the Virgin; the flesh of the Incarnate One; splinters, nails, whips, and torn flesh. The entire Gospel is enacted—physically, in the Catholic liturgy. Hence the ease with which the Catholic mind reaches for narrative. Tolkien believed he could not have written the saga if he had not been a Catholic. He trusted in his imagination in a way sadly rare among Protestants.

Tolkien's saga is also sprinkled with "sacramental": the lembas, the athelas (a healing plant), mithril (finely woven magical armor), Bilbo's sword "Sting": these aren't magic, much less omnipotent. But they do have *virtu*—spiritual character, excellence. Tolkien was used to holy water stoups, crucifixes, relics, the Rosary, and so forth, which stand on the cusp between the seen and the Unseen.

Third, good and evil in Middle Earth are indistinguishable from Christian notions of good and evil in our own story. To be sure, we do not find Gollum about today, but what does a soul en route to damnation *look like*? Whereas good and evil are usually veiled in our world (is that man a lecher or a good preacher?), in the stark air of myth, the murk is blown away and we get to *see*. Goodness, too, takes a shape (Tom Bombadil, Treebeard, Galadriel, Aragorn); and the matter need not be burdened with a homily.

Ultimately, the hobbits and the rest must struggle on in *faith*—substance of things hoped for, evidence of things not seen. But Tolkien, being a Catholic, would never smuggle in a paragraph to that effect. We must find it *in* the narrative, as Catholics do in the whole treasury of Catholicism.

Expensive Churches

The question before us, as I understand it, might be put like this: "What about splashy churches?" That is to say, ought the Christian church to pour enormous amounts of cash into erecting tremendous edifices to house its activities?

The question is not a new one. And before one has got through trying to arrange the issues that come crowding along the minute the question is asked, he has discovered that it opens out onto gigantic imponderables.

On the surface, the answer is clear. Indeed, it would hardly seem to admit of any discussion at all. Shall we build splashy churches? Of course not. Who do we think we are? Whom do we follow anyway? The pioneer of our faith never set about to upstage Nebuchadnezzar and Caesar. He never built so much as a lean-to for his followers or left any blueprint for such a structure. Let the pomps of Babylon and Rome memorialize themselves with golden images and arches of triumph, for they are all, precisely, Babylon and Rome. The pomps and triumphs of the kingdom of heaven are of such unlikely and unimpressive kinds as a girdle of camel's hair and a colt, the foal of an ass. Fasting in the desert. No gold, nor silver, nor scrip, neither two coats, nor shoes, nor staves. A borrowed room upstairs; a borrowed grave. Come—why waste time even raising the question?

Originally published in *Christianity Today*, August 17, 1979, 19–23. Reprinted with permission.

It seems to me that arguments against the proposal that we build big churches group themselves under at least four headings, although there are, no doubt, more than that. And underlying all of the four would be the whole prophetic biblical picture that would seem to rule out the enterprise to begin with. The headings under which we may group some of the arguments against our building huge and expensive churches would seem to be (perhaps on a rising scale of weightiness): taste, efficiency, imagery, and economics.

1. *Taste.* From a merely aesthetic and architectural point of view, what sort of harmony can we discern between what the Christian church is supposed to *be* and what these gigantic piles look like? Surely this is a basic principle of aesthetics and, hence, of architecture: the thing you are making ought to answer somehow to its *use.* The form articulated in the stone or brick or concrete (the World Trade Center, the Whitney Museum, the Opera in Paris) should address exactly the idea at work in the enterprise. Let us leave on one side for the moment mediaeval cathedrals and abbeys. The question being put to us here is whether *we* ought to be building big churches. The twelfth-century achievement is a *fait accompli,* and hence beyond our immediate reach.

But what about the churches that are being built now? Anyone with semi-civilized taste would have to grimace at most of them: great, looming, sprawling "plants", all landscaped and tricked out like suburban office parks. Alack! We perceive millions of dollars' worth of bricks and ersatz-Colonial woodwork, bland and functional, all announcing, "Get a load of the size of this operation." One wants to creep under the nearest cabbage leaf in sheer embarrassment.

But that is all a matter of taste. My point is simply to observe that the category of taste does, in fact, carry some possible arguments against building expensive churches. The fact that there are some churches being built here and there that might be candidates for genuine architectural immortality (Le Corbusier, for example) would carry us into later categories in this discussion. A corollary consideration, of course, still under this heading, is the awkward fact that we don't seem able very often to achieve good taste either expensively *or* cheaply; we are as likely to erect a botch if we scrimp as if we lavish. And the final, obvious factor is that for any Christian, taste is a highly ambiguous business in any event, since it seems to be more or less irrelevant to the category "sanctity", which is all that seems to matter when the chips are down—at least, if we take our cues from the Prophets, the Apostles, and the Lord's teaching.

2. *Efficiency*. Look at all that gaping space standing vacant for six days out of every seven. Think of the fuel being pumped into the furnace just to keep the cavern at 50 degrees. And the *classrooms!* Who can justify all this?

Of course, some churches can respond that they are, in fact, using the space quite efficiently and that countless meetings, both of parish and of community activities, occur all week long. Fair enough. The rejoinder to this often takes the form of a suggestion that homes and rented rooms about town might serve as well for most of what we house in these big plants. After all, the church is supposed to keep it simple. While I am not asked to settle that phase of the discussion, I suppose that if I were forced to take up a position here, I would want to raise the prior question of whether the church, locally, should ever be *big*. When you get two thousand people in the assembly, is it still possible to live the corporate, disciplined, mutual, sacramental life that is the apostolic pattern, and which we have no choice but to follow?

3. *Imagery*. This category is, perhaps, almost indistinguishable from the first category of taste. It seems to me, however, that there is a different nuance here, beyond

the merely immediate business of some congregation's erecting of an immensity that signals "Money! Success! Great fund-raising techniques!" to the local populace. We address rather the whole question of the image of what the Church is in history. Shall we have a pilgrim imagery, or a triumphalist imagery? Do we want to herald Christ as reigning gloriously over all the works of man or as kneeling with a towel? Do we hail human imagination with Annunciation, Transfiguration, and Ascension in what we build, or with *kenosis*, Nazareth, and Golgotha? Shall it be the prince Saint Vladimir or Saint Francis? Shall it be the rich Joseph of Arimathea or Martha of Bethany? Michael the Archangel or Mother Teresa?

At this point, many Christians may want to shout, Wait! We can't quite separate all that out. There must be some paradoxes there: Christ's majesty and his humility; Christ as conqueror and as servant; the Church as glorious and as pilgrim; the gospel as both the fulfillment and the antithesis of human aspiration; both gold and sackcloth as images that must be kept alive; the feast table that is also an altar; the sword and the healing hands; sceptre and towel; terror and comfort. We have a jumble of contradictions—all symbolizing the paradoxes roused by the appearance of the ineffable in the middle of our ordinariness.

But I am ahead of my argument. Here I would point out that there *is* an argument that proceeds from the problem of imagery. For what exactly does the Church wish to signal, if anything at all, in her buildings? Christians in Chartres, Bec, and Amiens had one idea. The First Church in Americasville that has just finished its $3 million plant has another. And Christians meeting upstairs in a rented Elks hall in Altoona have yet another.

4. *Economics*. What we mean is biblical economics. How on earth can we justify vast sums of money when half the

world is starving? The equation is outrageous. Have we never read the Prophets? Who among us wants to be found at Dives' table in this era of widespread poverty? But, alas, *all* of us sojourners in America are at Dives' table, strip down as we will. Can we not, then, conclude that the case is clear? In the light of such considerations, is there any doubt about the answer we should give to the question of erecting opulent church buildings? It would seem not. If taste, efficiency, imagery, and economics mean anything, then it would appear that the pouring of immense sums into church buildings is at least grotesquely inappropriate, if not immoral, in this age.

But we cannot quite leave it at that. There are at least two matters left dangling if we close off the discussion here.

First, there is the vexed question of what sum we should arrive at as a "Christian" ceiling for church building expenditure. If it is granted at all that there should be a roof over the heads of God's gathered people, and if all of them are not to meet forever in borrowed Elks halls, then how much shall we allot as a permissible per capita (or per communicant) outlay? Immediately, we meet a dozen sliding factors such as size of congregation, geographical location, labor costs, material costs, inflation, depression, desired durability of structure (grass? wood? adobe?), appropriateness to local culture (is it rural Idaho, urban Zaire, or suburban Mexico City we are talking about?), demands of the ministries carried on by the congregation in question, and willingness of the Christians to contribute offerings for the structure. Unless we grip things in some doctrinaire and bureaucratic headlock in the interest of Christian "economics", we will all hesitate to come up with a maximum or a minimum figure. Who knows what is appropriate?

From our editorial desks, it is easy to pontificate about how Christians all over the world are to budget their money. But then we stumble into a culture somewhere whose whole vision of what is supremely precious knocks into a cocked hat those ferocious prescriptions we thought we were inferring so precisely from prophetic biblical texts. Any reflective Christian would wish to receive hesitantly those shrill encyclicals handed out as "biblical" from theorists who claim to have found the right formula.

It is awkward, of course, that neither the Lord nor the Apostles ventured to hammer out an economic *system*. What was surely needed was the overthrow of the "system" under which humanity then staggered—as avaricious and unjust a system as any modern Marxist or capitalist has devised. But they seemed rather to appeal to prior principles—don't be greedy, give extravagantly, care for the poor and oppressed—that would work themselves out visibly in the Christian community, as a sign in Rome and Babylon of the kingdom of heaven.

Which of us has a warrant to walk up to a church building, point the finger, and say, "That is a sin"? That is the sort of inquisitorial righteousness the Pharisees excelled in, for they knew what was wrong with everyone and were prepared to assign guilt. How do I know, when I approach some painstakingly made and exquisitely crafted church building in Asia or Austria—or America—whether what I am looking at represents the pig-eyed egoism of some hard-sell preacher or the loving offering to God of the resources and labor of his people in this locale? My theories may shout one thing at me; I had better hold them tentatively and humbly.

I may *think* I know that the money in question should have been used for some other, more urgent purpose (and I must confess that most of the time I do think this). But one has to watch out when commenting on others' offerings— spikenard, and that sort of thing. This raises the second matter that must be stirred into our thinking before we close off the discussion. It is the mystery of the eternal in time; the mystery of the ineffable appearing in visible form. On this frontier we have awful paradoxes, and God deliver us from flattening them all out in the name of logic, pragmatism, economics, or even compassion. Here there will be things that defy our calculations. For example, there is a tabernacle made extravagantly, lavishly, wastefully even, of gold and acacia and fine-twined linen, for the inefficient purposes of the cult of a God named Yahweh. There were people who could have used those funds.

But here the objection may be raised that this is an Old Covenant item: everything has been superseded in the New. All that visible imagery is now brought to its fulfillment and enacted in the tabernacle of our flesh. It is charity of life, and not gold and acacia, that is to announce "holiness unto the Lord" now.

While this is true and taught in the epistle to the Hebrews, the whole thrust of the epistle—and, indeed, of the whole New Covenant—surely drives us into deeper, not shallower, channels. It does not end the offering of the works of our hands to Yahweh but, rather, places these offerings in the greater context of charity. It is not mere gold I am after, says the Lord, it is your heart. Learn to love me above all, and your neighbor next. And then make your offerings. All of your work—your domestic routines, your professional duties, your skills and your crafts, your sculptures and dances and poetry, along with your limitations and your sufferings and your gold and silver—bring it all to me. For in the oblation of these, you signal their redemption from the profanity that you brought on things by trying to seize them for your own in Eden, and you will herald the joyous return to the seamless goodness of Creation.

But how did we get from expensive churches to Eden and the hallowing of Creation? Was it not by reflecting on the mystery of the eternal in time? Heaven, in finding its way into our history, does not always do things the way our schemes might have thought it should. It calls us, for example, to feed the hungry—but then it asks us to bring lambs, bullocks, and doves to the altar, which is a waste of meat. Mary and Joseph could have put those poor turtledoves to much more obviously charitable uses. The woman with her costly ointment could have done better than to pour it out in a hysterical act of rhapsodic penitentiality and adoration. And, while the suggestion was made, it was silenced, and her waste was extolled and held up for the honor and emulation of all humanity forever.

The forerunner of the Messiah might have done better to preach insurrection against the system, since that, surely, was by far the worst evil abroad. But instead, he, and the Messiah after him, called on everyone to be baptized. That is most impractical and futile business, unless it is acknowledged that the visible tokens and vehicles of the eternal will not always make sense on a pragmatic accounting. The kingdom of heaven does not come always and strictly in plausible economic terms. It may do so, to be sure. But it will escape even that category from time to time—in spilled spikenard (a waste), or in a bunch of yellow roses taken to a shut-in (why not feed the old woman?), or in a song composed and sung as an act of praise (no bread is buttered), or (even) in a church built truly and visibly *ad majorem Dei gloriam*.

If, therefore, we begin our thinking about immense, expensive churches on the reasonable plane of logic and economics, we will arrive every time at the inevitable conclusion that no such structure ought ever to be built. The money can be put to better use; nay, it *must* be put to better use, as long as there is need in the world. But then we realize that, if we stick rigorously to this enormously plausible scheme, we have condemned at a stroke every single act of beauty ever offered in the wasteful business of worship. Bach ought to have been out helping others instead of cranking out endless cantatas. The workers of Chartres and Lincoln should have spent those generations doing something useful. Fra Angelico and van Eyck were indulging in a luxury while their neighbors' needs went unheeded. Every potter, every nun starching the fair linen, every silversmith and glazier and seamstress making something exquisite and extravagant, and every singer and dancer and actor and trumpeter is condemned by our serene inquisition.

Will our fierce economics, or even our arithmetic of compassion, quite compass the whole mystery? May heaven keep us from insisting on spurious and destructive dichotomies. Charity will appear at one moment in the plain white habit of Mother Teresa of Calcutta, and the next in the brocaded chasuble of her priest; at one moment in the chapped hands of Saint Francis and the next in the delicate hands of the illuminator; at one moment in the voice of the prophet crying "Woe!" to the rich and fat, and the next in the voice of the choirboy singing "*Ecce quam bonum.*"

It is all a jumble and a muddle, and none of it will fit. Which is perhaps our big clue. The drama of Love Incarnate is, precisely, a mystery, and you can't come at mysteries with either calculators or economics.

The Desert Fathers
and an Old Question

The other day, I pulled from my shelf a copy of Helen
Waddell's little book *The Desert Fathers*. In her introduction, she tells how various unsympathetic commentators
have taxed these fathers with having fled the world to seek
their own salvation, when what they ought to have done
was to lend a hand to make the world itself more livable
for the downtrodden. She mentions Rutilius, the fifth-
century Latin poet; Gibbon; and Lecky, the nineteenth-
century historian. "What ailed Rutilius and Gibbon and
Lecky is the Roman civic conscience; and to the Roman
civic conscience the exiles in the desert are deserters from
a sinking ship, fugitives from a rotting civilisation, concerned only for their personal integrity."

These ancient, holy, and celebrated troglodytes are
sometimes quoted as pursuing "the flight of the alone to
the Alone". This is not altogether unfair. But the remark
would be far from just, especially if we were simply to
leave it at that. To be sure, it is easy enough to find mad-
men in any ventricle that leads off from any quarter of
religion. Filth, eccentricity, even lunacy—make no mistake: You can find all this and more along the marches
of Christianity.

But to speak of the hermits of Egypt as having merely
ignored the world "is a kind of treason to the civitas Dei,"

Originally published in *Crisis*, July 1, 2007. Reprinted with permission.

says Waddell, "nor does it represent the whole of the Desert teaching. 'With our neighbour,' said Antony, prince of solitaries, 'is life and death.'" One Longinus (not the soldier with the spear at Golgotha) wanted to disappear into his cell for good and see no more men, in order to achieve holiness. "Unless thou first amend thy life going to and fro amongst men," the abbot Lucius told him, "thou shall not avail to amend it dwelling alone." The Venerable Bede, far to the north, testifies to the same thing when he speaks of Saint Cuthbert, who retired to Lindisfarne only after years spent among men: "The coming and going of the active life had done its long work upon him, and he rejoiced that now he had earned his right to climb to the quiet of meditation upon God."

The active life. That is one-half of a distinction that was a commonplace throughout the Middle Ages: the active life and the contemplative life. Which is better? We have all heard a thousand homilies on Mary and poor Martha. Pity the homilist who finds himself with that text for the Sunday. An element of confusion can be introduced into the matter at hand, at least for the laity (and, in my own teaching experience, for seminarians), by an insistent and almost exclusive stress on the vocabulary of "caring and sharing" and "service"—which, taken alone, are certainly worthy categories. Such a confusion cannot infrequently have a stultifying effect. I have noticed that very often the whole burden of the homily and the public prayers at the liturgy concern themselves with the agonies abroad, so to speak. I do not mean merely overseas; I mean trouble in the public realm, which, God knows, offers us only agony, for which our prayers must go up daily. But the Christian's real enemies are not usually "out there". The interior wrestling is not often over foreign policy, public injustice, or capers in the Senate.

But those grizzled hermits, they sought the face of God. What is there to seek? How much time should one put in on that quest? These men put in a lifetime. The reading at Morning Prayer this very morning, as I write, says this: "Who among us shall dwell with the devouring fire? Who among us shall dwell with everlasting burnings?" I do not think this speaks merely of hell. We are all going to experience that fire either as bliss or horror one fine day, depending on how we have disposed ourselves here. Hence the life of prayer, ardor, and obedience.

Hear the Angel Voices

For Orthodox and Roman Catholic Christians, the singing of hymns—at least in the sense in which hymnody is understood and practiced in the Anglican and Protestant churches—does not occupy exactly the place that it does in those latter two sectors of Christendom. The move away from the liturgy at the Reformation fostered an enormous efflorescence of hymnody. Martin Luther, Isaac Watts, Charles Wesley, and others brought to their congregations a treasury of hymns for which tens of thousands of Christian believers have been grateful.

There is, however, a treasury of hymnody almost unknown now, except, as it happens, in the traditional Anglican Church. For it is the Anglicans who, many years ago, found, opened up, and started singing the hymns from the early and mediaeval churches both in the East and in the West; Catholics, of course, have kept in a central place the hymns of Saint Thomas Aquinas, for example, *O Salutaris Hostia* and *Tantum Ergo Sacramentum*; and the Orthodox liturgy seems, at least to a Roman Catholic like myself, to be borne along on an almost ceaseless outpouring of glorious chant. But the phenomenon of vigorous congregational singing seems to be a particular specialty of the Anglican and the Protestant churches.

I myself grew up in that especially energetic quarter of Christendom known as Evangelicalism, and I must say that

Originally published in *Touchstone*, September 2011. Reprinted with permission.

it was there that I was tutored faithfully in Scripture and in a muscular personal faith in Jesus Christ. We sang—and sang—the strong hymns of Luther, Watts, and Wesley. It might almost be said that faith among us virtually lived and moved and had its being in "the great hymns of the Church", as we called them, meaning mostly eighteenth- and nineteenth-century hymns, although we very much loved Saint Bernard of Clairvaux's *Jesu, Dulcis Memoria*— "Jesus, the very thought of Thee / With sweetness fills my breast." We also drew upon a late-arriving genre of songs generally referred to as "Gospel songs", such as "Great Is Thy Faithfulness" and "O That Will Be Glory for Me", many of them drawn from the evangelistic campaigns of D. L. Moody and Ira Sankey.

When I became an Anglican in 1962, I discovered a whole world of hymnody that was new to me.

These were hymns from the early and mediaeval Church by such (to me) strangers as Saint Joseph the Hymnographer (ninth century), Saint Rabanus Maurus (eighth century), and Venantius Fortunatus (sixth century). It was as though the scrim that hangs between our ordinary mortal experience and *The Ineffable* were suddenly drawn aside.

"Father, we thank Thee who has planted / Thy holy Name within our hearts", from the Greek *Didache* of A.D. 110, was one of them, "The great Creator of the worlds / The sovereign God of heaven", from the Greek *Epistle to Diognetus*, A.D. 150, was another, and, from the high Middle Ages, there was Peter Abelard's "*O Quanta qualia / sunt illa sabbata*—O what their joy and their glory must be / Those endless Sabbaths the blessed ones see." These hymns struck a note that seemed to me to approach the *Mysterium Tremendum* itself.

The Eucharistic hymns from earlier centuries in the Church are particularly rich, among them "O Food of

Men Wayfaring", a Latin hymn from the seventeenth century, and "Draw nigh and take the Body of the Lord / And drink the holy Blood for you outpoured", from the seventh century.

There are two hymns that, in an especially notable way, seemed to me to open out onto daunting vistas of the sort that one comes upon in Saint John's Apocalypse. Saint Joseph the Hymnographer's ninth-century hymn, "Stars of the morning, so gloriously bright", and Saint Rabanus Maurus' "Christ, the fair glory of the holy angels" from the eighth century, draw us deeply into those vistas. It may not be amiss to quote a stanza or two from these two hymns for the benefit of readers who may not have come across them.

Saint Joseph's hymn speaks this way:

> "Who like the Lord?" thunders Michael the chief;
> Raphael, "the cure of God", comforteth grief;
> And, as at Nazareth, prophet of peace,
> Gabriel, "the light of God", bringeth release.
>
> Then, when the earth was first poised in mid-space.
> Then, when the planets first sped on their race.
> Then, when were ended the six days' employ.
> Then all the sons of God shouted for joy.

(It must be added here that the grandeur of these hymns is vastly enhanced by the tunes to which they have been set. They are worth hunting up in the 1940 Episcopal hymnal.)

In his hymn "Christ the Fair Glory of the Holy Angels", Saint Rabanus, after invoking the three archangels, beckons us all right up into the empyrean with this:

> May the blest Mother of our Lord and Savior,
> May the celestial company of angels,
> May the assembly of the saints in heaven,
> Help us to praise thee.

The point of all of this, of course, is that hymnody, under its own species, echoes what we find in the liturgy itself: we are set free from the shallow puddle of our own resources and experience and drawn toward the mighty precincts where *That Which addresses us* looms. The titanic Objective, we might say. Here, the whole matter of "testimony" and "sharing" recedes. What have we, poor gabbling novices, to say when Michael, Gabriel, and Raphael, and thrones, principalities, and powers (invoked in another stanza of Saint Rabanus' hymn) start up the chorus, led by the Theotokos herself?

W. H. Auden once remarked that the best hymns are "versified dogma". It may not be a bad recipe. Such hymns bespeak what we find in the *Te Deum* and the Akathist, and in such hymns as arose in the Church when men were accustomed to bow and be silent until, as it were, the angelic summons to us mortals to join in was heard.

God before Birth: The Imagery Matters

There is an ancient formula that goes like this: *Et incarnatus est de Spiritu Sancto ex Maria Virgine: et homo factus est;* which is, being interpreted, "and was incarnated by the Holy Ghost of the Virgin Mary; and was made man."

These words, at least the English of them, are familiar to any Christian whose church still recites the Nicene Creed. But even a Christian who has not come across this exact wording will be familiar with the doctrine it expresses. It is plain orthodoxy. All Christians believe it. The formula passes the test brought to bear by another ancient formula, the Vincentian Canon: *quod ubique, quod semper, quod ab omnibus creditum est:*—"what has everywhere, always, and by everyone, been believed". Here Mennonite and Byzantine, Salvationist and Latin, agree.

The difficulty with familiar formulas like this is, often, just that: they are familiar. We need to be jogged now and again so that what we are saying does not slip off into mere slogan. This is especially true of the affirmation in question here, for in this doctrine of the Incarnation, we speak of *the* point at which the mightiest mysteries touch our ordinariness. The whole thing was brought down to a point at our feet, as it were. "Eternity shut in a span", one seventeenth-century poet called it.

In these two short clauses, we find an enormous amount of biblical teaching crisply summed up for us. And the

Originally published in *Christianity Today*, December 17, 1976, 10–13. Reprinted with permission.

point in the whole drama of redemption that is bespoken here is one that, despite our fierce orthodoxy, we may miss: "... and was *incarnated* ... and was *made man.*"

In the early Church, people kept coming up with ideas as to how this teaching could be made more plausible. The notion of God becoming man—real man—was unmanageable. Of course, everyone was familiar enough with how gods had often *masqueraded* as men. And again, there were plenty of stories as to how mortals had been caught up and given a place in the heavens because the gods loved them very much or because they needed to be punished or rescued from some danger. But for Zeus or somebody to *become* a man was not one of the options. So one attempt after another was made to adjust the doctrine. One idea was that the Incarnation was one of those masquerades. Another was that the Holy Ghost had come on the man Jesus in a unique way and made him the "son of God" in some way not quite true of the rest of us sons of God. There were all kinds of variations on the theme, and most of them are still familiar to us. I myself grew up in an era when, as far as we could tell, our own fundamentalist church and the local Roman church were the only churches, out of thirteen churches in town, that taught anything like this stark Nicene (and biblical) doctrine of the Incarnation. Everyone else seemed to be still trying, two thousand years later, to say something plausible. We called it modernism, but it was, surely, a tired rerun of some very old notions.

It is not customary in Protestantism to speak of the Virgin as the Mother of God. The hesitation here is that this will make it sound as though she existed before God the Father somehow, and bore *him*. But that ancient title for her, *Theotokos*, the God-bearer, arose long before there were any universal schisms in the Church, to protect this idea that that which had become one with our flesh by being conceived and nurtured in the body of the Virgin was nothing other than God himself. The title was upheld by the councils of Ephesus and Chalcedon. The Incarnate was not a masquerade of God, a creature of God, an apparition, or a merely godlike hero. It was God.

There is a good difficulty about a doctrine like this that is true of all Christian doctrines. This good difficulty is that while what we say is clear enough for any ears to hear (God became a man; Christ died for us; he ascended into heaven), it is at the same time an impenetrable mystery. No one, not even the Angelic Doctor himself, can get to the bottom of it. We will be forever coming at it afresh. We will be forever working away at it, both here and in Paradise, although presumably the form that this latter "working away" will take will be adoration and not theology.

One aspect of this teaching is that, by virtue of this Incarnation, it may be said that *we wear* the flesh that has been hallowed and raised to glory by that event. The flesh that we bear was, and is, in a mystery, the flesh worn by the Deity. There is no other creature in the whole cosmos, so far as we know, that can claim this: no lion, be he ever so regal: no elf, be he ever so fair; no archangel, be he ever so mighty. It is our flesh alone that has been taken up. The Athanasian Creed, which goes back perhaps to the late fourth century, speaks of the Incarnation as "not ... the conversion of the Godhead into flesh, but [the] taking [of] the manhood into God."

This is what the Church celebrates in December every year. This is the mystery we try to come at with our feasting and caroling and giving. We come to the shrine where the great mystery lies, there in our flesh, and like the whispering shepherds and the adoring Magi, we know that in this small and unlikely drama being played out here in this inauspicious place, this stable, the shutters of the universe have been blown open for us, and we are being invited to peer through onto vistas of splendor only dimly guessed at in the songs and tales and prophecies of ancient seers, sages, and sibyls.

One of the questions that comes to us, though, is this: How do we wear that flesh day by day? The celebration comes and goes. We, like the shepherds and the Magi, must "return" from the shrine to our daily ordinariness. What does it mean, to us who have been to that shrine? The mystery that we beheld there is the mystery of our flesh raised to glory. We walk out now, clothed, as it were, in the image that has been raised to the pinnacle. Our flesh is the jewel in the crown of Creation. This again is why you often see, in the painting of the Middle Ages, the figure of Mary exalted to the heavens and crowned with splendor. The idea there is a theological one: human flesh, represented by Mary, since she is the one who uttered for us all the authentic response to the approach of the Divine Will, her great "Be it unto me according to thy word" (the response that we all, in our first parents, refused to make), is seen as redeemed and crowned with glory. And, to raise the awesome stakes even higher, the doctrine of the Ascension, which is the end in one sense of the part of the gospel drama played out on earth by the Incarnate himself, implies that somehow, in a mystery beyond all our powers to imagine, our flesh is now represented in the Tri-une Godhead. But at this point theological language falters.

So the question comes to us: How do we wear this flesh? Has it ever struck us that we are garbed in the most splendid raiment of all? That no archangelic wings or seraphic flames exhibit quite this particular glory, this glory of redeemed flesh—what has been called (by Dante, I think) *la carne gloriosa e sancta*, the holy and glorious flesh?

How does this affect our outlook? One note that it ought to introduce is the note of awe. That is, creatures who find out that it is *their* flesh that God has taken—and taken not just arbitrarily in order to get some random job done, but specifically to redeem and glorify *it*—these creatures can never thereafter take a cheap view of that flesh. The image that they bear is doubly noble. It is noble first because at the Creation it was said of them alone among all creatures that they would be formed in the *imago Dei*. But then at the Incarnation, in a glorious mystery of exchange beyond all attempts to compass it, they "gave", as it were, their flesh to him. That is an odd, and perhaps non-theological, way of phrasing it; but it is a mystery that anyone who has ever loved knows something about, namely, the mystery of exchange, in which no one can ever figure out who is doing the giving and who the receiving. Lovers know something that calculators do not. They know that giving and receiving are a splendid and hilarious paradox in which, lo, the giving becomes receiving, the receiving giving, until any efforts to sort it out collapse in merriment or adoration. (This, by the way, is why the political and 50-50 talk that "liberationists" bring to the sacrament of marriage fails so dismally; that tallying has nothing to do with what real lovers experience. And the love that is experienced and enacted in the fleshly sacrament of marriage is perhaps the most vivid metaphor we human beings have of the Divine Love that also deigns to enter into blissful exchanges of love with us creatures.)

Awe is hard to keep alive in one's imagination, since we live now under a mythology that rejects mystery. But it is not as though the Christian ought to float about in a state of perennial rapture, contemplating how splendid everything is. There are practical and specific points where, with his notion of the Incarnation, he will run headlong into conflict with ideas widely held by his contemporaries. If he does not reflect on his own Creed (*"et incarnatus est"*), he will find himself vaguely espousing these ideas because they sound nice.

For example, over against his own view of human flesh that he derives from the doctrines of Creation and Incarnation (and, indeed, from half the other Christian doctrines: Passion, Resurrection, Ascension—they all entail the flesh), he will discover that the general view of human flesh held by his contemporaries is, in effect, gnostic. That is, on at least two fronts now, the Western imagination is zealously attempting to disavow the notion that the flesh is good (which is what Christianity insists and gnosticism hates). The one front is that of Eastern mysticism, under which heading we find all sorts of Zen, TM, and other efforts to transcend the limits of bodily (read "hampered") existence. This is, of course, an ancient and widespread religious effort, and it seems to make particular sense in our own time, when we find ourselves, ironically, bored and destitute in the wake of doctrines that have told us the flesh is the *only* reality. The apparent glorification of the flesh that you find in *Playboy*, and in the more recent glossies that celebrate the idea that my body is my own to do what I like with, is a fraud, as Sodom and Babylon always find out. You can't stay alive on new moralities that tell you to do whatever you want (eat, drink, cohabit, etc.) whenever you want since there are no considerations bigger than appetite. "If you itch, scratch" is the catchy and convincing slogan. From this cloaca of mere carnality, mysticism offers an attractive escape, and it is not surprising that our era finds it appealing. A person, however, who believes that the way out of the mess has been shown to us by the Incarnate One will have a quarrel with any disavowal of flesh-and-blood ordinariness.

But the other form of gnosticism abroad now is infinitely more oblique, it is the especially contemporary notion that the imagery does not matter. Put another way, the idea is that what things *look* like is not significant. Human anatomy, for instance, is held to be purely functional. It is arbitrary, except insofar as it represents a useful stage in our evolutionary adjustment to our surroundings. We have lungs that are adjusted to the kind of atmosphere we live in: a happy development. And we have prehensile thumbs that permit us to make things, and reproductive machinery distributed so as to get the job done. But none of it *means* anything. To try to see it all as an image of anything is pre-scientific (goes the argument).

This starkly secularist line of thought is easily enough recognized by Christians. The trouble comes when Christians, having breathed in this mere secularism with every breath (who can escape it? schools, universities, books, journals, and television know no other view, and they pour it to us in season and out of season, line upon line, here a lot, there a lot), acquiesce unwittingly in this secularism. Oh, we're not secularists, we protest. We believe in the doctrine of Creation. We believe in the Incarnation.

Do we? Does our profession reach any farther than the formula on our lips? What about our attitude, for example, toward the notion that all this physical differentiation that makes men and women look different from each other has nothing to do with anything? All this imagery (these appearances, say) of masculinity and femininity, under which we mortals bear the *imago Dei*, is insignificant. What about that? The idea is that there is an entity "person" that somehow is truer and closer to our real identity than this random cloak of sexuality that we happen to be dressed in. Don't think of me as a *man*, for heaven's sake: I'm a *person*. Pray, don't speak of me as a woman: I'm a *person*.

Or, worse yet, don't ask whether I happen to be involved in the sacrament of marriage: it's not a sacrament in any case. It has nothing to do with anyone's personhood. It's a contract, and my spouse and I have worked things out in a very modern way that does not call either her individuality or mine into question.

The Incarnationist would understand the foregoing line of thought to be gnostic in that it introduces a disjuncture: it sets the thing itself (the personhood) over against the image of the thing (the body) and denies any real connection. The reality not only transcends the appearance (so far, a grain of truth), but, more than that, nothing at all is suggested about the reality *by* the appearance. The pattern of Creation, in other words, is more or less random. God had nothing significant in mind when he distributed his image among the two modalities man and woman. Nothing is to be inferred about what we *are* from what we *look* like.

Another variation on this gnostic theme would be the denial of the significance of the imagery in language. The pictures, for instance, by means of which God speaks to us of himself are connected with the reality in only a higgledy-piggledy sort of way—"culturally" is the usual word here. The images of Lord, King, or Father under which he spoke of himself have no connection with anything more far-reaching than monarchic and patriarchal Mediterranean antiquity. Heavens! He might just as well have chosen to speak of himself as an antenna if he had decided to wait a bit and come into an age oriented to high-speed communication, or as an androgyne to an age celebrating unisex. It's a question of culture. And the Incarnation? That imagery (of the Son) has nothing to do with reality, either. It is *ad hoc*, attached to a question of convenient communication. (It is worth noting that the gnosticism that urges the foregoing line of thought makes with equal fervor the point that in the Incarnation, God broke up all the *other* entrenched, established prejudices of antiquity. He missed his cues on this point alone. The Incarnate was a revolutionary, an icon-smasher, a rebel, a liberator. But he came, O rue the day, as a *man*. He missed his main chance.)

The question, really, is how far we are to carry our understanding of the Incarnation. All Christians agree on the doctrine, that's pat. The point that is being pressed here is that, just as the Church had to examine and deepen her understanding of this doctrine in other ages when plausible alternatives were offered (Arianism, Sabellianism, Patripassianism, Monophysitism, and so forth), so now, when once more efforts are abroad to revise or update the ancient and radical understanding of the doctrine, the Church ought surely to put her mind to getting clear just what she does affirm in this doctrine. If the Incarnation were, in fact, just *ad hoc*, and Jesus the Son may rightly be thought of by contemporary persons as Jesus the Daughter or Jesus the Hermaphrodite or Jesus the Person, then the doctrine and the tradition need to be scoured. We have been bilked. We need to excise from our thinking any notion that the imagery matters—that is, that there is any connection between physical appearance and actuality. No real clues have ever been given to us, after all, as to how we ought to think about things. Tastee Freez and Kool Aid will serve as bread and wine at the Eucharist, since everybody knows that Jesus wasn't made out of *wheat*. We may speak of God as Chairperson of the Committee of the Whole, since everyone knows that he's not sitting on any *throne* up there. We'd be more accurate to speak of him as Our Leader rather than Our Lord, since "lord" reinforces ideas that are out of date, not to say pernicious.

The imagery doesn't matter in the slightest, in the gnostic view. Or rather, yes it does, on second thought. It's just that it's all wrong. We'll have to get rid of *that* imagery (King, Father, Son) and bring in *this* imagery (Chairperson,

Parent, Child). Although even there we have a problem, since the latter two words smuggle in an idea of *family*, and if anything ought to be jettisoned now it's that old idea of family with all the pestilential hierarchical notions that tag along in its wake. Maybe Senior Citizen and Emerging Personhood would serve better than Father and Son—except that, again, "Senior" suggests hierarchy, and that's the worst idea of all. And we can't say "Elder" because that sounds as though God were aging. Oh dear—the imagery is crucial, isn't it?

Yes. It is. Perhaps Protestant Christians, whose vision of things has for four hundred years now been a radically propositional and non-visual one, need to plough back in and see whether there might not have been something about the whole drama that wants looking at again. The whole thing was played out altogether in material, flesh-and-blood terms. Creation, Incarnation, Passion, Resurrection, Ascension, Eucharist: they all, oddly, entail our flesh. The language of God's self-disclosure is shot through with unabashed images, inviting our imaginations, nay, compelling them, to think of him thus, and thus, and thus.

Has the time come for an updating? Ought we to separate the doctrine from the imagery? Perhaps the imagery was just cultural. Perhaps there is a seed of truth that needs to be separated out from the husk of all that culturally determined language and imagery.

Rudolph Bultmann and others would say yes. The Fathers would have said no. But, of course, Bultmann is our contemporary. He knows more than the Fathers.

Evangelical imagination has an important question in its lap.

Catharsis? Caritas!

In the mid-1960s, when my wife and I lived in New York, I used to pop in to Lincoln Center to take in bits and pieces of the New York Film Festival. It was all terribly heady. One wanted to be at the cutting edge. Au courant, so to speak. (I was young.)

The then-prominent names among the directors were mostly foreign: Buñuel, Renoir, Truffaut, Bergman, Fellini, Antonioni; a lot of the films were black-and-white. One didn't really think of the festival as mere entertainment. It was serious stuff, one told oneself. And indeed it was, from a given point of view. The films constituted a keen index, as it were, of modern sensibility.

My most distinct memory of these occasions is of the cinema buffs' remarks as they tottered, all agog, back up the aisle and left the theatre. Great rhapsodic breathings. Gasps of incredulity. *There's* catharsis for you! Now I know what Aristotle meant. Heavy.

It all started a train of thought in me that goes on until this day. And I speak as one whose livelihood for over fifty years has been the teaching of *belles lettres*. The concerns in these two fields, literature (in my case, the teaching of English literature) and cinema, are virtually synonymous. Literature, film, drama, music, dance, painting, sculpture, architecture: these would constitute what we commonly

Originally published in *Touchstone*, July/August 2012. Reprinted with permission.

call "the arts" and would themselves bespeak our awareness of the *significance* that seems to arch over our mortal
affairs and the immemorial human effort to find concrete
shape for that awareness. Dogs don't write poems. Eagles
don't come up with new choreography. Dugongs don't
create operas. Such attempts seem to belong to our species alone.

And somehow such activities seem to lie very close
to the center of human consciousness and aspiration—so
close, in fact, that finding the exact threshold between
the arts and religion is not always an easy undertaking,
since both evince this rum and dogged awareness that
won't leave us mortals alone. I am speaking, of course,
of imagination, which insists on finding a palpable *shape*
(incarnation, shall we say?) for its experience of existence,
whereas ratiocination seeks to get things articulated in discursive, propositional terms. (The question of the shape
taken by Reformed theology and spirituality, as distinct
from the ancient Orthodox and Catholic outlook, looms
at this point ...)

As I overheard the remarks on every side as we all left
the theatre after those evenings, a piquant question began
to suggest itself to me—piquant, since I was preparing for
a career in teaching *belles lettres* and might myself be called
upon to reply to some student's views on a question I am
about to raise in the following lines.

The word that stuck in my mind was *catharsis*. Rightly
understood, of course, this refers to a cleansing or purga-
tion. Aristotle speaks of this.

So: a cleansing or purging of *what*, exactly?

If we mooted the question at, say, a round table, the
participants being experts from the various arts and (perhaps more important) critics and philosophers of aesthetics
whose particular concern was to locate the phenomenon of

art among the truly serious human enterprises, we would find ourselves regaled with several points of view.

Perhaps the matter of *sensibility* would arise early on. But what a can of worms! How, for example, are we to urge that to love Bach's Goldberg Variations bespeaks a higher sensibility than to love the big band swing music of the 1930s? What we'd get would be a shouting match, with sociology and politics quickly commandeering center stage.

Do you mean to attach a pecking order of taste here, with Bach higher than swing? Come. That's just la-dee-da. The highbrows versus the unwashed proletariat, eh? Us ordinary folks versus some elite, is it? And who would wish to find himself defending quite such a division of things?

The same uproar would bedevil any possible discussion in this realm. Are Vermeer and Caravaggio "better" than what one sees in local art fairs? Is *Architectural Digest* better than *Beautiful Homes*? Are the waltz and foxtrot better than current "dance" forms? Is T. S. Eliot better than my verses here? Is Jane Austen better than Robert Ludlum? What a donnybrook.

We have lurched into very delicate precincts here. Obviously, we are talking about *discrimination*. The word has been throttled down to mere politics and sociology in our own time, but its more ancient usage, meaning the capacity to see, and to judge, a scale of values from better to worse, would be at work in the present discussion. But again, "better" and "worse" have themselves been ruled out of court in our time, in everything from taste to behavior to morals to values. The egalitarian notion presides.

But I have something fundamental in mind. Catharsis ultimately suggests the cleansing that will make me a better man. Schooled at the feet of Sophocles, Phidias, Orlando Gibbons, Shakespeare, Leonardo, Mozart, and Balanchine, surely I will, if I am operating on more than two watts, become a more whole man? Finer values. Breadth of sympathy. Acuity of taste. Chastened preferences.

Yes. All of that. But now I must put my Christian cards on the table. Will any such schooling make me a *better* man? There's the rub. Those last four phrases in the above paragraph certainly suggest qualities that seem to mark the civilized man—no doubt the man we would all like to know—nay, to be. Isn't it axiomatic that such marks distinguish me from the oafs and churls?

Well, perhaps, in a way. But something needs to be said on the point. We must press the thing further than civility, gentility, and taste, all of which, in their order, may be prized. But who is the *good* man?

Alas. Without canvassing the faculties of English departments in great universities whom I have known, I need go no farther than my own inner man. Alas again. No smallest tincture of vanity, irascibility, humbug, venality, cravenness, disdain, or niggardliness has been even slightly touched, much less expunged, in me simply because I love *Beowulf*, *King Lear*, Mozart, and Vermeer.

The joker in the pack is not faulty taste or ignorance of "the best that has been thought and said" in the world. Two cheers for Matthew Arnold, Henry James, and the critics. But they leave me where I was. The interior skirmish—the war, in a word—for me remains what it was.

The joker—one hesitates to be labeled a fundamentalist fanatic—is sin. The ancient curse. The thing that has beleaguered every man ever born to woman (and before: both Adam and Eve "fell"—not into bad taste, but into sin). Pride. Rebellion against the Most High. Iniquity. Guilt. All of the old, weary, shopworn tags.

We fundamentalists used to sing "What can wash away my sin? / Nothing but the Blood of Jesus." Oh dear. So proletarian. So Salvation Army. So tacky Sunday-night-upstairs-chapel.

No. So ancient, so Orthodox, so Catholic, so Reformation, so massively universal. The wine in the chalice: that, being the Blood of Jesus, alone can wash away my sin.

But how to introduce this embarrassing note into any serious discussion of aesthetics? Probably it can't, and shouldn't, be done. It's the wrong forum. But of course, every idea, every contribution, every sentence even, in such a discussion, skirts the final issue—namely, what sort of men do we want to be? Or, what is *better?* What is the desideratum—for the Regius Professor of Classics and for the tinker with his cart and for the farmer in the dell? Finer sensibilities? Well, that's not to be scoffed at. But what will make them all "better" men?

Surely it is, in the end, mere charity. *Caritas.* The greatest of these. Purity of heart. Love, joy, peace, long-suffering, gentleness, goodness, meekness, self-control, faith. Though I speak with the tongues of men or of angels.... Or so would urge Saint Paul—not, we might object, one of the panel at the Round Table. But is that a remark touching Saint Paul or the Round Table? The good saint is merely an Apostle, however. What remarks on the topic might we get from the Second Person of the Most Holy Trinity, who was incarnate by the Holy Ghost of the Virgin Mary and was made man?

Now you are swamping us with mere rhetoric. Revivalism. This is tendentious. Uncouth, really.

But as I left the theatre on those nights, I wondered which of us in the audience would, say, refrain from bedding down our current favorite or some chance encounter on Bleecker Street? Or would offer help to some dribbling derelict in Times Square? Or have the courage to demur in the presence of profanity? Or refrain from striking back at an insult? Or hold our tongue when calumny is being visited on someone whom we dislike intensely? Will Buñuel help? Truffaut? Fellini? Or, let's face it, Bach or Shakespeare?

One further point has occurred to me over the years as I have mulled over such questions. I have wondered whether the claim that the arts might make us actually *better* (more pure in heart, more righteous) people might be stopped in its tracks by recalling that, with every one of the arts, we are spectators. We are sitting in our armchair, or across the footlights, protected. We are *watching* King Lear in agony on the heath. We are *reading* about evil and hell in Milton, or about descending to the bottom of the Inferno, and thence up Mt. Purgatory and on into Paradise, with Dante. We *gaze* at Van Eyck's "Adoration of the Mystic Lamb" in Ghent.

But in no case are we actually *undergoing* the experience. Oh, indeed, we may weep great tears or gasp rhapsodically over the splendors of the music or poetry, but the tears we shed over Lear ("'Her voice was ever soft ...'") are nothing next to the tears we might shed over our own dead daughter. From the Christian point of view, suffering—and suffering alone?—seems to constitute the syllabus for us here in this mortal coil.

I take "the arts" seriously. The teaching of prose, poetry, and drama has been my livelihood. But I would be chasing an *ignis fatuus* were I to attribute to them anything that is actually salvific. Surely the Paschal Mystery alone is to be sought in that connection.

The Oldies Record

As a boy, I was never an aficionado of what was then called "the hit parade", the popular songs that were currently, and briefly, at the top of the list. There was a period, however, during my adolescence when I listened to these songs on the radio with some loose regularity. One program had a little signature ditty at the beginning of which the performers sang, "We'll sing the old songs, / We'll sing the new; / We'll sing the bright songs, / And maybe we'll sing the blue."

There were more bright songs in those days (this was the 1940s) than are abroad now. "Cruising Down the River on a Sunday Afternoon", "Lavender Blue, Dilly-Dilly", "Peg o' My Heart", and "Mairzy-Doats". Looking back now, one is agog at the sheer innocence that suffused these songs: How (thinks one in this jaded epoch) did such pallid songs ever galvanize the populace?

Recently I found myself also recalling the older songs that still constituted a sort of matrix for everyone's musical consciousness in that era. This "canon" existed prior to the then currently popular selections. It seemed coeval and coterminous with the mere business of being a person at all.

Virtually everyone could join in at any moment with "Just a Song at Twilight" or "Annie Laurie" or "Comin' through the Rye" or "The Blue Bells of Scotland" or "Sweet and Low" or "When Johnnie Comes Marching

Originally published in *Touchstone*, October 2008. Reprinted with permission.

Home". One sang these songs first at home, and then in school, and then forever.

The old canon was not a brief cultural oddity of the 1940s. The practice reaches back to the eighteenth and seventeenth centuries and, *a fortiori*, to Shakespeare's time and to the late Middle Ages, when the songs in the air extolled such gay sentiments as "Green Grow the Rushes-O" and "Sumer Is Icumen In." (I use that adjective [gay] deliberately, with its ancient definition. But how infinitely dismal that I should have to resort to this parenthesis.)

Whether in mediaeval Paris, eighteenth-century London, or Philadelphia in the 1940s, singing from the canon was as natural and unnoticeable as eating one's lunch or breathing. It was a staple of one's existence, as it were.

Recently I found myself jotting down a list of nouns that presented themselves to me as I thought over that canon. Those songs of the historic West extolled such notions as the following:

Innocence: Ben Jonson's "Drink to me only with thine eyes / and I will pledge with mine / But leave a kiss within the cup, / and I'll not ask for wine." We may compare this diffidence with what one vows to do in, say, the lyrics to rap and heavy metal songs.

Duty: "The minstrel boy to the war is gone, / In the ranks of death you'll find him;/ His father's sword he hath girded on, / And his wild harp slung behind him." The boy did not squall out his loathing for the Establishment that was sending him away from all that was familiar and loved by him (he was a Jacobite under a Hanover monarch, forsooth).

Domestic contentment: "Mid pleasures and palaces though we may roam, / Be it ever so humble, there's no place like home." We wince with embarrassment over such a treacly sentiment—treacly, it may be remarked, to imaginations seared by ennui and sophistication. (Readers may recall the earlier meaning of "sophisticated". It meant to adulterate something with impurities, as in "This wine has been sophisticated with vinegar.")

Fidelity: "Maxwelton's braes are bonnie, / Where early fa's the dew, / And 'twas there that Annie Laurie / Gave me her promise true ... / And for bonnie Annie Laurie, / I'd lay me doon and dee." The English-speaking world sang this song without smirking.

Purity: "O where and O where is your Highland laddie gone? ... He's gone to fight the battle for King George upon the throne, / And it's oh! in my heart, / How I wish him safe at home." (Another Jacobite here, doing his duty for his Hanover sovereign.) There is no hankering here for hasty (and explicit) carnal congress with the lad. "Where's the passion?" we might complain. Where's the authenticity? How vitiated it all seems. Shake the girl.

Soundness of mind (what the Greeks lauded as *sophrosyne*—a fundamental virtue): "Gaily the troubadour touch'd his guitar, / When he was hastening home from the war, / Singing ... 'Lady love, lady love, welcome me home!'" What the poor man needs is to have his libido unleashed. He needs to let it all hang out. Such lackluster yearnings he permits himself.

And there are many others, equally (to our ears) quaint and naive:

Hesitant delight in my lady, for one: "And 'twas from Aunt Dinah's quilting party / I was seeing Nellie home." What the boy wants seems very restricted, indeed: merely the delicate, nay, fragile, venture of accompanying her to her door. The delight anticipated in such an austere pleasure puzzles imaginations cauterized by debauchery. So pyrrhic. So timorous.

Courtesy: "If a body meet a body, / Comin' through the rye, / If a body kiss a body / Need a body cry?" These were very advanced sentiments, indeed. A kiss! How dashing! Pity the boy.

Sacrifice: "They were summon'd from the hillside, / They were call'd in from the glen, / And the Country found them ready / At the stirring call for men.... Keep the home fires burning." After Woodstock and Jane Fonda, we can only writhe with incredulity upon hearing such advice.

Joy: "When Johnny comes marching home again ... We'll give him a hearty welcome then, / Hurrah, hurrah! / The men will cheer, the boys will shout, / The ladies, they will all turn out, / And we'll all feel gay. When Johnny comes marching home." It is difficult to think of a rock setting for this child's garden of sentiment.

Peace: "Sweet and low, sweet and low, / Wind of the western sea.... Blow him again to me, / While my little one, while my pretty one, sleeps." The mother rocking the cradle: very destructive and atavistic sentiments to introduce into a culture having violently come of age under the baton of Betty Friedan and Germaine Greer. Everyone sang it without demurral, though.

Plain goodness: "A Spanish cavalier stood in his retreat, / And on his guitar played a tune, dear; / The music so sweet. Would oft-times repeat / The blessing of my country and you, dear." This calling upon patriotism will need the most rigorous scrutiny, surely, when patriotism has been exposed as a cover for imperialist ambitions?

Pure, melodious, unapologetic lyricism: "Hark, how the sailor's cry / Joyously echoes nigh: Santa Lucia! Santa Lucia!" After the Holocaust, Korea, Vietnam, and Iraq, not to say 9/11, this sort of capering insouciance seems grotesque, not to say sacrilegious. What authentically contemporary man can join in such a frolic?

And so our log could go on. I had jotted, besides the above categories: Stillness, Virtue, Civility, Grace, Dignity,

Gravitas, and un-self-pitying Sadness. Such words bespeak a state of mind—an ethos, really—that has traditionally been assumed to suffuse the very air of Western civilization, and of sympathetic common life.

The picture has now, of course, changed altogether. Even wistful septuagenarians may well find that they hear such sentiments with unease. Even the most nostalgic of reactionaries might find himself embarrassed to be caught singing these songs in public. Whatever the ethos was that fostered these notions over the centuries and that permitted adults as well as children to revel in them—that ethos has vanished with Ozymandias and the Great Auk.

I have only a sketchy view of the canon that supplanted the old one during the decades that followed Elvis, the Beatles, and the Rolling Stones. But things have changed, at least if one is to take one's soundings from passing pedestrians with headphones, from what gets piped into all shops in all malls, and from what seems to predominate both in programming on radio and television and in the "music" that introduces films and sports events.

The strains that emanate from the gravelly static one hears in those headphones and speakers in malls and restaurants seem harsh and violent (and even debauched?) to the ears of the traditional West. The cultural phenomenon called a "rock concert" would seem to draw upon and cultivate responses and notions hitherto thought by civility to be worth suppressing in public—and indeed, if one thinks about it, controlled watchfully even in the very recesses of one's soul.

Of course it is not merely a superficial question of musical taste. Music has from the beginning both arisen from, and formed, the ethos of the cultures in which we encounter it. Whence comes that odd and minimalist music that we hear in Japanese No theatre? What mean those flutes (not great horns, they tell us) that accompanied the Spartans into battle? What is the wellspring from which African tribal rhythms arise? Where did the Navajos get their modalities?

What are we to make of the rauschfifes, shawms, and gambas of the late European Middle Ages and the Renaissance? Palestrina, Victoria, Gibbons, Praetorius—what made them possible? Bach, Mozart, Strauss, Schoenberg, jazz, blues—what sort of a trajectory is this? Can we sort out the chicken and the egg here, distinguish which music expresses a culture and which forms it? I doubt if we can. None of these phenomena may be teased out and separated from the whole question of ethos: How powerful, nay, formative, is our music, culturally and anthropologically? And does it affect the moral imagination of a populace?

Halyards, Sheets, Shrouds, and Painters

The sailors among you will know what that title is all about. But it is not with those marine technicalities that I am going to start. Rather, I have in mind that painting by Georges de la Tour of a young woman (I seem to recall that it is the Magdalene) staring at a skull on her table. By our lights, the whole thing is macabre. That lady is headed for trouble, and what she needs is some upbeat counseling.

Anyone familiar with the two thousand years of Catholic forms of meditation will, of course, wish to lay a hand on the sleeve of the scandalized viewer and try to explain things. One may rummage in vain through the pages of a thousand contemporary books and articles on self-actualization and good mental health and fail altogether to find a syllable recommending what, to the Magdalene and hosts of ardent Catholics, is the very avatar of sound, sensible, solid mental health and freedom.

What we have there, of course, is a *memento mori*: a reminder of death. The idea is not that we need to wallow in "grim, ungainly, ghastly, gaunt, and ominous" revels about "tombs and worms and tumbling to decay" (my thanks to Poe for that glorious, alliterative line-up, and to Hopkins for the worms). The idea, quite sensible and wholesome if you think about it for more than the most rushed moment, is that unless you have a fixed, stark, and robust notion of

Originally published in *Crisis*, December 1, 2005. Reprinted with permission.

just what that lovely head of yours is going to look like one fine morning, the chances are that your life might fritter itself away, "distracted from distraction by distraction" (Eliot, *Four Quartets*).

Which brings me, oddly, to our halyards. Do not for a moment suppose that I look upon sailors as especially susceptible to distraction. Some of my best friends are sailors, to coin a brand-new phrase. I even sailed around the Caribbean in a little sloop, forty years ago, with two friends. I was most emphatically "crew", let it be stressed loudly here. The only thing I learned was that there is no such thing, God help us all, as a rope on board. There are halyards, shrouds, sheets, lines, a painter, et cetera, but to suppose that any of these is a rope is a solecism guaranteed to paralyze everyone on board with disgust and contempt.

But—to establish some sort of thematic connection here between Georges' painting and sailing—let me say that I live in a small town that has a splendid little harbor where scores of people moor their sloops, yawls, daysailers, and even ketches. Sailing is a noble activity. But, like all activities, it can ease itself toward being a sort of *summum bonum* for us mortals. It certainly has a definite cachet about it.

There is a phrase in Psalms that one comes upon every few days in the breviary, about "those who never think of God". It is alarmingly easy thus to "never think" since "the world is so full of a number of things / I'm sure we should all be as happy as kings." The thing is, it's not at all difficult to be as happy as a king while you are beating into a brisk northwest breeze with the spray twinkling and splashing over the gunwales.

But I pick on boats only because they are so beautiful and so obvious. My horse (there's foxhunting in the fields and spinneys just inland from us, but I don't hunt and have no horse), my books (this gets close to the bone for me), my backgammon, my therapist, my club, my very lawn and garden—anything can edge God over toward the margin. I could do worse than buy a cheap reproduction of old Georges' picture and mull it over.

Homer, Dante, and All That

An article on the reading of literature by Christians (that is, the reading by Christians of literature) is odd in that there are certainly no reasons for reading literature peculiar to a Christian's case. Furthermore, the thing that Christians see to be supremely important about life does not attach itself to culture.

If there are reasons why any human being ought to trouble himself with literature (and by literature I mean humane letters—serious poetry, drama, fiction, essay— and not philosophy, panegyric, tracts, journalism, and rubbish), they apply neither more nor less to a Christian than to anyone else. A Christian is, first of all, a human being. This sounds like heterodoxy at first, perhaps, in that we incline to feel that the call of God to us is *away* from human existence to a spiritual realm where we will be free of these old evil selves. But that is exactly the point: redemption is the redemption of *human* nature. It is not God's will to make us seraphim, rainbows, or titans. It is *men* he seeks. Human beings. Beings who will exhibit what he had in mind to begin with—this particular kind of creature, neither angelic nor animal, this excellent thing whose glory would be to choose to love him and to serve him under the special mode of flesh and blood. Indeed, his supreme unveiling of himself was under that mode. And there is to be no shuffling off of these dragging bodies in

Originally published in *Christianity Today*, October 25, 1968, 6–9. Reprinted with permission.

the end. The biblical description of the Last Things is of a *resurrection*—a reunion of flesh and spirit (form and content) from that grotesquery we call death, that obscene disjuncture of flesh and spirit that spoils God's creature man and into whose bailiwick the Son of Man ventured and whose spoliation he spoiled. So that a Christian is wrong to suppose that grace calls him away from human existence. It is precisely *to* authentic human existence (the kind announced and embodied in Jesus Christ) that he is called, so that he may embody for men and angels the special glory of his species. He is called away from *evil*, not human existence. It is evil—disobedience, pride, greed, gluttony, perfidy, cynicism, cowardice, niggardliness, and so on—that wrecks human nature, and God calls men to return to the glory first seen in one Adam, then lost, then restored by another Adam.

A Christian, then, is a human being, subject to all the laws (physical, political, moral, psychological) of that species, so that what is good for any man (vitamins, protection, fidelity, calmness) is good for him. The reading of serious literature is good for a man; hence it is good for a Christian.

This raises the other point mentioned in the opening paragraph—that the thing Christians see to be supremely important about life does not attach itself to culture (I mean culture in the humanistic, not the anthropological, sense—a man's intellectual cultivation, not his tribe). That is, a Christian sees the great and only issue in human life to be man's movement toward the perfection of love—what Saint Paul called being sanctified, or transformed into the image of Christ. This is the only thing that really matters, finally, so that a Christian sees every single thing in life— success, pain, fame, loss, education—as secondary to that. Why, then, it will be asked, are you talking as though *literature* were something important for a Christian? We've got our hands full with this business of sanctification and serving the Lord. We've no time for *cultchah*. We're people of one Book, and it's a book that contains all we need to know about life. Don't siphon us off to primrose byways of poetry and novels. Nobody ever needed that sort of thing to make him holy. You're not suggesting, are you, that an educated man has a better chance to be holy than an uneducated man? Whom did Jesus call? The philosophers? You have a rather sticky wicket to defend.

It is sticky indeed. These objections are convincing, and there is truth in them—namely, that it *is*, in the end, irrelevant whether a man is a scholar or a sailor. The City of God will be populated by men who, whatever else they happened to be doing on earth, learned the way of *caritas*. The credentials asked at the gate will not be books written, kingdoms conquered, or research accomplished. They will be obedience, purity, humility, faith, love. The shepherd, the duke, the housemaid, the tycoon, and the professor will stand, unshod, side by side, clad either in soiled rags or in the one garment of righteousness.

Why, then, an article in *Christianity Today* crying up the merits of literature? Haven't you just destroyed your own case? Isn't it, in fact, irrelevant and maybe even dangerous? No connection, it seems to me, can be established between culture and holiness. The following comments do not tend toward that idea. Certain rewards come to the man who will read serious literature. If those rewards commend themselves to the Christian's imagination, good. They are certainly no *less* applicable to him than to any other man, and they may, like any other equipment (muscle, money, brains), be brought to the service of either altar, God's or Satan's.

In the first place, we need to be clear about the nature of literature. Literature addresses the imagination, which is the faculty in us that enables us to organize the random tumble of experience into some sort of form and hence to manage it and savor it. Imagination is the source of all ritual. We shake hands, set the table for breakfast, lower our voices in a museum, or stand up for a woman: these are ritual formalizings of experience. Imagination is the image-making capacity in us, so that we speak of feeling like a wrung-out dishrag or of a man's brow as looking like a thundercloud or of the kingdom of heaven as being like a man planting seeds. And imagination is what makes art possible, because art is the transfiguration of the abstracts of experience (perception, emotion, ideas, and so on) into special forms (marble, melody, words), the idea being, not only that it is legitimate to handle human experience in this way, but, oddly, that in this way something emerges about human experience that is hidden from all the discursive analysis in the world.

There is a sense in which the imagination works in an opposite direction from the analytic faculty in us: it tends always toward concretion (the image), while analysis tends toward abstraction (the dismantling of the thing in question—blood, granite, neurosis). A Christian, of course, would see this tendency as enormously appropriate in a universe whose tendency is also toward concretion. The original creative energy, the Word, uttered itself in rock and soil and water, not in equations. And again, the ultimate utterance of that Word was in the shape of a man. Even the book given by that Word was not mainly expository and analytic but narrative and poetic and parabolic. Indeed, one suspects that the whole post-Baconian methodology (the sort of thing that leads us to think we are saying something *more true* about the solar system when we speak of gravity and centrifugal force than when we speak of Atlas holding the earth on his shoulders) may be leading us, ironically, *away from* the way things are. For its tendency is toward depersonalization and abstraction, whereas the Christian understands the original creative energy as moving always toward personhood and concretion.

In any case, literature addresses this imagination in us. It hails us with vivid cases in point of otherwise blurred and cluttered experience. Homer's heroic handling of jealousy, rage, bravery, cynicism, love, and endurance in the figures of Achilles, Agamemnon, Hector, Paris, Ulysses; Dante's cosmic geography of hell, Purgatory, and Paradise—what modern categories would reduce to abstractions like alienation, discipline, bliss; Shakespeare's probing of overweening pride in *Macbeth*, or of jealousy in *Othello;* Milton's shaping of the human experience of evil and loss into the *Paradise Lost*: these are familiar to us. We read them in school. And perhaps we remember a stirring in us, a brief glimpse of something that arrested us, or even a tidal wave of new awareness of what was at stake in human existence.

The world is full of such works of the imagination, all of them trying to see and utter and shape the human experience. There is Boethius' lovely *De Consolatione*, in which philosophy as a lady visits the discouraged man in his prison. (Boethius was, in fact, thrown into prison.) There are the dark and simple and noble Anglo-Saxon poems, from the huge *Beowulf* to the winsome *Dream of the Rood* (spoken by the Cross about its own experience of Christ's crucifixion), to the sad *Deor's Lament* (about the passing of everything dear), to the fragmentary *Battle of Maldon*. The Middle Ages are full of magnificent dreams and allegories, giving us powerful images of beauty and sin: *The Pearl*, about a man who lost his little girl and found her in Paradise; *The Vision of William concerning Piers Plowman*, one of the most overpowering allegorical descriptions of society, evil, virtue, and nearly everything else, written in the fourteenth century about that century but true in every point about our own. The sixteenth century produced the greatest drama our language knows (Shakespeare and his contemporaries) as well as unsurpassed lyric beauty in the work of Spenser, Sidney, and again Shakespeare. For someone who is looking for specifically Christian experience in his literature, the seventeenth century is the pot of gold. Virtually every major poet was Christian and made it his entire poetic business to shape his religious experience into verse: Donne, Herbert, Crashaw, Vaughan, and of course Milton. There were some naughty "cavalier poets" whose amorous verse is really very good, too.

The list could go on, of course, but it would be just that—a list—and would do little good. The point is that our language is full of works of the imagination, each of them uttering something of the human experience of life, each of them throwing some light onto experience, each giving some shape to it all. And for the man who will give himself to the austere luxury of reading it, there is that high guerdon of art, the heightening of consciousness.

By participating in the noble fictions of the human imagination, we enlarge our capacity to apprehend experience. There comes a sense both of the oneness of human experience and of its individuality. The figures of myth and fiction—Ulysses, Beowulf, Roland, Don Quixote—are not cards in a computer, but their experience is a paradigm of all human experience. As a man becomes familiar with the follies, sins, and troubles of the great characters in fiction and drama—a Tom Jones, Henry V, Jane Austen's Emma, George Eliot's Dorothea, Hardy's Tess, James' Isabel, Tolstoy's Anna—he realizes that here are profound probings by noble minds of the ambiguities of human experience, and his own appreciation of these ambiguities is sharpened.

Along with this heightened consciousness of human experience there comes an awareness of what was at stake in redemption. Minds that have been schooled in humane letters have been those that have often spoken eloquently to us of God: Saint Paul, Sir Thomas More, Erasmus, Melanchthon, Pascal, Newman, Mauriac, T. S. Eliot, J. R. R. Tolkien, C. S. Lewis. There is in them none of the stridence or flatulence that often marks the biblical exposition of men who have brought only their own myopia to the Word of God. (The point here is not that the Holy Ghost does not at his pleasure pick out someone whom scholars would call an ignoramus and through his mouth bring to nothing the wisdom of men. He does. But his freedom to do this has led altogether too many ignoramuses to assume that divine mantle and bleat their foolishness abroad in the name of the Lord; it will not do.)

The reading of serious literature, then, may increase our sense of participating in the human thing. It may enrich our sympathies, sharpen our focus, broaden our awareness, mellow our minds, and ennoble our vision. And it may energize that faculty in us by which we apprehend the world as image (which it is), the imagination.

Um, Praise Music

I hear from my young friends that there is a song abroad now, apparently widely sung, in which God is hailed as being "awesome". Which of course he is. But a tussle in my own imagination presents itself upon hearing this title. On the one hand, I can only extol the ardor that marks the piety of the thousands of young Catholics and evangelicals who sing this song and others in this vein. Who will carp? In this epoch when great cumulonimbus clouds of hatred appear to be gathering against the Lord and his anointed, what Christian will decry wholehearted Christian devotion, no matter from what quarter? Great zeal for God arising from a generation that has grown up in the present decades is a phenomenon that should bring solace to the stuffiest of us.

On the other hand (readers will have seen this demurral coming), one finds oneself asking about the immense treasury of Christian hymnody, going back at least to A.D. 110, which appears to have been lost altogether to the Church. The great thing to be said about the current genre of "praise music", we would be fervently assured, is that it expresses in popular language how contemporary believers *feel* about their *experience* of God. Perhaps feel and experience are the operative words there. And again, who will carp?

The word "awesome" is, I suppose, the fly in the ointment for the stuffy crowd (e.g., me): *Everything* is awesome

Originally published in *Crisis*, October 1, 2006.

now—Madonna, rappers, the TV series *24*, Tommy Hilfiger, Tom Cruise, and so forth.

But of course Christian believers of every stripe owe everything—the Church, Sacred Scripture, the Magisterium, and the Faith itself—to the Apostles, the Fathers, the Doctors, and the whole train of the faithful who have passed it all along. Hymnody is part of that patrimony. To be sure, the "awesome" troops will correctly point out that this patrimony has never been ossified. Every century has added to it (I speak now of hymnody) *in the language of that century*.

Yes. But a highly qualified yes, surely? And perhaps we come to the point here. Saint Joseph the Hymnographer (ninth century), Venantius Fortunatus (sixth century), Bernard of Cluny (twelfth century), and Peter Abelard (twelfth century), for example, all wrote hymns for their contemporaries. So did Martin Luther, Isaac Watts, Charles Wesley, and William Cowper—all Protestants whose hymns are finally trickling into Catholic use. But the language of these hymns was never drawn from slang; and the sentiments adduced tended to draw us all away from the precincts of chit-chat into the courts where the seraphim sing.

Put it another way: There is something at work in worthy hymnody, if we consult the first nineteen centuries, that arises neither from my current feelings about God nor from my daily chat. And beyond this, any era in the Church that has jettisoned the patrimony of hymnody that comes to it from its forebears has been impoverished.

This is a most difficult point to urge in our own time, when the breathless notion of "Now!" rules everyone's sensibilities. If the touchstone of praise is to be *how my generation feels*, where does this locate us all in those courts? Is there nothing to be gained by my setting on one side my own language, priorities, agenda, fancies, and impulses, and approaching the courts of the Most High seeking all the assistance I can get from the venerable throng of the faithful who have offered worship to Him for eons? Have I nothing to learn? Is there nothing that might be *ganz andere* (wholly other) from my imagination, fed as it has been by very loud, ebullient, and contemporary music and texts?

We might, for a start, join the second-century Christians in singing, "Father, we thank thee who hast planted / Thy holy word within our hearts."

The Parts Angels Play

One of the most haunting elements in the drama surrounding the Nativity of our Lord is the part played by angels. We are accustomed, of course, to the pictures and images of angels in Annunciation and Nativity scenes. Hence, it is difficult for us to keep alive much sense of awe, much less of dread, with respect to the sudden appearances of these glorious fellow creatures. But there they are, suddenly on *our* stage, arriving from that realm that is separated from ours, not by mere light years, but by whole modes of being. The fabric of our world has been pierced from the outside.

The term "fellow creatures" strikes a presumptuous note, however. Who are we, poor sublunary mortals and sinners, to claim fellowship of any sort with these bright immensities? If we share the humility and clarity of vision of the Patriarchs and the Prophets, we will do what they did: fall on our faces when these ministers of the Most High come near to us.

And yet the angels themselves, if we may speak thus, would insist that, glorious and terrible as they are, they are, precisely, fellow creatures with us. They are never to be mistaken for the Divine Majesty itself. They may be infinitely higher up the scale of being than we are; but between that whole scale of creatures and the Most High himself, there is a distance and a difference so utter that

Originally published in *Christianity Today*, December 1980. Reprinted with permission.

the distance between seraphim and flatworms dwindles to insignificance.

And, paradoxically, we creatures of mortal flesh here on earth—we humans—enjoy a dignity that no archangel or cherub, nay, or the seraphim themselves, enjoy. It is that this flesh of ours has been raised to incomparable glory by having been taken on by God himself in the mystery of the Incarnation in which, to borrow the language of the Athanasian Creed, we find not so much a bringing of the Godhead down to man as a taking of the manhood into God. For this reason, by the way, we find in the hymn "Ye Watchers and Ye Holy Ones" a human being addressed as "higher than the cherubim, more glorious than the seraphim". The words refer, of course, to Mary. While an angel was given the task of announcing to our flesh that it was to be glorified in the Incarnation, the task of bearing the Incarnate God was given to this flesh of ours.

But of course in the city of God it never comes to a matter of jockeying for position, of comparing credentials, or of sniffing at questions of dignity and precedence. No angel will ever quarrel with any of us about comparative dignity, and, until we know something we don't know now, our posture in front of them had better be prone.

I sometimes find myself peering into the dimness of what we mortals are permitted to know about angels. Of course, the first and perhaps most important thing to be observed is that our knowledge of angels amounts to almost nothing. We just do not know much about them. Insofar as they appear at all on the stage in the Bible, they are like the wind itself: we don't know from whence they have come and whither they have gone. Suddenness and peremptoriness seem to mark their entry: the drama is going along, quietly or turbulently—that does not seem to have the slightest effect on the angels' appearances. Then, all of a sudden, bang in the middle of the stage, dominating the scene utterly, there is an angel, with no apology or by-your-leave or any of the complicated protocol that might mark the entrance of a herald from even the greatest Oriental potentate.

The chief characters of the Bible find themselves hailed by these mighty spirits: Abraham, Jacob, Moses, Joshua, Gideon, David, Elijah, Zechariah, Joseph, Mary, and Peter. And in virtually every case the human reaction is at the very least one of awe and probably of terror. The Bible stories do not always describe the arrival of an angel as attended by dazzling light or braying trumpets, or the angel as particularly gigantic in size or specially frightening in appearance. Any of these qualities would arouse awe and terror in us mortals. But sometimes the story simply says an angel appeared to so-and-so. We have no reason to believe that the apparition had anything visibly terrifying about it. But we find that Zechariah or Mary or whoever it may be in the story in question is nonetheless filled with fear. What may we conclude from this?

Of course, any of us may experience a start if we look up from our dishpan or our desk and find someone standing next to us without our having been aware that anyone had come into the room. But in these cases, the shock is small and momentary, and then we say, "Ah, it's you"; or, if it is a stranger, we may say something like, "Um—can I help you?" wondering all the while how he got there and hoping that it is the meter man.

But to these angelic visitations, awe, fear, and even terror seem to be the appropriate and inevitable responses. And surely this is important. What we see in the reaction of these people in the Bible who found themselves confronted by angels will give us clues to some important aspects of the whole Christian vision.

For one thing, we see in Gideon and the Prophets and Mary and the others a capacity to *be* awestruck. Now that may seem a gratuitous observation. But to see the force of this, we might try, by *any* method, to arouse old-fashioned awe or admiration in someone who is at home in our century. What has happened to a generation brought up under the ear-splitting din and brutalizing cacophony of acid rock music played, always, at megadecibel levels? And what is the effect on us all of the stultifying avalanches of sheer information and diversion and entertainment—ever louder, faster, more colorful, and bizarre—that pour into our laps from television? What is the effect in our imaginations of breathless travel and of the ever more titillating pageantry furnished by cinema and glossy magazines? For people who live and move and have their being in the midst of all this, what chance has sheer otherness, sheer holiness, to flag them down? The capacity to be awestruck is rare. There is plenty of boredom and suspicion and surfeit and cynicism about, but very little understanding of "awe" or "admiration"—the ability to respond appropriately to sheer splendor or to be truly admirable.

To test this in a small way, one might try waylaying a sampling of passersby and asking them what their feelings were as they watched, say, the funeral of Lord Mountbatten on the television a year ago. (This event would supply us with a good case in point of what we were after because it was a spectacle that included as much imagery as any twentieth-century person is likely to see that is *like* the language of the Bible, namely, pomp and processions and trumpets and gold and so forth, all in the service of something entirely awesome and solemn.) Anyone familiar with Hebrew worship, or with the pictures in Isaiah or the Apocalypse, will have no trouble with this sort of thing. But what of your ordinary passerby in the Chicago Loop? If you could find anyone who had been interested in the spectacle at all, you might find that his reaction was, "Well, it was okay, but it's all a bit outdated, don't you think?"

The point here, lest it seem that we are getting too far afield from the angels, is that the little we do know about angels attaches to their very fleeting appearances on stage in our story and that, whether they come as shining lights or disguised as ordinary mortals, they seem to have about them an unmistakable quality of the ineffable. They come, in other words, from heaven. They come to us, as it were, *out* to us, from the Holy Place, from the precincts of the *Mysterium Tremendum*. What, we may ask ourselves, is our own capacity to respond to this sort of thing? What sort of vision and sensibility and sensitivity and awareness are we cultivating day by day? What will impress us and regale us and fill us with awe? Will it be Mick Jagger or Saint Michael? *Hustler* or the angel Gabriel? What are our tastes? There was something in Gideon and Zechariah and Peter that was already attuned to holiness, it seems, so that when it came upon them, they were able to respond with exactly the correct response, namely, awe. Fear. It is for heaven to say to them and to us, "Fear not." Until then we do well to tremble. That is the healthy starting point for us mortals. The cavalier and the sassy and the flip and the impertinent have no place at the door of the dwelling of the Most High from which these angelic visitants have come.

There is another point that seems significant. These people in the Bible who found themselves addressed by angels and who responded with the right response: How did they learn that protocol? Had Isaiah had a course in angelology? Had Peter been rummaging through occult lore and spiritism? Was Zechariah a priest at the shrine of Saint Michael? No. In every case, the response of these people seems to have been a by-product of a prior humility and goodness. These people loved and served the Lord himself. Hence they recognized holiness when it appeared in angelic form, and their reaction was appropriate. They were accustomed to bowing before the ineffable. By contrast, we might think of characters like Belshazzar and Herod: in order to flag them down and divert their attention from their orgies and obscenities, you had either to spell out their doom in letters that would admit of no mistake or to eat out their insides with worms.

It is an old notion in the Church (the Bible says nothing about it, though Paul may suggest it in 2 Thess 1:9) that the fire of hell may be the fire of the holiness of God experienced as agony by those who have never cultivated a taste (called sanctity) for that sort of thing. What was the difference between the Pharisees, on the one hand, and Simeon and Anna, on the other? The one group, ironically, had no capacity at all to recognize the thing when it finally came: they hated it. The others, the old man and woman in the temple, recognized and loved it immediately because they had kept their hearts with all diligence and were familiar with holiness, if we may put it that way. They knew how to respond to the approach of God because they had known him all along, not because they were particularly adept in occult lore.

This must be important. It is not for nothing that we are told so little in the Bible about angels. They are, if we may speak abruptly, none of our business most of the time. Our business is to learn to love God and our neighbor. Charity. Sanctity. There is our whole work, cut out for us. There are ten thousand utterly fascinating diversions possible— all sorts of things to siphon our energy and attention away from the task at hand—everything from brutish pursuits like sheer lechery to arcane refinements like angelology.

I myself am one who would like to make his pilgrimage to Saint Michael's Mount. The figure of that glorious archangel, doing battle with the Prince of Darkness: I love it. I love the vision of that mighty warrior, lordly and dreadful, fighting *for us*. There are very few pictures in all of myth and poetry equal to that of the archangel Michael riding out armed with the might of the Lord of Hosts, to crush Satan and his hordes. We may, it seems to me, let our imaginations reach as high as they can for imagery to bring to this event: all the flashing swords and snorting warhorses and glittering armor and fluttering pennons and sounding of alarums and excursions that ever regaled our childhood imaginations in tales of faerie and chivalry—those are all most appropriate.

And yet. And yet. Glorious as it is, we must take our cues from the way the story itself tells it. The Bible is the Book with the story in it. You have to follow how the author tells his story. You have to stick with his own emphases. You cannot go tooting off to write your own story and then call it his. And it is surely worth noticing that in Bible stories, almost no space is given to the angels. Their entries are sudden and brief, and then they exit. Michael himself is mentioned in only three books of the Bible, and in every case the reference is very brief and mysterious, as though we were given a glimpse through a cranny out onto huge vistas where heavenly dramas were in progress. Daniel mentions Michael as somehow assisting perhaps another angel (you cannot quite tell from the account) in getting past some evil power en route to Daniel with a message; in another place, Daniel refers to Michael as a great prince somehow charged with the defense of the people of God. Then Jude gives us a most awesome and tantalizing glimpse of the archangel fighting with Satan, if you please, over the body of Moses. What sort of a scene is that? How we would love to know; think of the thrill of that story! But no: we are not to hear it yet. It is not part of our story yet. And then just once Saint John the Divine, in the Apocalypse, pulls back the curtain and lets us have a glimpse of Saint Michael leading his angels against the dragon and prevailing. What oratorios could be written about that. What epics. But again, no.

It seems sufficient that we be aware that our story here is part of a gigantic drama in which all heaven, earth, and hell strive. A Christian is aware of living under titanic mysteries that arch and loom about his head. That much, at least, he is given to know. And in that drama the angelic hosts participate. The Bible never spells out much about them. There is a fascinating literature of angelology. Tradition lets us imagine nine orders in the heavenly hierarchy, starting at the bottom with angels, whose ministry seems to be very much toward us, right on up the scale, through archangels, virtues, thrones, dominions, principalities, and powers, to the cherubim who attend the worship of God, and the altogether mysterious seraphim. Even though most are mentioned in the Bible, the arranging of the so-called ninefold orders of angels is a neoplatonic business. We have no biblical warrant to make a cult of angels.

But it is salutary for us to mark and remember these glorious fellow creatures and their part in the divine drama. It does have an effect on us to know about them. It is humiliating for us to think of their splendor and encouraging and consoling to us to think that some of them at least are appointed by God as ministers on our behalf, and it is thrilling to look into the Last Things and see Saint Michael there fighting for us. But all crowns and diadems and wreaths of glory will be cast down at the Last Day before the sapphire throne on which the Ancient of Days himself sits and before whom the very seraphim cover their faces.

Our Bodies, Our Selves:
The Resurrection of the Body

Any orthodox Christian would go to the wall, so to speak, for the doctrine of the resurrection of the body, since it is included in both the Apostles' and Nicene Creeds, and more than that, since the doctrine is explicitly taught in Holy Scripture. It is not a controversial point like the mode of baptism or the nature of the presbyterate or the exact sequence of eschatological events. "I believe in the resurrection of the body", we all say, and there is very little room for ambiguity here. Saint Paul leaves no leeway at all on the point.

The doctrine may have some piquant implications, however, even for its doughtiest champions.

For a start, it is very far from rare for zealous Christian believers to be, unwittingly, what we might call "crypto-Manichaean", and the notion of the resurrection of the body knocks this tendency in the head.

Manichaean? But that is a full-dress heresy. *I'm* no Manichaean, you say. (For readers whose heresiology is somewhat rusted, we may recall that Manes, the eponymous third-century "founder" of the heresy, taught that the soul of man will eventually be set free from the prison of the body.)

On the face of it, Manes' teaching sounds sympathetic. A common religious tendency is to visualize some such final

Originally published in *Eternity*, March 1986, 18–21. Reprinted with permission.

flight from the shackles of the flesh and a disembodied bliss enjoyed in the vacuous ether of eternity. It is not uncommon among earnest Christians to hear that Christ has saved our souls. "Soul-saving" is a major industry. "Thank you, Lord, for saving my soul", was a popular chorus in the piety abroad in Christendom during my own childhood.

The difficulty with this picture is that it is not Christian. It is Platonic certainly, or gnostic, or quasi-Buddhist: but it is not Christian. Christ came to redeem us, and we are not ghosts or angels or wraiths. We are flesh-and-blood beings, made in the image of the Most High. No seraph may claim the august dignity that mantles us, since no seraph wears the flesh assumed by the Second Person of the Trinity when he came to earth. We do.

Hence, any picture of things that either denigrates our flesh or aspires to some future state when we all have gotten rid of our human flesh has confused Christianity with various merely transcendentalist points of view. Christian vision sees the fruition of redemption in that realm where our original wholeness has been restored—where we appear in that majesty and integrity that God had in mind when he made us to begin with. And we may be sure that it was not wraiths he was thinking of.

This doctrine of the resurrection of the body turns out to be of one fabric with the rest of the drama of redemption, when we think about it. In contrast to all the attractive "spiritualizing" religions, especially those from the East, which the West began so naively to turn to in the 1960s, Christianity is embarrassingly physical. Or, to be more accurate, we should say biblical religion rather than Christianity, since things began with the Creation and moved through the history of Israel, long before Christianity as such appeared on stage.

What we find in this drama is the God whose handiwork takes visible, tangible forms: ice, clouds, brooks, rocks, moss, hoarfrost, eidelweiss, tanagers, raspberries, dugongs, Adam and Eve, and "blood and fire and pillars of smoke", as Joel will have it. We gather all of this up in the doctrine of Creation. He made something. He, who is pure spirit, who dwells in light inaccessible, unfurled his wisdom in this panoply we call Nature. Very physical. No Jew and no Christian has the option of regretting the Creation the way the East does. It is good, says God.

But things do not stop here. When we lost our patrimony in Eden, then the God who had made it all, and us in it, set about restoring what we had forfeited. If he had been a different God, he might have waved a wand and put Humpty-Dumpty together again. But as it is, he did it differently, in keeping with who he is. Blood, stone altars, burned fat, shoulders of lamb and haunches of beef, incense, fine-twined linen, bells, pomegranates: the way of salvation was to lie through all of this. Very physical.

But that was primitive, we might object from our civilized and enlightened vantage point. You always get that sort of thing in the early stages; but religion evolves toward higher things—meliorative thoughts, and ethics, and improving sentiments.

Indeed, mere religion might thus evolve: but not Christianity. When all of that primitive smoke and blood was gathered up and brought to a point, not only do we not find it emancipated from the flesh: we find (alas for improving sentiments) *gynecology* and *obstetrics*. Annunciation. Nativity. Incarnation. Very physical.

But perhaps there is still hope for our higher faculties. Perhaps we may turn from the manger toward the truly central stuff: grace, atonement, justification, reconciliation. Surely these immensities—apparently so abstract— are the core of the gospel?

They are, on some categorical accounting. But those words refer to transactions that were carried out on the stage of our history via sweat, splinters, nails, thorns, blood, myrrh, winding sheets, and a grave. Very physical.

But the Easter faith! (says the modern Christian). There's where we emerge once and for all into truly grown-up religion. The religious experience of the early Christian community was such that the only vocabulary they could find to capture the intensity with which they felt the spirit of Jesus among them was the picturesque language of resurrection. And that is rubbish, says the orthodox Christian believer. Either something happened at the tomb, in the real world, before there was any talk of any "Easter faith", or the whole thing is a house of cards, and we would do well to give it a fillip and let it collapse. Saint Thomas will tell us that it was not an *idea* of nail-holes into which he thrust his hand; and Saint Peter will tell us that the fish they had for breakfast on the beach was not cooked by a ghost. It was all very physical.

And the tale does not end even there. Forty days later, the One they had known in the breaking of the bread (not, it may be noted, merely in devout memory) was taken up into a cloud and returned to heaven. Hmm. What does that mean? Language falters: trigonometry cannot plot the trajectory of that ascension: imagination casts about for a way of visualizing it all (*flesh* in the *Trinity?* Come!). However we may decide to imagine what Scripture and the Creeds speak of, it is a picture that deprives us of the luxury of jettisoning the flesh. If the doctrine of the Ascension means anything, it means that Christian vision knows no glory from which our flesh has been excluded. If we hesitate to bring the word "physical" to bear on that state of affairs to which the Lord ascended and to which he is bringing us (since who can say what "change" our vile bodies will undergo), we may at least say that Scripture goes to elaborate pains to prevent our thinking about it in disembodied terms.

We begin to see the seamlessness of the whole fabric of redemption when we reflect like this. The doctrine of the resurrection of the body is of a piece with all of it.

Are there any implications for us now, though?

Surely there are at least two. First, we find that these reflections kindle in us a lively sense of what medicine and psychology may refer to as the "psychosomatic". We distrust any picture of ourselves that introduces a radical disjuncture between our bodies, on the one hand, and, on the other, our "souls", or our inner identity or our deepest personhood. Some such distinction must, of course, be maintained, since Scripture uses the language of "spirit, soul, and body", and we know that our bodies can suffer disintegration while our inner man increases in joy. But if we suppose that the real us somehow merely tents in our bodies, and that these bodies have little to do with who and what we are, we go astray.

We can see immediately then, in the second place, what this does to such categories as sexual morality. The body is the epiphany of the person: that is, the body is the mode under which our identity manifests itself under the conditions of time and space. Any use of the body entails the whole person. When the body becomes the agent for random drug usage, for example, the whole person suffers. Ask any addict or ex-addict if his habit made no impact on his personhood. Ask any sufferer if his suffering stops at some mere "physical" disorder. By the same token, to recognize the body as the epiphany of the person is to recognize its sacred character. It is the form of a being made in the divine image. I have no warrant, then, to make merchandise out of anyone's body, my own or my neighbor's. The union of two selves (the outward and visible sign of an inward and spiritual grace) in holy matrimony cannot be parodied in extramarital congress without incalculable sacrilege and injury. It is hard to see this, of course. Our own epoch has made random sexual traffic so available and so attractive that no consequences at all seem to follow from indulgence at a moment's whim. But alas: the difficulty we have in seeing what is at stake is an index of our prior loss of the whole category of the holy. If we fail to see the body as the epiphany of the person, in all of the mystery and godlikeness of that person, then we approach the unhappy status of swine, who make no distinction between pearls and orange peels.

The resurrection of the body: it is a doctrine that repays sober meditation with very rich fruit.

Reawakening Wonder: Farther up and Farther in with C. S. Lewis

I had a professor when I was an undergraduate who made all the difference in my life. He laid a hand on my arm, as it were, and said, "Look!"

What he wanted us all to look at was whatever was in front of our noses. As he taught us Wordsworth and Keats, and English fiction, and then a bone-crunching course in Aesthetics, he had us all gasping and writhing and perspiring under the assault of sheer wonder. In every class hour, we were summoned by the great call, "Awake, thou that sleepest, and rise from the dead!"

He would harry us for being so besotted that we never paused, agog, at the sight of the squirrels that ran around the campus lawns. "If you stumbled across an aardvark on your way to class," he would complain, waving his arms about, "you would be agog. But think about it: an aardvark has nothing—nothing, I say—that is any more startling than what a squirrel has. Ears, nose, eyes, feet, tail: in what sort of torpor do you people drift about, that you can pass so somnolently by these exquisite little creatures?"

His point, of course, was that we had got accustomed to the squirrels. Hence we could no longer see them.

This touches on one of the oddities of our sublunary life. Sublunary. That's not a word that we come upon

Originally published in *StAR*, January/February 2010, 22–25. Reprinted with permission.

every day. It simply means "under the moon", which is where we mortals live, and it was used for centuries to refer to our ordinary life here on earth, as opposed to the life of the gods, or, in Christian terms, of the life with God in Paradise, where we will finally have won through to the capacity for pure, undying wonder in the presence of everything there is. This capacity to see splendor in ordinary things will never fade. This is because time will have been vanquished. For it is time, of course, with its corollary repetition, that cauterizes our capacity for wonder. We see something once—a bald eagle, say—and we are transported. But if we live in Vancouver and see these great monarchs every day, sitting in those stupendous fir trees, we get used to the spectacle. Bald eagles? Oh they're everywhere around here.

C. S. Lewis said that it was Beatrix Potter's Squirrel Nutkin that awakened in him the idea of Autumn. But surely by the time he read that book, he had lived through several autumns? It took those little sunlit watercolors of hers to awaken him to the haunting mystery of Autumn. It was Beatrix Potter's Mrs. Tiggy-Winkle that awakened me to sunshine on the hills.

I have a theory in this connection that there is a peculiar endowment vouchsafed to childhood, art, and eternity. In these three realms we come upon the weight of glory in things. Here we enjoy the undimmed capacity for wonder. The enemy of this capacity is time. But time stops in these three realms—childhood, art, and eternity.

For one thing, time chivvies us along. It hustles us. I have often thought of this in my travels. You get to some idyllic spot—the West Highlands of Scotland, the Cotswolds, or some high alpine meadow—and you think that here at last is what your soul has yearned for. The bracken and heather and gorse, the cozy pub lunches, the flower-sprinkled meadows and snowy summits—these seem to be the very precincts of felicity. But then you suddenly find that it is eleven o'clock on Tuesday morning, and tomorrow morning at eight o'clock your plane leaves London or Zurich. The hectic tyranny of sheer time.

And for another thing, time is the baleful herald of change. Things don't last. T. S. Eliot talks about how they're always putting up a factory or bulldozing a bypass in some erstwhile hayfield. And of course change is itself the herald of decay, decrepitude, and death. Golden lads and girls all must / As chimney-sweepers, come to dust, says Guiderius.[1] There is a house in the White Mountains of New Hampshire that has come down through six generations in my family. The bliss that rushed upon me in my early years upon arriving there each summer was almost insupportable. The silence of those fields and mountains and forests seemed to bespeak eternity itself. But then in 1950 they gouged Interstate 93 right through the Franconia Valley. Now there is unremitting din. Cars, SUVs, RVs, eighteen-wheelers, and, worst of all, straight from hell, the rocketing Harley-Davidsons, roar by day and night, just where my grandfather's hayfield used to be.

And then time *accustoms* us to things. We get used to them. Back to our squirrels: we no longer marvel at them as we might have done at the age of two. They fade into the drab domain of the commonplace. We no longer approach them with wonder. (The melancholy truth of the matter for me is that I now approach them with murder in my heart. They barge in and raid my antisquirrel bird feeders. They have disfranchised my chipping sparrows, tufted titmice, white-breasted nuthatches, and Carolina wrens.)

[1] William Shakespeare, *Cybeline* 4.2.262.

So—we poor adults ask ourselves—what will rouse us from our torpor? We cannot return to our childhood. But I have also, in this connection, mentioned art. I am speaking here most especially of painting and poetry.

For example, we get used to apples or peaches in a basket on the kitchen counter. As we come and go during the day, we scarcely notice them. In order to be flagged down by sheer appleness or peachness, we have to pop into the museum and find the room where they have hung Cezanne's paintings. It takes a still life to pluck us by the sleeve and bid us see apples and peaches. The hurly-burly of ordinary household life cauterizes our capacity for the wonder that is surely due these fruits.

Or, in this connection, you may perhaps recall Constable's painting of "The Hay Wain". Here is this great hay wagon being drawn by oxen across a shallow brook under tall shade trees. When we stand in front of that painting, we see the thing. Tranquility suffuses all. We find ourselves invited in to the domain of peace itself. The moment is arrested forever.

Poetry has this same office of awakening us. What happens to you when you hear Keats speak of the nightingale's song "that found a path / Through the sad heart of Ruth, when, sick for home, / She stood in tears amid the alien corn; / The same that oft-times hath / Charmed magic casements opening on the foam / Of perilous seas, in faery lands forlorn."[2] Or Tennyson when he tells us that "The splendor falls on castle walls / And snowy summits old in story; / The long light shakes across the lakes, / And the wild cataract leaps in glory. / Blow bugle, blow, set the wild echoes flying, / Blow, bugle; answer, echoes, dying, dying, dying. / O hark, O hear! How thin and clear / And thinner clearer, farther going! / O sweet and far from cliff

[2] John Keats, "Ode to a Nightingale".

and scar / The horns of Elfland faintly blowing! / Blow, let us hear the purple glens replying; / Blow, bugle; answer, echoes, dying, dying, dying."

Poetry will break your heart by restoring wonder to you with its incantations. It can pierce you with what C. S. Lewis called sehnsucht—that inconsolable yearning for— for what? One scarcely knows. It bespeaks ineffable joy, but at the same time leaves you desolate. You find that the joy that calls from those lines will elude you somehow. Time bundles you along.

Childhood and art seem to me to be the harbingers of eternity itself, which must be that domain where nothing fades, neither the thing itself, nor our capacity to see it— that is, to wonder. The passing of a thousand aeons, as time might tally it, will find us still ravished at things. Surfeit, sophistication, and ennui will have been vanquished, along with decrepitude, decay, and death.

Childhood, art, and eternity. These regions seem to be big with the promise that the capacity for wonder, which ebbs away as we mortals trundle through time, is not forever lost. We were alive with wonder in the dawn of our mortal life; we hear the faint echo of the horns of elfland when we contemplate a great painting; and we yearn with tears as we stand here, in time, outside the threshold of that far country.

C. S. Lewis' stories seem to bring us to that threshold again and again. Who of us has not longed to sit with Lucy by Mr. Tumnus' fire? "... and really it was a wonderful tea. There was a nice brown egg, lightly boiled, for each of them, and then sardines on toast, and then buttered toast, and then toast with honey, and then a sugar-topped cake."[3] Or again, we seem to see boiled potatoes for the first time as we read about Mrs. Beaver's kitchen, with the girls "helping

---

[3] C. S. Lewis, *The Lion, the Witch, and the Wardrobe*, 13.

Mrs. Beaver to fill the kettle and lay the table and cut the bread and put the plates in the oven to heat and draw a huge jug of beer for Mr. Beaver from a barrel which stood in one corner of the house, and to put on the frying pan and get the dripping hot."[4] It all plucks us by the sleeve. It is as though the veil is drawn briefly aside and we are given, briefly, to see with the clarity that properly belongs to things. The words "once upon a time" that invite us in to the ancient region of myth and faerie, act like a quickening spell.

And at this point you are all quoting to yourselves Lewis' words in "The Weight of Glory": "Do you think I am trying to weave a spell? Perhaps I am; but remember your fairy tales. Spells are used for breaking enchantments as well as for inducing them. And you and I have need of the strongest spell that can be found to wake us from the evil enchantment of worldliness that has been laid upon us. He is speaking here, of course, explicitly of the bleak spell that The Enlightenment has cast over us all. But I think he would permit my extending that spell to hint at our mortal condition itself. We become jaded. And that condition is the great enemy of Wonder.

Think of the later scenes in *The Voyage of the Dawn Treader*. You will remember that as the ship draws closer and closer to the East, a great silence settles in, and an insupportable clarity seems to suffuse things. "... they all found that they needed less and less sleep. One did not want even to talk except in low voices. Another thing was the light. There was too much of it."[5] The very water of the sea becomes pellucid. Lucy longs to talk with the noble lords and ladies down there on their great sea horses. There is obviously a hunt going on—a hunt such

[4] Ibid., 69.
[5] Lewis, *Voyage of the Dawn Treader*, 189.

as you read about in the tales of the kings of old. And when Reepicheep goes overboard, he finds that the water is sweet. " 'Sweet!' he cheeped. 'Sweet, sweet!' " When Caspian takes a drink, he says, yes, it is sweet. "I'm not sure that it isn't going to kill me. But it's the death I would have chosen if I had known about it till now.... It's like light more than anything else." Reepicheep remarks that it's drinkable light. "And one by one everybody on board drank. And for a long time they were all silent. They felt almost too well and strong to bear it."[6] Then they notice that the light, already too strong, is increasing. "But they could bear it", remarks Lewis.

And then, as they draw even nearer to the Utter East, "there rose a smell that Lucy found very hard to describe; sweet—yes; but not at all sleepy or overpowering, a fresh, wild, lonely smell that seemed to get into your brain and make you feel that you could go up mountains at a run or wrestle with an elephant."[7]

Certainly here we have Lewis, with every tactic at his disposal, awakening wonder in us. We find ourselves impelled to think, as though for the first time, of such commonplaces as water and air and stillness.

An interesting point arises here. The threshold between the commonplace in our world (air and water, for example) and the remote regions of felicity turns out to be very low. Ordinary things take on a thick individuality and appear crowned with splendor. Aldous Huxley stumbled upon this in his experiments with peyote in the 1930s. He testifies that under the influence of this drug, a chair is no longer a mere chair. He says, "A chair is a chair is Saint Michael and All Angels."

[6] Ibid., 199.
[7] Ibid., 207.

This summoning of things from the mildew of the commonplace back up into the clarity and luminosity with which they were endowed at the Creation, and to which they will be restored on the Last Day, is at work all the way through Lewis' work. I think this must be at least part of his reason for setting his tales either in the domain of childhood, in remote planets, or in a mythic pagan kingdom. In *That Hideous Strength*, on the other hand, we find ourselves down here in Edgestow, which turns out to be a town fraught with every refinement of vanity, duplicity, venality, pusillanimity, petulance, humbug, cynicism, fatuity, cruelty, and perfidy. But glory comes down upon things, not merely when the gods descend on Saint Anne's, but, equally if inauspiciously, in the commonplaces of daily life in that household, which turns out to be the last remnant of Logres. All the "family" there, *plus* Baron Corvo the raven, Pinch the cat, and Mr. Bultitude the bear, in their ordinary daily comings and goings, bespeak the same region toward which Jewel the Unicorn leads us in that joyous romp that takes us all Farther up and Farther in.

In this connection, of course, we all recall Lewis' sermon, preached in the Church of Saint Mary the Virgin in Oxford in 1941, to which he gave the title "The Weight of Glory". I think the sermon illumines the topic I have been working at here. We poor mortals have a hard time keeping awake. Time lulls us into stupefaction. In the dawn of childhood, our eyes have not yet been overcast with the film of the familiar. And art does its best to pluck us by the sleeve and say "Look!" And we suspect that the state of affairs known as eternity will find us fully awake.

In "The Weight of Glory", Lewis gives us a clue to the riddle. This is what he says:

And this brings me to the ... sense of glory ... as bright-
ness, splendour, luminosity. We are to shine as the sun,
we are to be given the Morning Star. I think I begin to
see what it means. In one way, of course, God has given
us the Morning Star already: you can go and enjoy the
gift on many fine mornings if you get up early enough.
What more, you may ask, do we want? Ah, but we want
so much more.... We do not want merely to *see* beauty,
though, God knows, even that is bounty enough. We want
something else which can hardly be put into words—to be
united with the beauty we see, to pass into it, to receive it
into ourselves, to bathe in it, to become part of it. That is
why we have peopled air and earth and water with gods
and goddesses and nymphs and elves—that, though we
cannot, yet these projections can, enjoy in themselves that
beauty, grace, and power of which Nature is the image.
That is why the poets tell us such lovely falsehoods ...
[But] if we take the imagery of Scripture seriously, if we
believe that God will one day *give* us the Morning Star
and cause us to *put on* the splendour of the sun, then we
may surmise that both the ancient myths and the modern
poetry, so false as history, may be very near the truth as
prophecy. At present we are on the outside of the world,
the wrong side of the door. We can discern the freshness
and purity of morning, but they do not make us fresh and
pure. We cannot mingle with the splendours we see. But
all the leaves of the New Testament are rustling with the
rumour that it will not always be so. Some day, God willing, we shall get *in*.[8]

My own guess is that most of us will feel that Lewis had
a part in making straight in the desert the highway that
leads Farther up and Farther in.

[8] Lewis, "The Weight of Glory", 12–13.

Newman and Lewis
on the Limits of Education

The philosophical map has altered. We live in a world wholly different from the world known by C. S. Lewis, by John Henry Newman before him, or by Francis Bacon in the Renaissance or Robert Grosseteste in the Middle Ages. Whether we wish to locate the wellspring of this latter change in the eighteenth-century Enlightenment or much earlier, it is a truism to point out that hardly a single one of our suppositions about the universe has remained unaltered.

It is hard to steer clear of platitudes when we speak of this enormous change from the world of antiquity, the Middle Ages, and the Renaissance to the world we call modern and even postmodern. We have got rid of the gods; we are not sure where to find truth; we are not sure that there is such a thing; there are no fixed values; there are no absolutes; human existence is a conundrum, and so forth.

The experience of this sea change has been scrutinized in a thousand novels, dramas, and paintings. Everyone from Dostoyevsky to Kafka to Updike, and from Gustav Courbet to George Braque to Claes Oldenburg, and from Pinter to Ionesco to Becket—our own epoch is rich in the artistic exploration of what it is like to be human when the very category "human" is itself problematic.

Originally published in *Crisis*, January 1, 1996. Reprinted with permission.

Obviously all of this is going to have its effect in the university. After all, the whole job of the university is to … is to … and there is the focus of the question. What is the job of the university? John Henry Newman thought he knew:

> This I conceive to be the advantage of a seat of universal learning, considered as a place of education. An assemblage of learned men, zealous for their own sciences, and rivals of each other, are brought, by familiar intercourse and for the sake of intellectual peace, to adjust together the claims and relations of their respective subjects of investigation. They learn to respect, to consult, to aid each other. Thus is created a pure and clear atmosphere of thought, which the student also breathes, though in his own case he only pursues a few sciences out of the multitude. He profits by an intellectual tradition, which is independent of particular teachers, which guides him in his choice of subjects.... He apprehends the great outlines of knowledge, the principles on which it rests, the scale of its parts.... Hence it is that his education is called "Liberal." A habit of mind is formed which lasts through life, of which the attributes are freedom, equitableness, calmness, moderation, and wisdom.

Various phrases through Newman's lectures catch our wary attention like small magnesium flares: "a pure and clear atmosphere of thought"; "an intellectual tradition"; "the principles on which knowledge rests"; and the notion that the branches of knowledge together form a whole. Is there any sense in which we would agree that "a pure and clear atmosphere of thought" presides in Cambridge or Ann Arbor or Slippery Rock? Does "a certain intellectual tradition" preside, say, in these English Departments, or in these Departments of Religious Studies? What, exactly, are the "principles on which knowledge rests", so serenely invoked by Newman? And what is that whole formed by all the branches of knowledge?

A certain embarrassment would descend over any forum today if such phraseology were put forward. On the other hand, it is often a salutary exercise to challenge our own most prized suppositions by testing them against alien ideas. Hence we should welcome gauntlets thrown at our feet from the likes of Newman and Lewis—from university scholars, that is, whose certainties were so vastly removed from our own certainties.

Some will wish to adjust the record here by pointing out that our particular hallmark is that we disclaim certainty. There can be no question of putting our certainties over against Newman's. The lines must be drawn, rather, between certainty and uncertainty. It is the mark of your modern, liberally educated, and therefore urbane man that he has jettisoned any hankerings after certainty and has learned to live, like Albert Camus, soberly and pensively, with bottomless uncertainty.

Our lines, then, should be drawn between the modern university, with its sovereign skepticism, and the old Western tradition represented by John Henry Newman and C. S. Lewis. In an essay entitled "Christianity and Culture" [in *Christian Reflections*], Lewis canvasses the question about the rival claims of religion and culture, with Matthew Arnold, Benedetto Croce, I. A. Richards, and others carrying the torch for culture's having supplanted religion as the agency for the betterment of mankind. Lewis marshals Aristotle, Plato, the Buddha, Saint Augustine, Saint Jerome, Saint Thomas, and Milton, as testifying to the inadequacy of culture alone to make us better people, that is, to make us virtuous. If it seems to have entailed a jump here, from education, or culture, to virtue, we may recall that the ancient tradition of education held that the *telos*, so to speak, of all tutelage was the virtuous man. [Lewis writes:]

> Finally I came to that book of Newman's ... the lectures on *University Education*. Here at last I found an author who seemed to be aware of both sides of the question; for no one ever insisted so eloquently as Newman on the beauty of culture for its own sake, and no one ever so sternly resisted the temptation to confuse it with things spiritual. The cultivation of the intellect, according to him, is "for this world": between it and "genuine religion" there is a "radical difference"; it makes "not the Christian ... but the gentleman," ... he "will not for an instant allow" that it makes men better.

Lewis here is considering Newman's claim "To perfect the mind is 'an object as intelligible as the cultivation of virtue, while, at the same time, it is absolutely distinct from it.'" Do Lewis and Newman mean to insist that I will be no farther along in the virtue sweepstakes after having immersed myself in the wisdom of Plato, opened myself to the force of *Oedipus Rex* or *Lear*, or learned all about Freud and Jung? To acquire knowledge with any trace of integrity—surely this is to hone my sensibilities and my perceptions, to broaden my sympathies, to develop greater sensitivity and discrimination, and to take on that gravity, moderation, and generosity that is the mark of the truly educated mind. And do not these qualities in some sense constitute virtues—or at least do they not contribute to the growth of virtue in me? It is nettlesome, really, to be told that I am no better a man for having gained this bachelor's or master's or doctor's degree.

When I lived in New York in the 1960s, I used to go to the New York Film Festival. Here was cinema that was serious, we told ourselves. The films probed our sensibilities and our values. Consciousness had been quickened, or so we felt. We were somehow chastened, purged, purified. As I was leaving Lincoln Center one night after a particularly heavy-duty film, I overheard a woman behind me in the emerging crowd effusing over how powerful it had all been and what a purgative experience it was.

I wanted to agree with her. But then *had* I been purified? In order to purify my inner man from all the venality and cravenness and duplicity and pusillanimity and parsimony and vindictiveness and vanity—not to mention concupiscence—in order to cleanse my innermost being from all of that, a very strong antidote would be needed. The intensity that is visited upon one sitting under the spell of good cinema or good theatre is a strong elixir, we might say; and we do feel chastened, at least emotionally.

Here is the problem. What is the connection between strong emotions and virtue? Intense emotions and insights do not always translate into an increase of actual virtue in us. The poor lecher dribbling into his scotch at the bar may admire virtue and may well have been deeply moved by the evening's performance, but somehow none of it empowers him to rise up, put one foot in front of the other, and head toward the virtuous life.

The university is the place where, at one remove from the hurly-burly of the marketplace, so to speak, we mortals have the task and the luxury of addressing ourselves to knowledge and culture—to the arts and sciences, to all that constitutes human endeavor, and to all that presents itself to our gaze. Astrophysics, psycho-linguistics, economics, computer technology, sculpture, logic: no region of inquiry is excluded. The increase of knowledge, the pursuit of data, the preservation of tradition, the passing on of the deposit—all of this and more is what courses through the corridors of the university.

But does it make us better? More informed, yes. But better? More able to control our environment, yes. But better? More powerful and more urbane, more discriminating and more aware, and more literate. But better? It is an awkward question.

Some such questions as these do, in fact, seem to tease us when we mull over this matter of the university. Are universities good places? I can remember thinking to myself, as I was working on my dissertation, "Now by rights all of us here in this English Department ought to be the best people around. After all, we have read *Gawain* and Proust and Edmund Spenser and John Donne and Emerson and Henry James. We are enormously civilized people here. We know sentimentalism when we see it. Our sensibilities are Olympian in their exaltedness."

Yes, I thought. But are we good? What does that professor there do about disorderly lust, for example? What do *I* do about it, for that matter? And vanity: Has the reading of *Piers Plowman* made this tutor humble and generous and pure? Has it made *me* humble and generous and pure? Has the reading of *Beowulf* or *Mrs. Dalloway* or *The Song of Roland* made us all noble and brave and true?

Which brings us back to Newman and Lewis. Newman insists that liberal knowledge is an end in itself and that we need no ulterior rationale for the perfecting of the mind. But he will "not for an instant allow" that any of this makes us better. Lewis, in the same essay quoted earlier, ventures the notion that culture is a storehouse of the best sub-Christian values:

> These values are in themselves of the soul, not the spirit. But God created the soul. Its values may be expected, therefore, to contain some reflection or antepast of the spiritual values. They will save no man. They resemble the regenerate life only as affection resembles charity, or honor resembles virtue.

Lewis, being himself a university man, defends the university, and the pursuit of culture, on the grounds that any good and true work on the part of us mortals is worthy. Here is how he puts the matter:

> Most men must glorify God by doing to His glory something which is not *per se* an act of glorifying but which becomes so *by being offered*. If, as I now hope, cultural activities are innocent and even useful, then they also ... can be done to the Lord. The work of a charwoman and the work of a poet become spiritual in the same way and on the same condition.

There is something vexing about these remarks if we wish to urge some special dignity for the university and its work, since Lewis' apologia on our behalf puts our work on the same footing as the work of the janitor and the woman with the mops. There is something perverse about such an apologia, surely?

We find Lewis' point in a sermon he preached in 1939 at Great Saint Mary's in Oxford:

> A university is a society for the pursuit of learning. As students, you will be expected to make yourselves ... into what the Middle Ages called clerks: into philosophers, scientists, scholars, critics, or historians. And at first sight this seems to be an odd thing to do during a great war.

Lewis then goes on to draw the analogy of Nero fiddling while Rome burns and points out that, from the Christian point of view, all times are like that: that is, at every moment of our lives we mortals have a question hanging over our heads that dwarfs even so urgent a situation as cities in conflagration. It is the question of heaven and hell. He acknowledges that university people can scarcely be asked to take seriously categories like heaven and hell, which seem to be the stock in trade of stump preachers and zealots. But, says Lewis, neither he himself, nor Saint Paul (who often gets the blame for talk of hell-fire) is responsible for raising such a specter. It is the Lord, Jesus Christ himself, who rings the changes on the topic:

> Human culture has always had to exist under the shadow of something infinitely more important than itself.... Men propound mathematical theorems in beleaguered cities, conduct metaphysical arguments in condemned cells, make jokes on scaffolds ... and comb their hair at Thermopylae. This is not panache: it is our nature.... We have to inquire whether there is really any legitimate place for the activities of the scholar in a world such as this. That is, we have always to answer the question "How can you be so frivolous and selfish as to think about anything but the salvation of human souls?"

He then points out the obvious, namely, that war or no war, hell or no hell, so to speak, we mortals are going to have to get on with the ordinary quotidian activities of eating and drinking and working and living.

> It is clear that Christianity does not exclude any of the ordinary human activities. Saint Paul tells people to get on with their jobs ... Our Lord attends a wedding and provides miraculous wine. Under the aegis of His Church ... learning and arts flourish. The solution of this paradox is of course well known to you. "Whether ye eat or drink or whatsoever ye do, do all to the glory of God." All our merely natural activities will be accepted, if they are offered to God ... Christianity does not simply replace our natural life and substitute a new one: it is rather a new organization which exploits, to its own supernatural ends, these natural materials.... There is no essential

quarrel between the spiritual life and the human activities
as such. Thus the omnipresence of obedience to God in a
Christian's life is, in a way, analogous to the omnipresence
of God in space.

And then Lewis weighs in with a remark that might
ruffle our scholarly feathers. He says,

> I reject at once the idea which lingers in the mind of some
> modern people that cultural activities are in their own right
> spiritual and meritorious—as though scholars and poets
> were intrinsically more pleasing to God than scavengers and
> boot blacks.... The work of Beethoven, and the work of a
> charwoman, become spiritual on precisely the same condi-
> tion, that of being offered to God.

What we encounter in the attitude of Newman and
Lewis is the outlook that sees everything *sub specie aeter-
nitatis*. On this view, God is not one among a number of
topics or headings. He is *the* topic. All topics crowd toward
him. All data imply God. There is nothing in this universe,
from the Christian point of view, that is not summoned by
that great bidding in the ancient canticle, *Benedicite, omnia
opera Domini*.

We find a paradox in the view of the university put
forward by Newman and Lewis. On the one hand, both
deny any special *cachet* to intellectual and cultural pursuits
and would hence seem to grant less dignity to the university than we ourselves might wish to grant. But, on the
other hand, given their Christian point of view, this locat-
ing of the university and its tasks in the same category with
all work, as that which may be made into an oblation to
the Most High—this crowns the enterprise with a dignity
and sacred character that exalts it far above the futility that
mocks work stained with the motive of career advance-
ment and destined for oblivion.

Both Newman and Lewis saw the whole human drama as positively humming with rumors of the divine drama. They believed that we mortals are never more royally ourselves than when we bow and offer the diadem of our humanity as an oblation at the Sapphire Throne. Because they believed this, they were able to speak of the university and its work as an activity most fitting to us mortals who owe our work and our very being to the God who is himself the source of all truth.

The Uses of Myth

We very often hear discussions on the topic "Christianity and Literature". Any such discussion, if it wishes to stay on the track, has got to acknowledge some high assumptions about myth—namely, that what we might call the *mythic mode* (that is, the mode of *showing and telling*, rather than of explaining and proving) is at the heart of the matter. The fountainhead of Christianity is not a moral scheme, a book of axioms, or a set of conundrums or cryptograms, as is the case with the world's religions: it is a drama, with a sequence of events, that was played out on the stage of our real, light-of-day history, in which the truth about things was embodied and enacted for us all to see. It was all shown to us, and told to us, in that drama. So that from the luminous intellect of a Saint Basil the Great, a Saint Thomas Aquinas, or a Pascal, down to the piety of a Sicilian peasant woman with her beads or the zeal of a stump preacher with his annotated Bible, all Christians are talking about a story: a myth, if you will, not in the modern sense of being a tale of marvels that never really occurred, but rather in the sense of being a narrative of events that themselves exactly embody and disclose high immensities and bright fixities.

The idea, for the Christian imagination, is that *the* drama, the only drama there is, really, and the drama that was guessed and strained at in the myths of the Greeks and

Originally published in *Mythlore*, Spring 1980, 20–23. Reprinted with permission.

the Norsemen and all other peoples, was, lo and behold, really played out for us in real history. This tale, or drama, is the fountainhead of all Christian thinking.

And the fountainhead of all literature is, of course, the incorrigible human inclination to take the clutter of mere experience and to order and shape it by working it up into narratives that will embody and disclose the truth about that experience for us and, in so doing, give that experience back to us transfigured—transubstantiated, even— into splendid and blissful forms. The literary or artistic imagination—let us call it the poetic imagination—sees that if you want to come at the nub of things you have to *re-create* them somehow over *here*, in some visible or audible form (in verse or mime or fresco or liturgy or sculpture or something). Somehow, we can't get things nailed down by means of propositions, questionnaires, or explanations. We must *show* them, exhibit them, enact them, celebrate them, recreate them. Hence all storytelling, all portraits, all still lifes, all singing of ballads, hymns, love songs, or dirges, all fanfares, all effigies, all processions, and so forth: these are cases in point of us humans trying to get a handle on the significance of things. They all, one way or another, bespeak the mythic mode—the mode of articulating significance by showing and telling rather than by explaining and dismantling.

Presumably all of us here would offer some such rationale for the mythic mode if we were called upon to say something in its behalf. We would try to point out to our interlocutors that we are not arguing for some particular viewpoint: rather, we would urge that you can't talk about the human phenomenon at all without affirming that the whole thing is "mythic", as it were—that we are myth-prone creatures; nay, that we are not only myth-prone, but that the only option open to us at all vis-à-vis our experience of existence is to re-create, or re-present, it to ourselves mythically. Otherwise, we land in sheer inanity and stultification. No doubt this would be the reason why we find a deep skepticism in ourselves about the modern reading of human existence: it is a radically analytical reading, and sooner or later that reading is going to drain the sap from existence, so that you are left with a civilization that does not know what to do about morals, about birth or death or anything in between. The sap that energizes and vivifies the tree of life rises from depths beyond the reach of any analytic plumbing—depths that pagans, Jews, and Christians have always recognized as being mysterious and which they have always approached, not with clipboards, questionnaires, computers, and caucuses, but with incense, blood, chant, and sackcloth.

But I am straying from my topic here, which is the uses of myth. We may begin by saying that myth as we usually think of it, that is, as narrative, is one of the modes that participates in this all-encompassing mode of which I have been speaking. That is, the telling of stories is itself one of many manifestations of the thing that shows up in all art, liturgy, costume, and cult. But not all stories strike us as being mythic. We feel that that term ought to be reserved for a special category of story that does not include all journalism, topical satire, popular fiction, and so forth. And so it ought. I would like, then, to mention four things that ought to be true of narrative before we call it truly mythic. I think that the *ises* of myth will be implicit in the discussion of these characteristics of myth.

First, when we speak of myth, we ordinarily refer to a narrative that is very remote in its setting. I was going to say that it had to be about the far away and long ago, but somebody would raise the question of science fiction and tales of the future and argue that those are mythic, too, and we would get into a discussion that I don't want to get into here. So let me say that myths have to be about the very remote (and this would take in planets and galaxies, if that is your taste). And we can all agree that traditionally this remoteness has been very much in terms of the far away and long ago. "Once upon a time in a far-off land" is the perfect beginning for a mythic tale. We don't want our myths beginning "At eleven A.M. yesterday in Cincinnati, a beautiful princess awoke and looked out the window at the smokestacks." That won't do. Why not? Well, because myths don't happen in Cincinnati, and they don't happen yesterday morning, or, for that matter, at eleven o'clock on *any* datable morning. And what's more, you can't have smokestacks in myths. You have got to have a noble lady awaking in a palace and looking out at the rosy-fingered dawn; and never mind exactly where the palace is or what year it is. If you nail it in to history and geography that closely, you have wrecked it somehow.

Some of you may have had the distressing experience of whisking along the autobahn in Germany and seeing signs indicating that you were driving through the Black Forest. The Black Forest? Great Scott—the Black Forest is a dark wood with gnarled oaks stooping low over your head, and you go through it on a dim path, on foot or at best on a horse. Elves peep at you, and crones pass by muttering, and hags beckon from their hovels, and hermits say Mass at tiny chapels. The Black Forest forsooth. This 1976 version is a keen disappointment. Why? Because the Black Forest of the fairy stories does not exist in terms of real estate in the Bundesrepublik Deutschlands. The same thing is true when you fly in a jet over Baghdad or Samarkand. Alas—I wanted to arrive at Baghdad at twilight, on the back of a camel, with the sky all crimson and the turrets pointing into the deepening indigo of the dusk, and the whine of reed pipes and the waving of diaphanous veils and the smell of incense. I somehow didn't fancy myself coming into this *airport*. If I had to fly in, I at least might have come in on a magic carpet.

Myth has to be remote somehow. There is a reason for this, I think. It is because myth hails the deepest recesses of our imaginations, and in order to do this, it must hail us with story and picture detached from the clutter and the hurly-burly of daily ordinariness. Myth takes us to a distant time and place (and my own suspicion is that it has got to be the distant part because we have a memory of Eden back there) to show us the pictures and tell us the stories that are there in that distant, basic region. Tolkien could not have had his Dark Riders sputtering up in helicopters, or Gandalf arriving at Minas Tirith in a Cadillac. It wouldn't do.

Secondly, however remote the region of myth is, it has got to be rooted in the same soil that our experience here is. That is, you can't have myths about creatures who have nothing in common with us at all, or about a realm that is unimaginable to us. There has got to be time, for one can't grasp sheer eternity or simultaneity; and there has to be *space*—we can't grasp a realm of pure dimensionlessness. There have to be intelligent, speaking creatures—you can't have myths about geometrical points or non-beings; and there has to be good and evil in terms that we can recognize—we are stuck with ideas about mercy vs. cruelty, and veracity vs. mendacity, and cynicism vs. hope, and lechery vs. chastity, and so forth, and no matter how you stretch or reverse or manipulate the moral scale in your tale, you have got to make it recognizable to us mortal men. Otherwise, you lose us.

In the Greek myths, for example, the Medusa was a horrible monster with snakes for hair. Well, it goes without saying that Medusa was evil: you can't have snakes for hair and be good. Or again, in Tolkien, the Dark Riders first show themselves as black-cloaked figures riding huge horses, sniffing the ground, and apparently ghost-like in that there does not seem to be anything inside those black cloaks. Well, there is no way, with a description like that, that a storyteller is going to get us mortal men to believe that those creatures are *good*. Certain shapes and characteristics mean *evil* to us. So the myth has to be rooted in the world that we know, where babbling brooks and soft flutes and sunlit meadows and misty mornings and lovely maidens and clear-eyed knights mean goodness, and where stinking pools and throbbing drums and beetling crags and murky midnights and hags and leering trolls mean that something is wrong.

Thirdly, real myth has got to invoke the high things. The high things? I use that term because I am not sure what else to call them. I am referring to such high things as majesty, courtesy, nobility, splendor, goodness, courage, sacrifice, and purity. What's that list all about? Nobody believes in all that any more. And that is just my point. You can't write novels and film scripts and serious dramas about majesty and purity and so forth, because you are writing for a world that thinks that business is gone with the wind, and the goner the better.

But the human imagination cannot live with this. You have doubtless read novels of the future—*1984* and *Brave New World*; in them you can see what happens when we try to live without the high things. And any Christian affirms this: he is committed to a vision of reality that is full of majesty and splendor and purity and joy and courtesy. And so he knows that a world that scorns these things is somehow damned. He believes what the prophets and poets knew, that the cities of the plain, that get themselves emancipated from the high and ancient things, are damned cities. He knows, for instance, that be we never so ferociously egalitarian, there is a majesty in the cards, for God is not the chairperson of any ad hoc committee: he is the king, crowned with gold, the Ancient of Days. And he knows full well that the mediaeval painting of God the Father as a bearded valetudinarian sitting on a throne, crowned with the tri-reghum, is closer in to the truth of the matter than any notion of him as Our Chairperson which art in heaven, or even as the Ground of Being.

Majesty is in the cards, then; but we live in a world that knows nothing at all of this, indeed, that disavows and hates this idea. Hierarchy, the corollary to the idea of majesty, is a sincerely detested idea in our day—and sections of Christendom have run hell-for-leather to hook themselves onto the bandwagon that is rolling loudly along toward the egalitarian city of man, or, rather, the city of persons; and they think it is a paradise, but alas, it is called hell. And how are we to keep alive the notion of majesty in our imaginations unless somewhere in there we keep telling stories that show us majesty? When we've got it all democratized and equalized and purged and disinfected from the old idea of hierarchy and majesty, pray God that there will be some old nurse somewhere who will still tell our children stories that begin, "Once upon a time, there was a great king."

And nobility and sacrifice and high courtesy and purity are all in the cards, but there is no imagery in the modern world by which we may speak of these things or keep them alive. So we have to have old tales that bespeak a world in which those things make sense. Our democratic landscape furnishes us with nothing that will enable us to keep keen and bright in our souls the vision of what any Christian suspects the City of God is like. Somebody has to

be telling stories about these things, since you can't argue
for them on the TV talk shows and in the columns of the
popular magazines. A stiff challenge for a writer of fiction
nowadays might be to write a story for us about a modern,
liberated woman, and to make her one-half as splendid
and mighty and ravishing and feminine and free as Tolkien's Galadriel, Sophocles' Antigone, Dante's Beatrice,
or Shakespeare's Portia. Or again, to tell us a story about
heaven, but instead of making it the city of the Great King,
with towers and jewelled gates and thrones, to make it a
commune with a rotating chairpersonship.

You may have read C. S. Lewis' space trilogy. At the end
of the first story, when the hero comes back to the planet
earth, he is talking with his friend about his extraordinary
and glorious and blissful experiences on the other planet,
Malacandra. Naturally, the idea of telling about his adven-
tures comes up, but he demurs: What good would it do?
Nobody would believe such things. No, says his friend;
but we must tell about them anyway, since, although we
may not get a believing audience, we will at least have a
body of people who have *heard a story like yours*. That is,
there will now be people familiar with certain ideas, and
with certain ways of looking at things.

And, fourthly, real myth stays very much in the realm
of externals. That is, the stories don't impress you as being
"deep" in psychological or moral "insights or in character
development, or in subtleties of plot and so forth." It is all
quite straightforward adventure, with one event following
another, the hero moving from this ordeal to this one, and
from this adventure to the next one, the landscape changing all the while from deep glades to caves to rocky defiles
in the mountains to dappled meadows, and so forth. Very
childish, apparently. And a lot of attention is given along
the way to plain things like rocks and trees and moss and

water and crusts of bread and flagons of wine and bowls of thick cream, and velvets and homespuns and brocades, and iron and steel and wood and earthenware. What's all that about?

Do we not see here a tremendously important thing—a thing, actually, that all of our lesser arts strain to get at one way or another, namely, the completely successful fusion of idea and image? That is, rather than the author having to talk to us, as it were, and lead us to the depths of significance in his work by what he interjects into his tale, we have instead the phenomenon of the "externals" of the story—the rocks and fabrics and scenes and situations—carrying on their own shoulders, sans any "authorial" assist, the entire burden of significance. So that it becomes, not a matter of any deep or heavy passages in myths, but rather of our being taken into a landscape where the scenery and situation are themselves an exact map or pattern of the reality being talked about—a reality that we lesser men have to come at by writing moral or psychological or philosophical essays, or moral stories or psychological novels. Or, put it another way: the spectacle is all you have, and all you need to have. In Perseus fighting the Medusa, you have a perfect and complete picture of a kind of struggle with evil that a thousand essays on evil don't give you quite so vividly. Or in the heroic and lonely stand of Gandalf before the gates of Minas Tirith, against the massed hosts of the Nazgul and their minions—do we not have there a picture that drives straight to the center and wellspring of our beings and opens up to us more vividly than a thousand meditations can just what heroism and purity and authority are?

I think we can see an attempt at the same thing at work in the visual arts. Take a painting of the Annunciation from the Middle Ages: here is the Virgin, crowned and sitting under gilded Gothic arches, with the winged angel approaching her. Do we suppose that Fra Angelico or Roger van der Weyden thought that it might have looked like this in first-century Nazareth? Not a bit of it. What, then, were they trying to get at? Was it not that they were trying to get a *picture* or *significance* that all glory is here when God comes to his handmaiden? Here is the transaction when our poor flesh is raised to the pinnacle of glory. How do we propose to visualize this to ourselves? Well, crowns and Gothic arches are one way of coming at the mystery.

But I would be giving a wrong impression if I seemed to be arguing that all the rocks and trees and scenes in mythic tales are supposed to suggest some sub-surface allegorical significance to us. They are not puzzles or conundrums, where we end up with little charts interpreting the myths for us, with rocks equalling obstacles in our allegorical gloss, and water equalling refreshment, and swords courage and dragons evil. The items in a mythic tale don't equal anything cued; they are themselves. The point about them is that we can see, visibly and vividly, in them situations that echo unmistakably moral and psychological situations that we know about from our own experience.

In fact, C. S. Lewis has pointed out that there is an odd sense in which the myths give real trees and rocks and eagles back to us in a fresh and vivid way that we might miss if we had "only" the daily trees and rocks and eagles that we see in the rush of our workaday lives. That is, having been taken into some ancient oak grove, all cool and twilit, with gnarled roots clinging to the lichen-covered rocks—having been taken in there in some myth, we have new eyes to see the oaks and rocks around us that we probably don't see at all, left to our own unaided imagination.

Well, perhaps this brings us back around to our original question. What are the uses of myth? Myth, in our sense here, is a special kind of narrative—a narrative that evokes the high and far-off and that gives us adventure taking place in a noble setting, among noble characters. The Greek myths do this, and the Nordic myths, and the Arthurian tales. And Tolkien has done it in our own time. But his choosing to do this was an odd thing, when we have such a rich and sophisticated literature already going in the twentieth century. *Why* did he do this?

Besides his confessed love of this sort of thing, and his stated desire simply to tell a story, it must be said that the kind of thing he wanted to evoke for us could only be evoked via this kind of narrative. In the brawling tumble of modernity, whose landscape is blasted with the ash heaps of technology and participatory democracy and the power struggle and chairpersonships and litigation and miles per hour and pragmatic banality, how do we propose to keep alive in our souls such notions as majesty, splendor, courtesy, nobility, sacrifice, renunciation, fidelity, chastity, virginity, and so forth? They don't fit in our landscape, and there are few raw materials in our landscape from which we can fashion pictures of them. Hence, somebody in there has to keep on telling tales of realms in which those things make sense. We can't win debates on virginity anymore: but perhaps we can tell tales of a high and blissful order of things where virginity makes overwhelming sense. And so with the other things that you find in myth but that you can't find in our imaginative landscape. Any Christian suspects that those things are there forever. One way or another, we have to tell the story about them.

The Evangelicals—Part I

The other day, my wife and I found ourselves talking about a friend who is on the (very large) staff of ministers at a big, energetic Protestant church near Chicago. The conversation turned to the whole phenomenon of such churches, and it struck me that it might be something to the purpose to try to explain all of this to Roman Catholics, who most certainly have heard about "the evangelicals". Who are they? What's the difference between a Protestant and an evangelical? Any number of such questions tend to perplex curious Catholics.

Evangelicalism is not a denomination like Presbyterian, Baptist, or Episcopalian. The word refers, rather, to an outlook on the part of some millions of Protestants in America and England—and, by extension, in the rest of the world, which has been the object of English and American missionary work. I should mention that the word *evangelische* in Europe merely means Lutheran. But in America, the evangelicals believe the ancient Creeds, with no diluting brought about by what Pius X saw coming down the pike, namely, Modernism. The big Protestant denominations, with the exception of the Southern Baptists, have pretty well gone over to some form of Modernism, which questions the authenticity of the Old Testament and, in many cases, entertains the most somber doubts about Our Lord's miracles—most notably, his virgin birth and his Resurrection. The evangelicals will have none of this. Like

Originally published in *Crisis*, April 1, 2006. Reprinted with permission.

orthodox Roman Catholics, they take Scripture and the Creeds to mean that Mary conceived Jesus without help from any Roman soldier (that is the usual canard) and that his physical body left the tomb on Easter. Evangelicals also cling fiercely to Luther's notion of *sola scriptura*, which holds that nothing but the Bible (no Church, no Tradition, no priesthood) is fundamental to Christian life and belief. That is why your evangelical friends, upon learning that Catholics venerate (not worship) the Blessed Mother, will want you to quote them a text from the New Testament supporting such a practice. So far, evangelicalism is indistinguishable from old-fashioned, orthodox Protestantism.

In order to clarify the distinction, we have to go on to speak about the evangelical outlook and attitudes. For one thing, evangelicalism constitutes an enormously muscular—doubtless the most muscular—wing of Protestantism. The sheer facts account for this. In the usual run of things, the liberal (Modernist) Protestant churches, while commanding all the headlines in the *New York Times* and ruling absolutely from all of their denominational headquarters and in seminaries, have a melancholy way of dwindling, whereas one can't stop the evangelical churches from growing and bursting. It is nothing for an evangelical church, founded five years ago by some ardent minister out of his own back pocket, to swell to thousands and find it necessary to split into two, then three, then four, congregations.

One such church is the Redeemer Presbyterian Church in Manhattan. A man called Tim Keller started this operation some years ago, and it is very likely the fastest-growing—and, I would guess, the most intelligently energetic—church in New York. Actually, the world now is full of such churches. The "mega-churches" are all evangelical, although many cautious evangelicals are far from certain as to what view to take of them. They look like corporations to an outsider.

We have perhaps brought things to a point, if not of completion, at least of introduction. Next month, God willing, we may continue this brief sketch of a phenomenon that we Catholics will do well to ponder. As a convert myself from evangelicalism to the Church, I ache to see evangelicals enter into the riches of true Catholicism.

The Evangelicals—Part II

To continue the discussion of evangelicals, begun last month: Catholics are somewhat aghast at the sheer energy that is at work in the evangelical churches. For one thing, the evangelicals never need to have any sort of yearly canvass for funds. You can't stop them from giving lavishly. Catholics think you are doing handsomely if you ante up 10 percent of your annual income; evangelicals empty their pockets. For another thing, evangelicals talk incessantly about their faith. In random conversation, over the telephone, in endless Bible study and fellowship groups, they speak in familiar terms to each other about "the Lord". A Catholic may find himself staggered by this happy volubility and wonder what has happened to the *mysterium tremendum* in all of the chat. On the other hand, your evangelical may likewise find himself nonplussed by the Catholic's embarrassment when it comes to nattering about the faith. (This is why many evangelicals wonder among themselves whether Catholics are "saved" at all: How can they say they believe something about which they are so unwilling to pipe up?)

The Catholic's question about this easy familiarity with "the Lord" is difficult to answer, since the founders of Protestantism—Luther and John Calvin, and even Ulrich Zwingli and Menno Simon (of the Mennonites)—would have found it odd. Their clientele did not seem to have been quite so happy-go-lucky about things. The habit

Originally published in *Crisis*, May 1, 2006. Reprinted with permission.

may have arisen in the wake of the great John Wesley's preaching in eighteenth-century England. He preached the necessity of intelligent conversion (as opposed to infant baptism) and set his people on a course of ardent, Bible-based spirituality. But if the habit did not appear then, it most certainly did in the wake of the mass-meetings of the nineteenth-century evangelist D. L. Moody. (It may be worth noting for some confused Catholics that an "evangelist" is merely a man who preaches the gospel—while an "evangelical" is a Christian who finds his home in the sector of Protestantism of which we are here speaking.) As a result of Moody's preaching, an enormous number of eager believers was added to the ranks of American Protestantism, and they, with their leaders, were more than ready to speak quite informally about their faith.

At their meetings, they were (and are) much given to offering "testimonies", which take the form of one's standing up in a meeting and talking in an impromptu way about "what God has been doing for me these days". These testimonies are heavily laced with Scripture quotations, which fact leads us to yet another characteristic practice of the evangelicals that ought to interest Catholics: the discipline of "Scripture memory". Beginning as a child, at your Sunday school and vacation Bible school, you are given lists of Bible texts to memorize, usually with the reference for each one attached to your recitation the next day. So, a tot will stand up and say, "John 14:6, 'Jesus saith unto him, I am the way, the truth, and the life: no man cometh unto the Father but by me.'"

Readers will ask what all of this "saith" and "cometh" is about. It betrays the version of the Bible from which I and all generations of Protestants from the 1950s back to the seventeenth century memorized these texts. It is the King James Version, properly called the Authorized Version, translated from the Hebrew and Greek and published in 1611 at the behest of King James I of England. I have heard Catholics refer to this Bible as "the Saint James Version". King James was not, so far as we know, a saint, although (another memory verse of mine) "Man looketh on the outward appearance, but God looketh on the heart." Thank God for that!

The Evangelicals—Part III

This will form the third entry in a somewhat unplanned series that I stumbled into two months ago. I found myself wanting to say something helpful to readers of *Crisis* about that notable and energetic sector of Protestantism loosely known as "the evangelicals", but I ran out of space in my first column and spilled over into a second and now a third.

In the last two columns, I pointed out that evangelicalism is not a denomination. A man may be a Presbyterian, an Episcopalian, a Methodist, or a Baptist and not be particularly evangelical. The word refers to an *outlook*. The evangelicals, many of them in these denominations, actually believe the Creeds quite literally, as do all orthodox Catholics. They will have no nonsense about the Virgin Birth being a pious fiction, or the Resurrection referring only to some vaporous survival of "the spirit of Jesus" in his followers. Most of the big official Protestant denominations allow for great liberty on these points, and nearly all of their seminaries have long since gone over to what Pius X called Modernism. To this extent, then, we may say that the evangelicals constitute an energetically traditional and orthodox presence in Protestantism.

But there is an enormous phenomenon among them that leaves Catholics scratching their heads. This is the "independent" churches. Since the evangelicals do not believe that the Church is a visible institution founded by the Apostles, with an apostolic priesthood and hierarchy, but believe

Originally published in *Crisis*, June 1, 2006. Reprinted with permission.

it to be merely the worldwide aggregation of all individual believers in Jesus Christ (called the "invisible Church"),
they, of course, can start up a church every hour on the half-
hour. They don't even need an ordained minister to do so.

A "church", for them, is just a group of Christian believers
who want to gather together for "fellowship" and preaching, and perhaps, from time to time, a "communion service" (this would answer to the Mass, but in their view the
bread and wine stay just that, brought into play as a memorial device). Bill Jones may be the pastor, and, if things flour-
ish, the group will move out of somebody's living room and
into some local facility. And then, as happens more often
than not, since these evangelical churches *grow*, they will
build an enormous building to house the hundreds, and
often thousands, of people who have turned up to join the
assembly. The "mega-churches" grow this way, and their
facilities often look more like airports than churches.

A Catholic will be huffing and puffing at this point.
"But you can't just *do* that!" Well, they do. And here is
where the rub comes—hundreds of thousands of Roman
Catholics find their way to these churches and emerge
gasping, "I was a Catholic until I was fifteen, and then
I met Jesus!" or, "I was raised Catholic, but I became a
Christian when I was twenty", or, "I was Catholic until I
was thirty, and then I was born again."

We may protest. But there it is. What has gone wrong?
Have their parishes fed their sheep on pap—"caring and
sharing", and other Hallmark card sentiments? If this seems
too severe, then we may look where we will for answers.
Evangelicalism, from the Catholic point of view, is a sort
of para-church phenomenon, and there is much that we
would wish to tell them—about sacraments, the Eucharist,
apostolicity, the Magisterium, and so forth. Meanwhile,
we may do some sober reflecting.

High on Books

The following is not so much a systematic or exhaustive bibliography as a brief list, assembled at the request of the editors, of books that have instructed me in the whole matter of liturgy and sacraments and that have opened up immense and splendid vistas of Christian vision not commonly accessible to strictly Reformational imagination.

The Golden String by Dom Bede Griffiths. The autobiography of the man to whom C. S. Lewis dedicated his own autobiography. It records, with luminous integrity and gracefulness, Griffiths' pilgrimage first to faith, then into the Roman Catholic Church, then into Benedictine monasticism. His description of what the liturgy means is magnificent.

The School of Charity and the Mystery of Sacrifice by Evelyn Underhill. The book contains two long essays, the second of which is a guide to what is going on in the liturgy by a woman who had written much on mysticism and the spiritual life before she became a believer.

The Descent of the Dove by Charles Williams. A brief, layman's history of the Church, written by this vastly energetic and resourceful friend of C. S. Lewis'. It convinced me that the Holy Ghost has indeed been operative in the Church for two thousand years, in all sorts of odd ways not admissible to my own rather smallish categories.

Originally published in *Eternity*, March 1978, 16. Reprinted with permission.

Apologia Pro Vita Sua by John Henry Newman. No apology need be furnished for this towering Christian classic. It is Newman's pilgrimage from devout evangelical faith to Rome.

An Essay on the Development of Christian Doctrine by John Henry Newman. A highly controversial essay in which Newman attempts to show that the natural fruition of what is fully and plainly implicit in the Gospel is to be found in the Roman Catholic Church. One does not have to accept his case to find the book vastly informative and challenging.

The Shape of the Liturgy by Dom Gregory Dix. This is the great encyclopedia on the history and development of the liturgy. Enthralling reading and almost guaranteed to stun any honest mind with the validity of the liturgy.

For the Life of the World by Alexander Schmemann. A virtually indispensable book, quite brief and in paperback by an Orthodox theologian, describing with thrilling clarity and patience just what the sacramentalist outlook on the world is.

A Spiritual Aeneid by Ronald Knox. The spiritual itinerary of one of the most urbane and brilliant minds ever to emerge from Eton and Oxford. (Knox is familiar to evangelicals as a translator of the New Testament.)

Christian Celebration: The Mass by J. D. Crichton. A step-by-step explanation for the benefit of old-fashioned Roman Catholics on what the Vatican II liturgical changes mean. Protestants ought to find it instructive and exciting, leading them to ask, "Well, if this isn't what the Lord's Supper is all about, then what *is* it all about?"

The Sacred and the Profane by Mircea Eliade. Basic. Most helpful in opening up the whole topic of mystery and the sacred to Protestant imagination.

God in Search of Man by Abraham Joshua Heschel. Written by a rabbi, the noble vision of the holy in this book will overwhelm many Christians with the unhappy conviction that they have hitherto settled for a tawdry, tacky set of religious wares.

William Cowper:
Selected Poetry and Prose

edited by David Lyle Jeffrey

If anyone still knows the name of William Cowper (pro-
nounced "Cooper") besides graduate students in English,
it will be Protestants who may on occasion find themselves
singing one of his hymns, most notably "Oh! For a Closer
Walk with God", although under the seismic wave of
"Praise Songs", this hymn may have been lost along with
the entire treasury of English-language hymnody.

In good eighteenth-century fashion, Cowper wrote
immensely long poems, not all of them easily readable to
modern readers. However, if one sticks to the job, he will
discover sentiments, articulated gracefully and earnestly,
that spring from the center of Christian piety and devotion.

The reader who happens to be Christian in his outlook
may gradually find that Cowper's "quaint" way of speaking
turns out to be the very mediator of hitherto unthought-of
avenues of prayer and meditation.

Cowper had a terrible life, if we are speaking of his soul.
Brought up an Anglican—his father was a clergyman—he
was bedeviled for virtually the whole of his adult life with
what he felt to be culpable doubt of the most bottomless
order. More than once he was consigned to the "mad-
house". His troubles would nowadays, of course, be assigned
to clinical depression.

Originally published in *Crisis*, January 1, 2008. Reprinted with permission.

He made gestures toward suicide three times, feeling that he had somehow committed the Unpardonable Sin. Good friends had to look after him and take him in for most of his life. He appears to have won some serenity before the end.

The first poem included in David Lyle Jeffrey's brief, helpfully footnoted anthology may be taken as representative of his long works. It is entitled "Truth" and offers a close scrutiny of man with all of the temptations and guilt that beleaguer us mortals.

In the course of the poem, Cowper lets fly at what he sees to be the faults of Protestantism, for example, parsimony and humbug, with "Yon ancient prude [who] sails with mincing airs, / Duly, at clink of bell, to morning prayers," followed by her little servant, "The shiv'ring urchin, bending as he goes, / With slip-shod heels and dewdrop at his nose ... [who] Carries her Bible tucked beneath his arm, / And hides his hands to keep his fingers warm."

But the poet also takes aim at the papist with his "Book, beads, and maple-dish.... Girt with a bell-rope that the Pope has bless'd." Any person who has the least capacity for enjoying poetry at all may find great pleasure here.

Cowper wrote endless playful, but usually poignant, lyrics as well as these long poems. We find a twelve-line threnody "On a Goldfinch, starved to death in his cage", and "A Tale", lauding bleak and barren Scotland for the love that we (English) may learn from her, most notably from the heroic mutual loyalty of two Scottish chaffinches.

My own favorite of these bagatelles is "The Diverting History of John Gilpin", in which we have a London linen draper whose horse runs away with him, thus furnishing great hubbub and glee over the countryside through which the horse obliges poor John to gallop.

There are some nettlesome oddities about the volume, which perhaps ought not to be laid at Jeffrey's feet. For example, the classical Latin subscripts from Horace and Virgil are not translated, and while on one page we are told that "Britain's oak" refers to "oak-timbered ships", on a later page we are left to our own resources with the phrase "go snacks", whose very syntax, let alone the allusion, is opaque.

But far more vexing than these minuscule items is the fact that there is no index. This seems inexplicable in a volume of verse. How is a reader ever to find the selection he wants? I had to leaf through the entire book to find various items I wanted.

One can scarcely attribute this sort of thing to Jeffrey, who is a most accomplished scholar and is to be commended on this judicious selection from Cowper's work.

No doubt Cowper's greatest legacy is his contribution to the famous "Olney Hymns", which he and the converted slave-trader John Newton wrote. My own favorite (included here) is one that might invite shudders from modern Christians. In it we hear that "There is a fountain fill'd with blood / Drawn from Emmanuel's veins."

The point here, certainly, would be the Precious Blood that all good Catholics, Orthodox, and Protestants adore as supplying their eternal salvation. For bringing such a poet out of obscurity, Jeffrey deserves the thanks of all.

Finding the Landlord: A Guidebook to C. S. Lewis' *The Pilgrim's Regress*

by Kathryn Lindskoog

The Pilgrim's Regress has never been a favorite of C. S. Lewis' books with his reading public. It is unabashedly allegorical, for one thing, and if allegory is too obvious or slavish, it can become boring. Many readers perhaps fear that they will be thus bored if they persevere with the reading of this book. But no doubt the principal reason for the public's skittishness about *The Pilgrim's Regress* is that it is so allusive and seems to presuppose one's having mastered almost the whole intellectual history of the West.

The latter fear is not altogether unfounded. If there is any legitimacy to it, Kathryn Lindskoog has done the work that ought to dispel it.

There are too many books and dissertations about Lewis; most of them will prove, mercifully, to be ephemeral. My own guess is that this work by Mrs. Lindskoog may well find a secure place among the few books that ought to remain on the shelf next to Lewis' own work.

The work is nothing if not thorough. We begin with an excellent literary biographical sketch, in the sense that it is brief and does not mire us in the thousand details that might be diverting, or interesting, but are not strictly necessary to the single course Mrs. Lindskoog is following,

Originally published in *Cornerstone*, January 1996, 23, 29. Reprinted with permission.

namely, to illumine Lewis' text itself. Lewis' early (and persistent) experience of "Joy" is explained and illustrated for us with an economy and clarity that is wholly satisfying. Both scholars and ordinary readers will be the beneficiaries of Mrs. Lindskoog's amazing knowledge of, apparently, every line of Lewis' entire oeuvre, and her mastery of the relevant material in letters, diaries, and so forth. She marshals all of this with an unprepossessing ease that is a rarity in scholarly work.

The approach to the text itself is systematic—almost delightfully so. You begin on page 1, and you are told everything that you might need to know. Latin superscripts are all translated, every image is explained, and allusions are cross-referenced either by way of suggesting their actual sources in literature or at least of hearing echoes. Scripture, myth, philosophy, and culture are all touched by Lewis' allegorical imagery, and we are assisted at every point. (Again, one is amazed at Mrs. Lindskoog's exhaustive knowledge of things: she is a polymath. She has smoked things out of D. H. Lawrence and Clive Bell, who did their work at a polar distance from Lewis' world, as well as out of Spenser, Bunyan, and the Bible.)

The experiences of John, the protagonist, lead him from fear through desire and lust, and thence through rationalism, thrill, Romanticism, squalor, and the barren uplands of "Northern" philosophy (not to be confused with the "Northernness" that so haunted Lewis in connection with the tales of Balder, Siegfried, and the Norse gods). The itinerary—West then South, then North—is pursued for us, with the points on the compass and the landscape itself being explained. If this sounds pedantic, or perhaps even patronizing (come: I don't need to be held by the hand in quite this solicitous way), then one has not yet put himself into Mrs. Lindskoog's hands. There is no pedantry and no patronizing. All is helpful, clear, and to the point. It would not be stretching a point to venture that this study of *The Pilgrim's Regress* turns out to be as helpful an introduction to Lewis' entire life's work as any book that has yet been written on him and his work. I myself would be happy to give it to anyone as a first book on Lewis—always urging, as would Lewis and Mrs. Lindskoog, that the point, of course, is that one get on into the original text itself.

The Franklin Trees:
A Late-Summer Night's Dream

by Jonathan Nauman

T. S. Eliot speaks of the "fear in a handful of dust", the idea being that if we could see the thunderous worlds of sub-atomic activity even in such an unlikely heap as a handful of dust, we would be stricken.

The same thing is at work in the great paintings. The artist—let us say Vermeer—fixes upon a kitchen, with nothing at all going on in it. A maid stands there with a ceramic milk pitcher. Nothing of interest here—or rather, everything. The painter sees luminescence and sublimity in this vignette that the rest of us would have missed.

Orthodox and Catholic Christians encounter the same thing day by day in the liturgy. We find a man, bread, wine, and a pre-set script, but the eye of faith sees here that the scrim between the temporal and the eternal has become very thin. Cherubim and seraphim are, in fact and not in fantasy, in attendance.

Literature, most notably children's literature, often bespeaks this oddity, namely, that Ultimacy—or Glory perhaps—lurks very nearby. In one story, we may be whirled off by a cyclone to Oz; in another, Peter Pan is the avatar. (I myself think that those two examples trivialize things and fall into frivolity and bathos.) In another

Originally published in *Touchstone*, September/October 2010. Reprinted with permission.

tale, we find that a wardrobe full of fur coats backs up onto Aslan's Country, and in another we are summoned to the Third Age of Middle Earth. In the novels of Charles Williams, we find heaven and hell under every bush, in the form of the Holy Grail, or a cube of the primordial matter of the Creation inscribed with the Tetragrammaton or the Platonic archetypes.

It is worth noting that in such tales, where the treatment is serious, what goes on beyond the scrim of ordinariness is clearly of the same fabric as the quotidian conditions in our familiar world. Serious fantasy never depends on sheer extravagance for effect. A certain reticence, even humility, seems to govern things in the worthy examples of fantasy, as though one stood in the presence of great glories and could not play hob with things.

The book in question here, Jonathan Nauman's *The Franklin Trees*, exhibits that reticence. On the surface of things, we find ourselves, as it were, in the world of the Hardy Boys: plain, decent, believable schoolboys going about their business in upstate New York. The business, however, entails a small prank—just a forgivable trick played on their teacher. But the prank opens the gate onto that domain where our commonplace actions and motivations and relationships appear illumined by the radiance of Truth itself.

In the commonplaces of ordinary life, we are most often "protected from heaven and damnation" (Eliot again) by the pall of the ordinary. But when the light of Truth breaks through to us, we find that hell and heaven, or shall we say vanity, malice, grudge, parsimony, and pusillanimity, on the one hand, and courage, candor, nobility, generosity, and Caritas, on the other, lie under every bush. And what did we ever suppose were the wellsprings of our ordinary encounters with each other anyway?

Our hero is a boy called Jim Canby. His friend Alan Prince accompanies Jim up to a certain stage in the action. A thoroughly believable—and interesting—story unfolds. But presently we (and Jim) wonder just what footing things are proceeding on. Almost imperceptibly, strangeness filters onto the stage. Reality—commonplace, tangible "reality", that is—seems to be being called in question.

For one thing, there are the Franklin trees. Their delicate blossoms seem to exude something more than their fragrance. Is it light? Do they have the power to unveil the past perhaps? The boys react as normal boys would. Doubt, curiosity, hesitation, fear, wonder—how does one react to these blossoms?

And then there is the question of dreams. Jim's dreams seem to bear a somewhat questionable relation to light-of-day circumstances. And not only that: one wonders whether they are perhaps piercing the scrim that keeps the commonplace safely commonplace. It is all handled with great skill by the author. There are never effects for effects' sake.

There is an old estate, complete with gardens, gates, walls, and an old house with tall staircases and echoing rooms and a dark attic. And an old woman. Who is she? What is her story? Where are we? In the present or in the past? Or both?

But a review must stop on the hither side of giving things away.

To my mind, this tale does indeed take its place among the works mentioned in the opening paragraphs of this review. The "machinery" of the action is controlled with the tact that marks off worthwhile stories from mere sensationalism. Before we are through, we have been hailed with "the Permanent Things". There is sin (there is no other name for it, finally) in its civilized guises of bitterness and vengefulness and vanity and jealousy. And there are the saving graces of courage and decency and purity of heart and forgiveness.

The Lady Julian tells us, "All shall be well, and all manner of thing shall be well." That would be an intolerable bromide if it weren't bought at the price of great sacrifice. Jonathan Nauman's story leads us into the precincts where these immensities touch believably on the life of a young upstate New York schoolboy.

Foreword

I have never met Gregory and Maureen Floyd. And yet I consider them to be among my most cherished friends. We have spoken on the phone many times and exchanged letters. I have listened (with unabashedly flowing tears) to Gregory's tape of songs that he wrote not long ago.

About what? And whence this odd friendship? Ah: there is the key.

It is all about the sudden death of their little boy John-Paul, struck by a car in front of their house in a quiet cul-de-sac, and killed instantly. His brother David was with him and was also hit, but survived.

All of us, I think, and especially us parents, would place the death of one of our children at the top of the list of unimaginable horrors. War, famine, betrayal, estrangement, death—these are all there on that list. But there is something about the poignance, the grotesque irony, and the clashing contradiction that swirl about the death of a small child, especially an angelic child, which John-Paul happens to have been—there is something about this that complicates and intensifies and batters at our grief in a unique way.

Gregory Floyd, in the book you are about to read, has charted, with remorseless candor, immense courage, and acute notation of every nuance, the progress (if that is the word) of the grief that overwhelmed *him* in the days,

Originally published in *A Grief Unveiled* by Gregory Floyd (Brewster: Paraclete Press, 1999), xi–xiv. Reprinted with permission.

weeks, months, and now years, that followed John-Paul's death. I say overwhelmed him: Maureen is very, very much at the center of the picture. But Gregory confesses over and over that he, the father and man, cannot quite enter wholly into the fathomless mystery that marks the grief of a mother. This couple knows, if anyone ever has, what it means to be one heart and one flesh in the holy sacrament of marriage. And yet death, that great Enemy, has among his cruel tactics the power to drive a wedge even here, so that there is a dread sense in which each must bear his own grief, even in the midst of bearing one another's burden.

The following record is a very rich one. Gregory Floyd is a man who knows God, like Job or John the Baptist. Hence, there is nothing saccharine or tawdry here (it is so easy to gild death with sentimentalism), nor any pyrotechnics. It is a straightforward and unsparing record—unsparing of the reader as well as of the writer, I might add. Nothing is swept under the rug. No platitudes are brought into play to ameliorate things. The boy is dead. An outrage has torn at the fabric of the universe. An obscenity (yes—an obscenity) has stained Creation. Mere palliatives and placebos won't do. We go down into the valley of the shadow of death with this family—nay, we might even say to hell, following the Pioneer of our Faith as he descends on Holy Saturday to the extremity of the mystery.

There is an interesting note that strides like a motif all the way through this account. It is this: No matter how high-flown or deep-probing Gregory's reflections and cries of agony are, and no matter what spiritual immensities are invoked, we are never, for a single page, removed from the immediate, tangible, physical reality of John-Paul's death. There is no threshold between the spiritual and the physical here. The one bespeaks the other. This is because Gregory is a sacramentalist and, hence, is utterly at home in those precincts where the eye of faith sees the eternal in the temporal. We never leave that little boy, eventually buried in his coffin, for two minutes. There is an incomprehensible disjuncture, of course, between the simultaneous facts of John-Paul's body in the cold earth and his being safely home with Jesus and his Blessed Mother—even in the "lap" of the Father, we are told more than once. But this is not a contradiction. The disjuncture stretches our faith and toughens it, getting us ready for that great Consummation of all things when we will see how everything fits.

The reader will find himself pricked by the needle-sharp perspicacity of Gregory's insights, and also of his probing and doubts. He (the reader, that is) will find himself drawn into somber reflections about the mysteries of God—of God as loving Father (then why did he let this happen?) and as Sovereign (then why did he let this happen?). He will find himself challenged by reflections on Scripture that penetrate far beyond the cavalier reading we are likely to give Scripture when all is going brightly for us. And dreams—lots of dreams. What about dreams in the life of a Christian? It becomes clear that more than a few of them come from a Source infinitely higher than anything poor Sigmund Freud ever fancied.

And what about "healing"? How fast should it occur? Are there temptations to dawdle or to hold on to one's grief as a sort of cockade in one's hat, giving one special status? How does one orchestrate one's own broken heart while still having to be fully father to a houseful of surviving children and husband to a grieving mother?

The prose in this book is often positively gnomic (a nice, ancient word suggesting compact, incisive, "repeatable" lines). For example: "There is a difference between early grief and later grief. Early grief is acute; later grief is more diffuse. Early grief smacks, stings, punches; later grief is more gentle. Early grief is a stalker; later grief is a companion. Early grief is crags and crevices; later grief is furrows softened by the passage of time."

One more thing: the songs. Here we find lyrics wrung from the depths of a bereaved father's heart—songs of sorrow, of love, of wistfulness, but then of hope and even—yes—joy. I have had the privilege of hearing these evocative lyrics sung when I set aside one Sunday afternoon to listen to Gregory's album, *Angel in Disguise*. When it was finished, I rang Gregory to tell him how much it had meant to me. But he had to interpret my sobs, for I could not speak.

Read this book, and be drawn along the Way of the Cross.

The Roots of American Order

by Russell Kirk

The key words in the title of Russell Kirk's book, "roots" and "order", are germane to any Bicentennial reflections on what America is and where it is going.

The political left has pre-empted the word "radical". Indeed, a case can fairly easily be made that as the word is used in popular politics now, it means merely "drastic". It pertains to a view of things that, while proposing sweeping changes in social and moral conditions, seldom has the patience and modesty to go to the *radix*, the root. In other words, "radical", at least as we know it in the United States now, means its own opposite: superficial (viz., the student revolts of the late sixties, or the various brands of "new" politics that appear weekly).

The other word in Kirk's title is equally germane. Order. Any society—feudal, Maoist, or Jeffersonian—has to have some understanding of the nature of its own ordering of things if it is going to preserve and defend that order. Order is what makes moral and social existence—in fact, existence itself—possible. Chaos and anarchy stand, not just over against moral and social order, but over against existence. Mao knows this as well as Genghis Khan.

In this study, Russell Kirk goes all the way back. His thesis is that order is necessary to any existence called

Originally published in *Christianity Today*, July 1976. Reprinted with permission.

human and that this order is moral. He asserts that this thesis has been demonstrated in history.

Kirk begins historically with "The Law and the Prophets". The Old Testament is not always included in discussions of American democracy. Indeed, popular imagination often sees, no doubt, an antinomy between this democracy and the dreadful, absolutist, supernaturalistic, legalistic, Yahwist order in ancient Israel. But this is to miss our debt to Israel, which is at the very least the understanding that *God* is the source of order and justice and that what binds a healthy society together is covenant, not just between man and man, but between those men and God. The Prophets kept alive the ethical meaning of human existence by their shrill denunciation of sin—not just of fornication, as is often suggested in caricatures of the Prophets, but of all forms of violence, corruption, oppression, indulgence, and so forth. A great legacy from Israel to us is the notion of *man under God* and the corollary notion of the impossibility of any humanly constructed utopia.

The history of Greece furnishes us with a "cautionary tale" of class conflict, disunity, and internecine violence. "The ancient Greeks failed in this", says Kirk: "they never learned how to live together in peace and justice." Kirk argues that, while Plato and Socrates were not direct influences on our founding fathers, yet their vision was there, in the fabric of Western tradition, "reminding some men that there endures a realm of ideas more real than the realm of appetites ... insisting that if men's souls are disordered, society becomes no better than a cave or a dust storm." On the other hand, "the Greeks' conviction that religion and culture must be bound up inseparably with the city-state went against the grain of American individualism.... The Greeks would have been astounded that such a nation–state [as America], unconsecrated to the gods, could endure for a decade."

Our debt to the Roman ideas of *ius civile* (law for the franchised citizens), *ius gentium* (for all the people), and *ius naturale* (fundamental principles founded on ethical norms) is well enough known, and Kirk emphasizes this. His account of the decline of Rome, with the insoluble problem of centralization, the increase of taxation and bureaucracy, and the draining off of the ancient religious order into the vagaries of emperor worship and the mystery cults, is self-evidently relevant to our own experience. Over against the public moral decline stood the lonely figure of Marcus Aurelius, the Stoic emperor, whose view did not carry the day.

The Christian order, such as it was, supplanted the Roman order in the West. The chaotic nature of the "Christian" centuries itself may bear out the Augustinian canon that we live in a sinful world and that there is no salvation to be looked for from the political order. To the Christian outlook the American Fathers owed their ideas of individual worth, of the equality of all men before God, and of the limitation of earthly authority. The mediaeval patrimony of law, of slowly developing representative government (especially in England), of the effort to achieve a balance between church and state, of language, of commerce, and of learning (viz., the great universities) "was so much taken for granted by the men who founded the American Republic that they did not even trouble themselves to praise it so much as they should have done", Kirk observes.

The American Fathers shared the Reformers' rejection of the Renaissance as a blending of "licentious paganism with corrupt Catholicism". But among the legacies of the Reformation to America, we must also include the great energy and individualism that characterized the formative years of our civilization.

In seventeenth-century England, we find Hobbes, whose influence on English and American thinking was enormous, divorcing as he did politics from religion; and Bunyan, celebrating the meaning of individual life as a pilgrimage toward God; and Locke, urging the ideas of natural contract and the right to property. In our own colonial order, we find a growing toleration of religious and philosophical outlooks, a rejection of aristocracy (notably in South Carolina), the rise of representative assemblies, and the appearance of Deism, which, despite the influence of Wesley, Whitefield, and Edwards, eventually dominated official American imagination. In the eighteenth century, influences that Kirk touches among others are those of Hume (politics as the art of the possible), Blackstone (the notion of precedent as a determining factor in jurisprudence), and Edmund Burke (civil liberty comes, not from Nature, but from experience, convention, and compromise).

There is very little similarity between the American and the French revolutions, in Kirk's view. The American Revolution attached itself always to history and experience rather than to slogans and utopian ideas. Our Constitution reflects the tension between order and freedom and presupposes religious belief. Our Fathers insisted on a government of laws, not of men.

Kirk advances his last chapter with a small demurral. It is entitled "Contending against American Disorder". This might appear to be going beyond the terrain he set himself in his title, but, he argues, it is necessary "to say something about the troubled reality of order, and the idea of order, in nineteenth-century America." This is fairly familiar to most of us, but Kirk provides an angle on it that very, very few of us will have encountered in our schooling.

He advances the name of Orestes Brownson as perhaps the most perspicacious critic of nineteenth-century America. Brownson, a New Englander, moved through most of the varieties of American religion (Congregationalism, Presbyterianism, Universalism, Unitarianism, and the like) in his search for authority. He was finally received into the Catholic Church, a very *un*-American move in those days. But his move makes sense, though it may have cost him the attention of American historians. He criticized the *merely* democratic suppositions that were at work in American imagination (suppositions that no orthodox Christian can quite buy), and he insisted on a fixed moral order as necessarily underlying any healthy political life.

Kirk has chosen an astute commentator on American life for the ending of his book. Brownson's observations need no updating.

Two things remain to be said. First, Kirk has included a large chronology, bibliography, and index to his book—always welcome in a work of this magnitude. Second, anyone who wishes to reflect and talk on the topic "America", and especially any Christian who wishes to do so, will do himself a favor if he reads Kirk's book.

Of More Than Routine Interest: Ten Ways to Destroy the Imagination of Your Child

Here is a book that will send a reviewer—and all decent-minded readers—groping for superlatives. Indeed, I find it difficult to refrain from cluttering my review with mere rhapsodies, which might be warranted, but which do not throw much light on things.

Anthony Esolen mounts a crushing and delightful riposte to the whole array of theories on the rearing and education of children that preside in current American culture. Ironically, however, the note he strikes, far from sounding the sullen tone often marking the work of those who (justly) find themselves appalled at those doctrines, is *joyous*. Sprightly, lucid, exultant: such words touch on the spirit of the book.

Early on we find a crucial distinction between, on the one hand, the modern notion that what the child needs above all is to be set free from the iron grid of dull memory work (dates and names, etc.), so that he is free to float in the ether of free-wheeling "creativity", and, on the other hand, the ancient notion that memory places a child within a lineage in which he is a very recent arrival. The latter approach helps the child to avoid the trap of hubris. Esolen marshals everything from Icelandic sagas to *Ray's*

September 29, 2013, *The Imaginative Conservative* (originally appeared in *Modern Age* and the *Intercollegiate Review*, reprinted with permission).

New Higher Arithmetic (1880) to demonstrate this point. The tedious burden of numbers and facts and dates (says modernity) can quell a child's creative spontaneity. Esolen responds by extolling the numbers and the facts. He suspects—with good reason—that an untutored "creativity" most often lures a child into the fen of mere banality and solipsism.

At this point Esolen considers the modern anxiety that hovers like a nanny over children's education. He suggests waggishly that one tactic for protecting your child from the threat of brittle and demanding reality might be, then, to keep your child indoors, since outdoors, what with its winds and waves and woods and loam and curious little paths, with the vast sky flung overhead like an azure canopy, might vitiate his conviction that he is the center of everything. Don't let your child discover the psalmist: "When I consider the heavens, the work of thy fingers, the moon and the stars which Thou hast ordained ..." or G.M. Hopkins' "What wind walks! What lovely behaviour / Of silk-sack clouds...." The danger here is that your child might be beckoned out into That-Which-Is-Bigger-than-He, thus planting in his mind the humbling idea that all of this immensity exists quite apart from whether it *pleases* him or is *convenient*.

The next theory (or "Method Two" in Esolen's litany of the tactics proposed by contemporary educational canons) warns us against allowing a child to play unsupervised games of his own devising. The great thing is to ensure that he is "socialized into a managed world". Over against the old spontaneous world of Hide and Seek, Red Rover, Cops and Robbers, Jump Rope, or Leap Frog, all of which seemed to have sprung any-old-how from the rough-hewn nature of childhood itself, linking children with centuries of play, we now find the great pall of

Planning, issuing from the ponderous and shadowy committees who "know" what children need.

In this connection we find Esolen unexpectedly putting the case in favor of machines. Machinery is *dangerous*, say the experts: safety, safety, safety, at all costs. We might, in such a book, have expected the usual jeremiad decrying the rattle and filth of the Machine Age. But Esolen is no Luddite. He reminds us that machinery is a Good Thing: refrigerators ("ice-boxes", they once were called) obviated the whole business of sawing ice and hauling it from ponds; washing machines lightened the backbreaking work of washboards. He points out the fascination of backhoes and pile drivers that invite a child to ponder such contraptions, thus saving Esolen's argument from being a mere encomium to The Past.

The old, unedited fairy tales and folk tales, which opened out onto a totally unregulated domain, patently dangerous for a child's emotional health, simply won't do. We can't have the wolf gobbling up granny, or Cinderella's sisters having their eyes pecked out by helpful little birds. All too gruesome—the modern theory being that the child must never be asked to cope with the gruesome. I must confess that I myself might wish to tax Esolen on this point—amiably, to be sure. But *his* point is that those old tales, at times gruesome, roused a child's imagination. They saw life in all of its peremptory starkness. They never *applauded* the gruesome. Furthermore, the figures that showed up in those stories were patently good or evil. Esolen remarks here, "It has been a great victory for the crushers of imagination to label such figures 'stereotypes,' and add a sneer to it, as if people who used them in their stories were not very imaginative." Current educational theories, with the moral vision that suffuses them, suppose that at all costs everything must be nuanced. Since there are no eternal fixities anyway, we can never presume to judge people—whether thieves or cruel stepmothers. Esolen's rejoinder here is that in the realm of faerie we do, in fact, come up against intransigent figures—or better, archetypes: orcs, Dark Riders, dragons, wicked stepmothers. That's what the genre is about. It is in other genres of literature—serious drama, or post-eighteenth-century prose fiction, say—that we undertake the nuanced psychological scrutiny of human behavior.

Speaking of the (praiseworthy) case of traditional romance novels, we find this: "Some years ago, the romance novels were populated by women dying to swoon into the arms of Dangerous but Gentle Men, who only needed a Loyal Woman to bring them back into Decent Society. Now what they need is a Strong Woman, a Lady Lawyer, or an Adventuring Careerist—the clichés will shift from decade to decade, but the fullness will remain. Remember to foster banality."

If we were to forge straight on through Esolen's swashbuckling (but wholly fair) assault on modern theories of child-rearing, this review could run to insupportable length. We have so far canvassed only four of the ten aspects in Esolen's critique. Heroes and patriots—what about them? Who is the "hero" now? Sex: What has become of Odysseus' shy and exquisitely delicate ode to Nausicaä, whom he might have seized and ravished on the spot if he had been weaned on contemporary cinema? Or the Scot William Douglas' musings on Annie Laurie: "Her brow is like the snow-drift, / Her neck is like the swan, / ... And dark blue is her e'e, / And for bonnie Annie Laurie / I'd lay me doon and dee." Or gender: Could Milton have gotten away nowadays with his unabashed extolling of Adam's delicate plea to Eve, who, in demure and maidenly hesitancy, has fled from the approach of the Masculine? Or

Sigrid Unset: surely editors now would have incredulously blue-penciled these lines: "The child grew red with pleasure, for she knew well that her father was held to be the comeliest man far around; he looked like a knight, standing there among his men." Fie.

This book, in my opinion, qualifies for the *New Yorker*'s category, "Of More Than Routine Interest". Far more. The work is remorselessly perspicacious, prophetic, serious, amusing, and vastly refreshing.

A Conversation with
Thomas Howard and Frank Schaeffer

Tom Howard is an old friend. He has also been something of a mentor not only to me but to a whole generation of Protestants who have found their way into the historical Church. Tom's book *Evangelical Is Not Enough* played a major role in my spiritual journey from Protestantism to Orthodoxy. Tom is a gifted scholar. To his many loyal friends, however, Tom is much more than a Ph.D., professor of English, and writer. To those who know him, Tom is a gentleman, a man of letters, and a self-effacing example of Christian piety, not to mention civility.

I first met Tom in the early 1960s at L'Abri Fellowship, the Protestant retreat and study center in Huémoz, Switzerland, founded by my parents, Francis and Edith Schaeffer. I was a teenager and Tom a young man. I remember being impressed by the fact that Tom came from one of the most "influential" Protestant families in America. (There are indeed hierarchies even in Protestantism!) His father and grandfather were revered editors of a well-established magazine.

Tom's arrival in our community caused quite a stir, since in addition to his distinguished family, Tom had just published an immensely successful book, *Christ the Tiger*. Tom's book was taking the more literary elements of the Protestant, evangelical community by storm. As

Introduction by Frank Schaeffer, editor of *The Christian Activist*. Reprinted with permission. Copyright ©1996-2003 Orthodox Opinion, Ltd. All rights reserved.

the years passed, from time to time I would hear news of the illustrious Howards, particularly of Tom Howard's writing and his sister, Elisabeth Elliott, and her work as a famous missionary and author. Whenever Tom and his distinguished family became the topic of conversation, they were always spoken of with love, respect, and reverence.

I was pleasantly surprised when, in 1980, my wife and I discovered that in moving to the North Shore area of Boston we had coincidentally become virtual neighbors of Tom Howard. Tom and I became reacquainted and found we shared a deep interest in sacramental forms of Christian worship and that as such we both had a growing interest in Roman Catholicism.

During the early 1980s I would sometimes drop by Tom's house as a guest and participate in what became his famous "beer and bull" sessions. These were casual discussions carried on amongst various Protestant, mainly evangelical, men who, for one reason or another, had developed an interest in the historical Church and sacramental worship. Most of us were at that time refugees from evangelical churches and were attending various Episcopal churches and/or Anglo-Catholic parishes. We looked to Tom as a guide to the extent that he seemed the most likely to "pope" first (in other words, to become a Roman Catholic). Tom's erudite intellectual ability, his love of the English language, his warm personality and good humor did nothing to diminish our interest in Roman Catholicism. If a staunch evangelical Episcopalian like Tom Howard was seriously considering a move to Rome, it gave the idea a certain respectability even for us ex-evangelicals with all our anti-Catholic prejudices.

In 1985, Tom was received into the Roman Catholic Church. His conversion cost Tom his job teaching English at the evangelical school of Gordon College. Nevertheless, several of Tom's friends followed him to the Roman

Church. Several others did not. I was one of those who did not. Ironically it was Tom Howard who first directed me toward the Orthodox Church inasmuch as I learned through him of the writings of such contemporary Orthodox authors as Alexander Schmemann. Over the years, Tom had also talked about some friends of his, especially Peter Gillquist and something called the "Evangelical Orthodox". At that time, except for Tom, I had never met a Protestant or Roman Catholic who took the Orthodox Church very seriously. (Several years later, when I myself was becoming Greek Orthodox, I found that those "evangelicals" Tom had talked about, like Peter Gillquist and Weldon Hardenbrook, had been taken into the Antiochian Orthodox Church.)

As I began to move toward Orthodoxy, Tom was vocal in his encouragement. I realized that Tom had not only struggled with the same questions I had, questions that can be summed up as one question—What is the Church?— but that Tom Howard had seriously considered joining the Orthodox Church. I was chrismated into the Greek Orthodox Church at Christmas of 1990, five years after Tom became Roman Catholic. Tom and I have remained close friends. I have always been curious to ask Tom about certain points related to his decision to become Roman Catholic rather than Orthodox. The following conversation, "interview", goes a little way toward answering the question of why Tom Howard, or anyone else seeking the historic Church, would join the contemporary Roman Catholic Church rather than become Orthodox. It also, to my mind, illumines some important truths concerning the pitfalls confronting both the Roman and Orthodox communities in regard to modern, self-destructive liturgical and theological innovation.

❧ ❧ ❧

FS: What is the history of your work as an author?

TH: When I was in my early thirties, in 1967, I wrote a book called *Christ the Tiger*, a sort of young man's spiritual pilgrimage through some lurid worldly patches. The upshot of the book was that I did not throw in the sponge on Jesus Christ or Christianity. Christ triumphed over my somewhat devious ways in my twenties. *Christ the Tiger* caused something of a splash in evangelicalism.

FS: What came next?

TH: After *Christ the Tiger*, I wrote *Chance or the Dance?* about a Christian way of looking at reality. Any Orthodox, Roman Catholic, or evangelical Protestant person would agree with this book; that the universe represents a "dance", it's choreographed, it's orchestrated, it's not just random and haphazard. It was written from the point of view of literature and the arts. Then I wrote a book about the Christian household called *Hallowed Be This House*. Then I wrote a study of some of C. S. Lewis' fiction and another book about his friend, Charles Williams. [Editor's note: Thomas Howard is considered one of the foremost experts on the life and work of C. S. Lewis.] And finally I wrote a book called *Evangelical Is Not Enough*, in which I try to trace my own pilgrimage from good, sturdy, Bible-centered Protestant evangelicalism into a form of Christianity that was at least liturgical and sacramental and historical, namely, the Anglican or the Episcopal Church. Since that time, I've only written a couple of small books.

FS: Have you written any books on your journey from the Episcopal Church to Roman Catholicism?

TH: Yes. There is a small book called *Lead, Kindly Light*. The title is borrowed from a phrase in a hymn by the nineteenth-century literary and theological figure Cardinal Newman, who was himself a convert to the Catholic Church from Anglicanism. He wrote a hymn when he was on the ship coming back to England from Italy at some point in the 1840s. He was in agony about the possibility of having to become Roman Catholic, and he wrote a well-known hymn, well-known now that is, called "Lead, Kindly Light". "Amid the encircling gloom lead Thou me on." I borrowed that title for the record of my itinerary into the Roman Catholic Church. Most of my story had been already told in the book *Evangelical Is Not Enough*, but, of course, at the time I wrote that, I was still an Episcopalian.

FS: Your grandfather was a famous evangelical missionary; you have a well-known sister in evangelical circles; talk about some of these evangelical Protestant figures in your family, present and past.

TH: Well, for about a century, from the middle or latter part of the nineteenth century until about 1950 or 1960, there was in the family ... or let me put it this way, the men in my family were the editors of a journal that was, during that time almost, you might say, "the Bible" of Protestant fundamentalism. It was called *The Sunday School Times*. It was a venerable and trusted journal. My great-grandfather was the founding editor. Then my great-uncle succeeded him in the early twentieth century. My father succeeded him in about 1940. They were the custodians of this paper, and I think I was slated to be the next editor, but by that time I had begun to move in the direction of sacramentalism and the liturgical churches, and also, the paper being a somewhat old-fashioned and venerable institution, it simply didn't survive the post-WWII explosion of new Christian enterprises, new ventures, like the appearance of *Christianity Today*, and lots of other journals. So after my father retired, the paper closed. With me having become a Roman Catholic, an amusing item is that my parents and my four older siblings were all missionaries to Roman Catholic countries! My parents, in the 1920s, were Protestant missionaries in Belgium. My oldest brother in Northern Canada, near the Arctic Circle, is a missionary to Roman Catholics. My sister, Elisabeth Elliot, was in Ecuador. A brother of mine, Dave, in Colombia, South America, and another sister is in the Philippines. So here are all these evangelical missionaries to Roman Catholic countries, and then I end up becoming a Roman Catholic myself!

FS: What was the reaction of your family, especially with your distinguished missionary background, when you began to move out of "respectable" evangelical Protestant circles, first into the Anglican and Episcopalian churches, then beyond that toward Roman Catholicism?

TH: Well, it was 1960 when I was received into the Church of England, or the Anglican Church, and that was all right with my parents because at that time there was a very, very strong "evangelical" wing in the Church of England— John Stott, J. I. Packer, lots and lots of "good men" who were good friends of ours and allies—so my move into the Church of England was not alarming to anybody. Then my father died, and I moved on into what they call Anglo-Catholicism or "High Church" Anglicanism, where the liturgy looks much more Catholic. Nobody was alarmed. Then in 1985, when I was received into the Roman Catholic Church, my mother was very old by that time and didn't have a firm grip on things, so it didn't bother her. My brothers and sisters were all absolutely magnificent. Not one ripple between us, not one blip on the screen. They obviously have their own strong convictions, but it hasn't resulted in a shadow coming between any of us. Some of them are more than sympathetic to my point of view, although none of them have been received into the Catholic Church.

FS: Your wife, Lovelace, has recently joined you in the Roman Catholic Church.

TH: Yes, I was received in 1985, and she was received in 1995. People sometimes ask me whether there was tension, whether that was difficult, and actually, the answer is no. It was a wonderful thing to watch. As I came closer to the threshold of the Catholic Church, obviously we did need to talk things through. Lovelace is a very holy and wise and godly woman. She began to read about the Roman Catholic Church. One of her real spiritual mentors became Saint Francis de Sales, the Catholic bishop of Geneva just after Calvin's era. He won back to the Roman Catholic Church tens of thousands of converts to the Reformation after Calvin. He's a magnificent writer on the spiritual life, and he really was my wife's spiritual mentor. She also read a number of other authors, including Cardinal Newman, his book on the idea of development in Christian doctrine. It was a major milestone for her, as it had been for me. Lovelace was received into the Roman Catholic Church one year ago [1995]. The Archbishop of Boston, Cardinal Law, was personally very pastoral toward me and toward Lovelace. He received her himself at the cathedral on Easter morning. I would say she is the happiest woman in Christendom right now.

FS: Let me go back to your own journey from Protestantism to Roman Catholicism and, without going into every twist and turn, if you were putting together a lecture about this journey, what would your outline be?

TH: It began, I think, and I am happy to admit it, aesthetically. I saw and yearned for, deeply yearned for the beauty of the liturgy, the sense of mystery. As a young boy I knew that it was there in the Episcopal Church, and so I would admit those early steps were aesthetic. I wanted the beauty of the Renaissance polyphony, the vestments, the incense, the music, the tremendously rich hymnody, and also the magnificence and authority of the old Anglican Book of Common Prayer. So I became an Anglican while in England. That was really the first step for me toward the Roman Catholic Church, the major step.

FS: Didn't you spend some time studying in England?

TH: Actually, I was teaching at a boys' school there, and that is when I was received into the Anglican Church. That was around 1963. Then I came back to the United States, got my doctorate, and married Lovelace.

FS: Where did you do your doctoral studies?

TH: I did my M.A. at the University of Illinois in Champagne-Urbana and my doctorate in English literature at NYU, so my wife and I lived in Manhattan from 1965 to 1970 and were Episcopalians there and had our children baptized as Episcopalians. But I would argue that any thinking Episcopalian, because he is in a church that makes historic claims—which makes claims of apostolicity and so on—sooner or later is going to have to settle the question

of the Church. I would say that unless he, by some strange
alchemy, heads in a Protestant direction, he is going to find
himself on the threshold of either Byzantium or Rome, so
to speak: of either the Orthodox Church or the Roman
Catholic Church.

In my own case, I read and read and read and read, and
I would have said back in 1985 when I was received into
the Catholic Church, and I still would say, that I would
never quarrel with a man who has become Orthodox as
opposed to Roman Catholic because there is a sense in
which (I have to say it half-shamefacedly) I gave up on
the questions. You see, I had read Kallistos Ware, George
Florovsky, Alexander Schmemann, Thomas Hopko, John
Meyendorff. I had read all these authors and totally could
see the Orthodox point of view. I don't remember the
fine tuning, but I eventually concluded that if these two
ancient sees, the East and the West, cannot unscramble the
questions that lie between them, and obviously at root it's
the question of Peter, that I, a solitary layman, can't get
them unscrambled either.

I pray every morning for the reunion of the Church,
on God's terms, not ours, and I will be the happiest man
in Christendom if that can ever get itself sorted out. But
meanwhile, I am a Western Christian, I am a Roman
Catholic.

But you were asking me the steps. I think, as I say, it
began aesthetically, but it came down to these questions
of history, apostolicity, and authority, and then eventually it boiled down to one question: What is the Church?
I think anybody like yourself, or me, particularly from
Protestant evangelicalism, because we, as you would tes-
tify, we were serious about the faith—it matters, it was
our whole life, it's ultimately serious, it's nothing to play
with—I think we took these questions very seriously. An

evangelical eventually wakes up and says, "Look, I've got Jesus. I've got the Bible. I've got the faith. I love the Gospel. We've got zeal, we've got creativity, we've got energy. We've got everything. But what is the Church? WHAT IS THE CHURCH?" That question became relentless for me. What is the Church? I am one of the ones who was eventually received into the Latin Church. However, I was very much shoulder to shoulder and side by side with Peter Gillquist and the other evangelicals who were received into the Antiochian Orthodox Church. You, one of my trusted friends, Frank, became Greek Orthodox, and, as I say, you people are my allies, not my enemies.

FS: Let's say that we could roll the clock back, and you were still in the midst of the last couple of years of your journey to the Roman Catholic Church, and you were talking to a Protestant friend who was also asking himself the burning question: What is the Church? and he said, "Tom, you're my good friend, but I've got this other friend, Frank Schaeffer, and he's telling me that you're a good fellow, Tom, but that a fuller expression of the ancient faith can be found in the Orthodox Church." Obviously, in good conscience, you would be telling that person your point of view, and no doubt as someone on the way into the Roman Catholic Church, you would make some effort to steer him in what you would consider to be the right direction. How would you make the Catholic argument to the truly inquiring person who has come to the stage of saying, "I want liturgy, I want to be in The Church, I'm standing on the threshold, and yet there is something holding me back, I'm looking at both Orthodoxy and Catholicism." You must meet people like that all the time.

TH: Oh, sure, and I've lost any number of them to Orthodoxy! (Laughter) I would do the following, and I would push it only so far, and then I would let go, because it would not make me sad to see them be received into the Orthodox Church. I would simply put the case for the way the Roman Church took shape in those early centuries. You had the bishops around the Mediterranean eventually sort of say, "*Roma locuta est, causa finita est.*" (Rome has spoken, the case is decided.) The question is laid to rest. I would recount that. And, in a sense, that is the watershed. It was in that epoch of the Church around the Mediterranean taking shape that the Petrine See emerged. Also, of course, the Roman Catholic Church does attach enormous weight to the unique things that were said to Peter as "prince of the Apostles". The binding in heaven and earth, the threefold command "Feed My lambs", which wasn't explicitly given face to face to other disciples, the uniqueness of Peter in the New Testament Church. The Roman Catholic Church attaches an enormous weight to all this, and they see a seamless metamorphosis or growth from that to Peter's successors in Rome—Linus, Cletus, Clement of Rome, and so forth. I would push it that far. I would mention the scriptural texts, the "Petrine texts", and simply make that historical sketch. After that I would probably tiptoe offstage, because an Orthodox can give a Roman Catholic some bad moments. For example, if he presses home the question, "Where did you people get the filioque? That wasn't added until, what was it, the eighth century in Spain somewhere?" Interestingly enough, I've never found a Roman Catholic theologian who has much of an answer to that. So as far as I can tell, in the West we have to say yes, they scotch-taped that on. Although obviously Roman Catholic theology would say it's a true understanding of the Trinity. I would not be one of the ones who would go to war about someone becoming Orthodox, as I said.

FS: Let me ask you a question that is in a way more relevant, because we each have to get up every Sunday morning and must decide where to go to church. Just to give you a bit of background from my own experience, one of the reasons I did not become a Roman Catholic but became Orthodox is because of the state of modern American Roman Catholicism. After all, I don't live in Florence in the fifteenth century, any more than I live in Byzantium in the eighth century. I live in Newburyport, Massachusetts, in the 1990s. The question of where I go to church next Sunday is very relevant because it's not a small question, especially if one puts an emphasis on the sacraments and on liturgy. It's a lot more than "Where do I hear next Sunday's sermon?" Anyway, one of my problems with contemporary American Roman Catholicism, it seems to me, is that the contemporary Roman Catholic scene has been deeply corrupted by left-wing political thought. This in turn has opened the door to all kinds of liturgical innovation, wherein, for instance, if I accompany my son to Mass in the private Roman Catholic high school he happens to be attending now, I'm as likely to see things that will scandalize my Orthodox sensibilities as I would be if I went to a local "liberal" Protestant church. Tom, you being someone with your eyes open, I just wonder what your feeling about all this corruption of the modern American Roman Church is. Surely you must have, if not misgivings about the Roman Catholic Church, certainly you must have misgivings about the contemporary American situation? I subscribe to a paper called *Adoremus*, and I happened to read an article of yours in it. As far as I can tell, this paper is put out by faithful and loyal traditional

Roman Catholics who lament the devalued currency of modernized American Roman Catholic liturgy in the same way that an Orthodox would. Correct me if I'm wrong. What's the history of this?

TH: There are two or three levels on which that question, which you have put very well, needs to be addressed or answered. The history of that is the liturgical corruption in the Second Vatican Council. From about 1960 to 1965, I think it was, enormous changes were made. One can get the documents in a paperback book, and actually, if you read the text, it was very, very wonderful scriptural stuff. A Protestant evangelical reading it would say, "Praise the Lord! Look at all this!" What happened after that, though, because the West was going through the convulsions of the Vietnam War, the hippies, the whole radical New Left movement, the sexual revolution— violence and change and anarchy were abroad—was catastrophic. Thousands, maybe millions of Roman Catholics, including nuns, priests, monks, sort of said, "Yippee! The windows are open! Anything can happen now!" And, of course, thousands of monks and nuns drained out of the monasteries and the convents, and a lot of liturgical fiddling began to take place. A new order for Mass in the vernacular (in French, English, German) was promulgated from Rome, and it was still a perfectly orthodox Mass, but people took whatever small bits of elbow room were given, or took room that they weren't allowed, and simply ran off with the Mass.

Today you'll have a priest come to the front of the church at the beginning of the Mass and instead of saying, "In the name of the Father, Son, and Holy Ghost", say, "Hi, nice day today. Good to see you all here." And you're off and running with that terrible music, that chatty modern Roman Catholic way of doing the liturgy, and this is dreadful! You mention *Adoremus*. What that paper is trying to do is not to go back to the old Latin liturgy, but simply to return to that authentic thing which Vatican II brought to pass and which, in some senses, was left in the dust by people just picking up and going haywire with it in the 60s and 70s. This does bring up a key point in answer to the bigger question that you're asking. A Roman Catholic like myself or anybody else, who looks around on the local scene or even the national scene in the American Roman Catholic Church sees things that he doesn't like—various forms of feminism, various forms of heresy, this, that, and the other thing . . .

FS: Of which, by the way, you would feel a lot of Roman Catholics have succumbed to . . .

TH: Oh, indeed, but I myself would be—I mean, I'm happiest with the third century, so to speak—but, you see, a Roman Catholic's situation is different from a Protestant's. A Protestant looks at the collapse or the draining away of orthodox religion and has nowhere to turn. A Roman Catholic has still got the Petrine See in Rome. It is of the esse, the essence of the Church. A Roman Catholic believes that there is a scriptural promise that heresy will not be taught from the Roman See; "You are Peter. On this rock I will build My Church, and the gates of hell will not prevail against it." The Church, says Saint Paul in Timothy, is the pillar and ground of the Truth. Not only are we not hearing heresy from John Paul II, we are having a ringing, glorious affirmation of the faith.

To a Protestant or Orthodox, the next question might be, "Well, what about all the wicked popes in the Renaissance?" And the very interesting and piquant point about that is, yes, indeed, there were wicked popes—Dante has half the popes in hell—but not one of them changed one jot or tittle of the theological or the moral teaching of the Church. Whereas other benches of bishops, which shall be nameless, in our own day are applauding homosexual promiscuity, adultery, and everything else, themselves in a frolic through Sodom and Gomorrah. Not one of those wicked Renaissance popes ever said, "Yes, I have lovers backstage here, and this is a deeply Christian style of life." They knew they were going to hell. They knew they were sinning. So as a Catholic, I feel that my position is not any better or worse than a Catholic Christian in fourth-century Hippo, tenth-century France, fifteenth-century Germany. There has always been heresy abroad.

I happen right now to be reading Saint Augustine's huge book, *The City of God*. He says that you are going to have good and bad in the Church. For us Protestants, particularly us Protestant evangelicals, our answer to trouble in the Church was split, split, split, split, split. Start a new church every hour on the half-hour in the interest of "orthodoxy"! Well, both the Western Catholics and the Eastern Orthodox would say, "You can't do that." Saint Augustine said to the Donatists, who were the "evangelicals" of his day, "Hey, guys, your desire to purify the Church is a good desire. But you can't do what you are doing. You can't split the Church." I believe that the gates of hell will not prevail. If it gets down to me and John Paul II (of course, it won't!), I believe that the gates of hell will not prevail.

I think one other thing needs to be said here on the question you raise. It's an article of faith that heresy will not prevail. It took Athanasius years to get Arianism out of the Church. You will have found this in Orthodoxy. There is a very, very profound and authentic breed of piety, you might say, in Orthodox or Roman Catholic bosoms that is unrecognizable to a Protestant evangelical. If a Protestant evangelical can't get somebody to say "I know Jesus is my Savior" or, "I have accepted the Lord Jesus Christ into my heart", he has doubts about that person's salvation. But the world is full of old Greek crones and babushkas, Sicilian peasant women, you name them, who wouldn't be able to find the Letter to the Colossians if you handed them the New Testament, and yet they are there day by day, standing before the throne with their prayers. Charity is being formed in them. I think that's a huge element that gets missed, that an evangelical can look at his neighboring Orthodox or Catholic church and say, "But those people don't know Jesus. They can't stand up and give a testimony." But, I think your experience has probably been the same as mine, Frank. The longer you live in the milieu of the historic Church, you realize, my word, this is authentic Christian piety here.

FS: You said that the beginning of your journey to liturgical worship was the aesthetic quality in the liturgical practices of the Anglican and Roman Catholic Church . . .

TH: I know what you're going to ask. You mean, how well is the Roman Catholic Church doing on the aesthetic front?

FS: Correct.

TH: Why Catholics can't sing? Indeed. That's a very, very good question. There is a great deal to be deplored, or at least regretted, and almost everybody realizes that.

FS: Well, tell me a little about what that is, for people who haven't been in a Roman Catholic church for the last thirty years. What's going on?

TH: Well, I might put it this way. When I was an Episcopalian, I used to drag people to the Episcopal liturgy in the hope that would convert them, and it did. They were swept away. There are scores and scores of my former fundamentalist students who are, as I speak, Episcopalians because I took them to the Episcopal liturgy. It was so beautiful. But now if somebody wants to come to a Roman Catholic Mass with me, I might say, "Oh, er, I don't know whether you … you don't really want to come", and so on. The Roman Catholic Church is very much like the Lord. There is no form or comeliness. When you see it, there is no beauty that you should desire it. Now, perhaps that's a little bit too ferocious. Of course, there is still a great deal of true beauty here and there, but the specialty of particularly American Roman Catholicism is not gorgeous liturgy! The music is either nonexistent or of a very, very, very poor quality. Terrible! There is a lot that could be said there. Very often the Mass is said in a chatty or offhand way. There is a general, what seems to an Orthodox, evangelical, or Episcopalian, a general lack of reverence.

FS: What about all this business where altars have been taken out of Roman Catholic churches, and the place has been covered with linoleum and the crosses are gone? To me, the modern American Roman church is a building that looks something like a United Nations meditation room wherein someone who acts like a not particularly talented talk show host …

TH: An emcee …

FS: Yes, an emcee at a used-car-dealer convention, is presiding as "priest". Somebody is up there with an electric guitar. Someone claiming to be a "nun", wearing no habit or visible sign of an order, strolls in and says something. Kids serve the Eucharist, or it seems to me they are serving it—maybe technically they are not. What is all this about? What's going on in your churches? For someone who has an aesthetic sense ... Of course, our readers ought to know that I've known you and your taste in literature, and so on, a long time, so you know, my feeling must be, well, Tom Howard's flesh must be crawling!

TH: Well, I think the answer to that is fairly straightforward. That is, as in so many other situations, there is a spectrum. That is to say, some of the scouring out of churches, the removing of the statues and the ornateness, was perhaps in the interest of something good. That is, they had gotten cluttered and so on, and of course the Benedictines have always had extreme simplicity in their churches, so, in one sense, the presence or absence of art in a Catholic church, or decoration or whatever, is not necessarily of the essence. A statue in a Western church does not have the meaning or place that an icon in an Eastern Orthodox church has. So that would be a problematical question. Do we like it or don't we? The one thing that is the absolute "tuning fork" or "litmus test" or, should we say, presence that makes a Catholic church a real Catholic church is the tabernacle with the consecrated host in it. So whatever the rest of the enterprise looks like, whether it's trashy and tacky or gorgeous, those are secondary questions. After all, Bethlehem was a jerkwater town. The manger was the worst accommodation in the town. There was only one thing to be said for it. God was there. And as an Episcopalian, of course, it mattered to me. I wanted to find the best music and the best preaching and the best architecture. So you shop around. You go tooting around. As a Roman Catholic, I go around the corner to my local parish. Locally I have good Christians to fellowship with, fellow believers. There's no nonsense there. It's a fairly plain parish. Not a fancy Mass. Interestingly enough, the present "pastor", as they now call our priests, restored some of the statuary to the church. But again, a Roman Catholic would have a robust sense of what is the taproot here. What is really important? What is essential and what is peripheral? And what you were mentioning, of course, the terrible music or even haywire ways of doing things, as I say, that would represent a spectrum from legitimate changes—which do or don't matter—all the way over to license, to things that are really doing a disservice to the faith. On the question of music, which I suppose we all have, I simply have to speak as somebody who loves Gregorian Chant and Renaissance polyphony. Okay, I admit, that is a question of taste for me. I cannot insist on Palestrina. I am not happy with what they call these "praise songs". It's a whole new genre, a whole new ilk of music that has overtaken the Church, and that evangelicalism is now full of, too.

FS: Wouldn't you say that the evangelical movement, to this extent, has succeeded in "Protestantizing" American Roman Catholicism?

TH: Yes, to a very significant degree.

FS: Speaking of which, I know you stay in touch with your Orthodox friends, and, from time to time, you go to an Orthodox liturgy or service or Vespers or Compline, whatever it might be. Is what is going on in the liturgies and the prayers and tones of the Orthodox Church something that is attractive to you? Do you like the traditional Orthodox forms?

TH: Enormously! Enormously! As a matter of fact, I don't even know the exact musical designation, but whatever one hears in that particularly Russian, I think, music in the Orthodox Church where they have three or four people around a lectern who are carrying the choir part, I'm thrilled by that. When I walk into an Orthodox church, which I did just the other night for a great Compline, one is indeed immediately aware that one has stepped into the presence of what Saint Paul would call the whole family in heaven and earth. You have stepped into the precincts of heaven!

As a Western Catholic, I ... is envy a proper word? Indeed, indeed, I love the Orthodox Church's spirit. I think the Orthodox Church, many, many centuries ago, discovered a mode of music and worship that is timeless, that is quite apart from fashion, and that somehow answers to the mystery and the solemnity and the sacramental reality of the liturgy. We don't have that in the West. If we have anything that is analogous to it, it would indeed be Gregorian Chant, and that is hopefully experiencing something of a renaissance as we speak.

FS: There are a number of Orthodox writers and thinkers who are at some pains these days to point out that great swatches of the Western Church, at one point, were not "Roman Catholic" in the sense that you would think of that today. For instance, the Celts, a lot of the churches in Britain, France, a lot of this goes back to a classical form of Christianity that was neither "Eastern Orthodox" nor "Western Roman Catholic" but simply the early common Christian inheritance. There would be a belief that a lot of the character of the modern Roman Catholic Church is something that does not belong to the common Christian era. I know there is a debate over that, but given the fact that you yourself find Orthodoxy so congenial in its worship, do you think that it's a loss that so much of Western Christianity has taken on the characteristics of the sort of free-form, make-it-up-as-you-go-along Protestantism? Is there a truer tradition, one that is more truly indigenous to Europe and, by extension, to Western Christians everywhere?

TH: As you say, that would be one of the two or three absolutely taproot questions between the East and the West. I guess that the Roman Catholic answer would lie along the lines that John Henry Newman pursues in his book called *The Idea of Development in Christian Doctrine*. A Roman Catholic would perceive a legitimate and an organic growth in the churches until it was universally acknowledged that the Petrine See is the Apostolic See. On the Celtic question and so on, yes, one reads Saint Ninian, or reads about him, and that the Council of Whitby in A.D. 664 was where the question of the date of Easter was settled and the Celtic churches acknowledged the authority of Rome there. Obviously, the discussion between let's say a Roman Catholic historian—a Latin Church historian—and an Orthodox historian would soon get out of my league. I would simply have to be a listener. But it does, I suppose, come back to a Latin Christian attaching significance to the question of Peter.

FS: Which is what it always comes back to?

TH: Yes, it does.

FS: And you feel comfortable in accepting that?

TH: Yes. Yes, I think Peter is the sacrament of the Church's unity. The Petrine See is the sacrament of the Church's unity. Peter is the Vicar of Christ, who is, indeed, the head of the Church. And, you know, in trying to write this recent book that I'm writing about my own Catholic experience, I find myself saying, and it surprised me, it was true.... You know, Peter is only Peter. For instance, both you as an Orthodox and I as a Roman Catholic would put the Mother of God, the Theotokos, as really the preeminent human being. Obviously the Patriarchs, the Prophets, the Apostles, the Evangelists, the Martyrs, the Fathers—they all bore witness to the Word, but Mary bore The Word!

FS: You may or may not recall this, but many, many years ago, you and I were talking about the great dearth of liturgical practice and our problems in our local Episcopal communities, and so on, and you said to me, "Well, there is this little group of guys in California who came out of Campus Crusade led by someone called Peter Gillquist, whom you know from your days back in L'Abri Fellowship in Switzerland. You really ought to see what they are doing." This was at the time when the "Evangelical Orthodox" were on the verge of coming into the Orthodox Church. Ironically, it was you who first made me aware that there were other evangelicals out there who were thinking along these lines. Now, some twelve years later, here I am in the Orthodox Church and you are in the Roman Catholic Church, and yet obviously, as you indicated earlier in this interview, there was a time when you were thinking seriously about Orthodoxy for yourself. I think there is some irony in the fact that you became Roman Catholic and yet some of your writing, such as *Evangelical Is Not Enough*, some of your contact with Peter Gillquist, for instance, played a role in bringing a number of converts like me into the Orthodox Church.

TH: Yes, and as you say, there is an irony, quite a piquant irony there. I guess it comes back to this elusive question: Why did I head West, so to speak? It's a little bit hard to know what the chicken and the egg were. I think, number one, I did indeed, with as much integrity as I could muster, I did indeed realize that I could not finally sort out the question of the division between the East and West, the Petrine question.

FS: Do you think that some of it was cultural? I mean, if we are really being honest, you come from a Western tradition, you live in the United States, not in Greece. I wonder if your background had been slightly different, let's make a completely unlikely scenario here, but picture, somehow, that you were a professor teaching English literature in Thessaloniki, and you happened to have married a Greek woman thirty years ago. It doesn't seem very far-fetched to see you in the Greek Orthodox Church today.

TH: No, it doesn't. Would I be so stuck to the Petrine question?

FS: Or let's say that you had been teaching at the University of California at Santa Cruz, and right up the street was Saint Peter and Saint Paul Orthodox Church with Father John Hardenbrook, or Father Peter Gillquist and company, and that you had been doing your "beer and bull" discussions there. It's a little hard for me to see you being Roman Catholic today.

TH: My very strong guess is that I probably would, indeed, have become Orthodox. Of course, then I would have to ask myself, but would my own understanding of the Petrine question then be a different one? And all one can do is to say, I have tried to take each step with integrity. I will very often, when someone comes to see me or writes to me, who is on the threshold of apostolicity—or asking the question, what is The Church?—I have more than once told them that it may indeed be the case that they really ought to look seriously into Orthodoxy because I think again, heavy duty theology or ecclesiology aside, I think in some ways it's less of a step for a good biblical Protestant evangelical to come into the Orthodox Church. In some ways it looks more strange—the icons, the architecture of the church, and the ethnicity—but there is something more immediately visible and transparent about Orthodoxy. To an evangelical, the Roman Mass can seem merely rote. Also, a Westerner has got the whole history of historical difficulties—the wars, the mutual burnings at the stake, the hostility. An evangelical grows up being anti-Roman. He doesn't grow up being anti-Orthodox. The Orthodox Church does not exist for most evangelicals. So there is no trauma when the evangelical embraces Orthodoxy.

FS: Wouldn't you say another point of similarity, even though it wouldn't be obvious at first, is that the Orthodox Church has a conciliar tradition in which no one bishop ever claims to speak "ex cathedra" or "infallibly" as the pope does?

TH: I think that, indeed, is probably the bottom line. It would be a toss-up, if one can speak irreverently, it would be neck and neck between the pope and the Virgin Mary as to which is the more difficult for the Protestant! Of course, a Protestant evangelical is going to have just as much trouble with the Orthodox view of the Blessed Mother of God. Even there, however, when the Orthodox Church speaks of the Dormition of the Mother of God, it is in contrast to the Western Church that has defined the dogma of the Assumption. The Protestant looks at that and says, "Hey, I think I can live with the Dormition (which of course entails the Assumption), but the Orthodox Church doesn't promulgate these things as dogmas."

FS: But don't you feel from your own point of view that, if I was going to argue with you, which is inconceivable considering how long we've been friends, not to mention what a reasonable person you are, Tom—I'm not reasonable, but when I'm with you, I catch that disease and become almost reasonable (laughter)—but if I were going to argue with you, I'd say, "Isn't there something refreshing about the Orthodox tradition of not being so dogmatic, where you have the idea that the teaching of the Church lives within the liturgical tradition and not everything has to be set down in black and white?" After all, Tom, the Eastern Orthodox view of the seven ecumenical councils is almost one of default. Whereas the Church already believed these things, the councils were simply called to rectify heretical belief. From our Orthodox point of view, it would have been better had this "dogma" never had to be set down at all and it had just been maintained in the liturgy. In terms of your own personal sensibility, doesn't the Western Augustinian, rationalistic, Aristotelian approach—however you want to put it—fall short? Don't you think that the lack of dogma is one of the things that speaks well of the Orthodox tradition, that it has not gone down the rationalistic Western path?

TH: Well, of course, that is a good question. It is interesting to me that it is in some sense the Greek Church that sees the whole West, Latin and Reformation, as being Hellenistic or staggering along under rationalistic, Aristotelian categories. The only rejoinder that a Roman Catholic can mount to this particular question is simply that regarding Christian truth, all syllogistic categories fail. They collapse. They stop short of the Mystery. Nevertheless, reason is a God-given faculty. Certain numbers of things can be said and even defined. Probably again what we would need is an ecclesiologist here or a theologian. But probably the Roman Catholic view of those ecumenical councils is very close to the Orthodox view. Namely, indeed, Chalcedon, or Nicea, or Constantinople did in fact find a phraseology on which we may lay our case.

FS: Let me change the subject. There is a new biography out about C. S. Lewis called *Jack*, published by Crossway. Who is the author?

TH: His name is George Sayer.

FS: I believe he was a friend of C. S. Lewis?

TH: Very much so. They used to take walking holidays together.

FS: I have not read the whole book, but someone drew my attention to a certain section describing a holiday where George Sayer, C. S. Lewis, and C. S. Lewis' wife, Joy, went off to Greece. C. S. Lewis attended some Greek liturgies and a Greek wedding. I was quite surprised that Sayer quotes C. S. Lewis as telling him that of all the liturgies he'd ever attended, he preferred the Greek Orthodox liturgy to anything that he had seen in the West, Protestant or Roman Catholic. Then he went on to say that of all the priests and monks that he had ever had the opportunity to meet, the Orthodox priests that

he ran across in his sojourn in Greece were the holiest,
most spiritual men he had ever met. C. S. Lewis referred
to a certain look they had, a sense.

I know you are a scholar and an expert on C. S. Lewis,
so I'd like your comments. I find it odd to read this pro-
Orthodox statement stuck in the middle of a biography
being sold by a Calvinistic, Protestant publishing company.
This brings up a point: Isn't it strange that C. S. Lewis is an
"evangelical hero" when he certainly cannot be described
as Protestant, let alone "evangelical" in the classical sense?

TH: You've put your finger on a very, very interesting
point. I had an article in a Roman Catholic magazine
called *Crisis* several months back on this very point: on
C. S. Lewis and his evangelical "clientele". Not only is it an
irony, it is a contradiction. Lewis would have been appalled
by the evangelical adulation of his work. He would have
been horrified, even enraged by a lot of what he would
see today in American evangelical circles. He was not a
free church evangelical. C. S. Lewis was a sacramentalist,
an Anglican who really did not want to pursue the ecclesiological question farther than he did. He resisted, rather
angrily sometimes, the Church questions. But he was not at
all attracted to Protestant evangelicalism or even [Anglican
evangelicalism]. Actually I can bring it in closer than just
George Sayer's speaking about C. S. Lewis' attraction to
the Greek Orthodox liturgy. Lewis himself, and I probably
can find the quote for you, in one of his letters, I think it's
in *Letters to Malcolm*, speaks of having been at an Orthodox
liturgy, and he said he loved it. He said some stood, some
sat, some knelt, and one old man crawled around the floor
like a caterpillar! He absolutely loved it! Lewis' good, very
close friend J. R. R. Tolkien, the man who wrote the hobbit books, was a very devout Roman Catholic and tried

hard over the years to budge Lewis across the line. He got nowhere. Lewis would not speak about Church questions. We only know for sure that C. S. Lewis loved the Orthodox Church, though, of course, he never joined it and remained in the Anglican Church.

FS: Speaking just as a layman, it seems to me that the "theology" you get out of *The Chronicles of Narnia*, *The Great Divorce*, *The Screwtape Letters* is Orthodox. I was recently rereading *The Screwtape Letters*, and Lewis has a section where Screwtape (the lead demon writing to the little demon, Wormwood) says something like, "In misleading your Protestant convert, the best thing to do is get him to pray extemporaneously, make sure that above all he does not pray the liturgical prayers his mother taught him, let him think that everything he says is original." When I read C. S. Lewis, I hear an Orthodox voice. I hear a sacramentalist and liturgical traditionalist writing. How do evangelical, let alone fundamentalist, Protestants read C. S. Lewis and think that they are reading someone who is on "their side"?

TH: Maybe I'm being a little bit naughty, but the answer is, probably the same way they read the Bible! You and I would say the Apostolic Church is there, in its seed, in the Bible, but apparently it's possible to read the Bible as a Protestant for sixty or seventy or eighty years and never see it! By the same token, Lewis' evangelical American "clientele" simply don't get it. When C. S. Lewis speaks of the Blessed Sacrament, they don't hear it. When Lewis speaks of the prayers of the Church, they don't hear it. When Lewis speaks of auricular confession, which he practiced, they don't hear it. I think when Lewis smokes a cigarette or drinks his whiskey, they don't see it, either; not that

that's on the same level as his ecclesiology! (Laughter) C.S. Lewis would have been very, very ill at ease with his eager North American free church clientele. Very, very ill at ease and out of his metier.

FS: Let me change the subject. Within the Orthodox community right now, coming out of places like Holy Cross Seminary Press, certain professors at Saint Vladimir's Seminary, certain scholars and laymen and laywomen—really only a handful of people—there is a movement to come up with various so-called common translations of Orthodox liturgies and prayers that would supply the English-speaking Orthodox, whether Greek second generation or convert, with a "common liturgy" and a "common translation" from the Greek or from Church Slavonic to English. It's been my observation, as someone somewhat familiar with some of the liturgical problems and innovations in modern Roman Catholicism and also, of course, the liturgical problems within the Episcopal Church, that in the introduction of vernacularized English, the use of "politically correct" English in terms of gender, referring to "mankind" as "humankind", or changing the Creed "for us men and for our salvation" to "for us humans and for our salvation", this type of nonsense, that the Orthodox are opening a Pandora's box they scarcely comprehend. To someone from my background, who has seen the bad results of this type of innovation before, a lot of Orthodox seem to be rather naive about liturgical "innovation", seem to think that it is a matter of no consequence. But I wonder from your experience, both in the Episcopal community and now as a Roman Catholic who laments some of the liturgical innovations in your own community, if an Orthodox scholar at Holy Cross was saying, "What harm is there in changing this, that, and the other? What's the problem with this?

Why can't we use modern, 'politically correct' English everywhere?" What would be your general comment?

TH: I guess my answer, or rejoinder, also as a teacher of literature, would be to say that words touch on reality! They are the only way we have of getting a grip on reality. The liturgy is made up of words and gestures. When God came to us, he came as The Word made flesh. Words are crucial! They are essential! If you are affirming in your liturgy a God who might just as well have come as woman, then you're off and running with gnosticism. I would be one of the increasingly rare people to see that the substituting of "humankind" or "personkind" for "mankind" is a mistake. Not because I think that men are better or more important than women, but because I think that way of speaking of the whole species of Homo Sapiens cuts to the very center of reality. I think, on the other hand, womanhood, femininity, probably is indeed the custodian of our humanity. We men would botch it hideously if it weren't for the women here to keep us human. But all of this is by way of saying that if I were Orthodox, I probably would be in there with you thumping the tub for a frame of mind that attaches enormous weight to how things are said. Certainly the ecumenical councils had to. What's the difference between homoousion and homoiousion, this sort of thing—God of God, Light of Light, Very God of Very God, begotten not made, being of one essence with the Father. It matters how you say things! Liturgical modernization is like the frog in the boiling water. If you raise the water temperature, change it one degree at a time, by the time it's boiling the frog doesn't know it but he's also dead! I think that is what is being done with language in the Church, particularly in the Western churches, and, as of seeing you today, I now discover that there is something percolating like that in the Orthodox Church. My heart sinks! I look to the Orthodox Church, sort of wistfully and hopefully, and say, "Don't you guys change, for heaven's sake!"

FS: Don't you think feminism has been particularly insidious in its assault on the English language, to politicize it and use it as a political "tool" to bring about political change in a kind of backdoor manner of mind control?

TH: Yes. I don't think there's any question this is so. My guess is that the feminists would be the first to agree with that. The only historical analogy I know to the politicization of grammar is the fascist Mussolini. It had something to do with the second-person pronoun, singular or plural, in Italy in the 1930s. That's the only analogy that I know of for what the feminists are trying to do to the English language today. It's what the fascists tried to do in Italy.

FS: It seems to me that a lot of the energy for "modernization"—making things "trendy", "updating" them in the Roman Catholic Church, in the Protestant community, in the Episcopal Church, and now within some of these modern liturgical translations coming out of Orthodoxy—that the energy comes from wanting to stay in the "good books" of one's feminist colleagues on campus, one's token feminist on the "liturgical committee", whatever. It seems to me the majority of the faithful are not asking for these changes. It's always an elite, it's always from the top down, it's always scholars with a bee in their bonnet. You're a scholar, Tom. Is my suspicion true?

TH: I think there is no question that it is relatively small cadres who initiate and foster moves like this. I mean it only took four thousand Bolsheviks to overthrow the Czarist empire! I think what we have seen in the churches in the last twenty or thirty years in terms of language, sensibility, and now political correctness was begun by a smallish cadre, although, alas, one finds that certain ideas catch fire in a certain era. Feminist "political correctness" certainly has swept all before it in our own time. I think when you get an era like this, for someone like me, the real regret comes in the realization that there is no going back. The language will never, never return to what it was before. I deplore what has happened to it, but I have no hope at all that it will ever be restored.

FS: Wouldn't you say, though, that one of the areas where something historical and meaningful can be maintained— something that is true and sane and beautiful—would be in the Orthodox Church?

TH: Absolutely! The liturgy of the Church is crucial, and that's why these questions, particularly for the Orthodox and Roman Catholics more than others, are very, very important. Being a Roman Catholic, of course, I am not only consoled but I am energized, delighted, lifted up, whatever one wants to say, by the faith, the belief, that you are never going to find the Roman Catholic Church, the Apostolic See, teaching error. You may get what Walker Percy calls "nutty theologians", and indeed, we have more than our share of them. But eventually, when the chips are down, the gates of hell are not going to prevail. If the last trump holds off for another ten thousand years, the Church, the Orthodox Church, the One, Holy, Catholic, and Apostolic Church, in some modality will indeed be here. And because I'm a Latin Catholic, I believe that Peter will still be with the Church. But, you know, with you as an Orthodox, I probably would agree with 89.6 percent of everything you'd say about the Church!

FS: When it comes to liturgical innovation, modernization, vernacularization, my guess is that you and I would
be in 100 percent agreement.

TH: Yes, certainly in terms of sensibility. Absolutely. And
theologically. There is nothing in the Orthodox liturgy
at which I demur. There is not one single point. It may
be that the prayers, for example, might not include the
bishop of Rome, or something like that, but there is no
liturgical and ecclesial point at which I have to demur as a
Western Christian.

FS: A large number of ex-Episcopalians are retreating from
the modernized Episcopal Church—wherein there has
been radical liturgical innovation and wherein homosexuals are being ordained, et cetera, et cetera, we all know
the problems—they are running to the Orthodox Church,
some are running to the Roman Catholic Church. But a
growing number of Roman Catholics are also distressed by
what they regard as the mistakes of modernization within
Roman Catholicism and liturgy, some of the modern bishops, what's happened to the orders. They do not think that
Vatican II was the right thing to do. They don't say that
it was simply "misinterpreted"; they feel more than that,
that it was a terrible mistake. For instance, Father Alexei
Young, who is now an Orthodox priest, writes on that
subject quite passionately. Are you aware of the fact that
there are many Roman Catholics who are moving toward
Orthodoxy in the hope of escaping what they feel is the
modernization of the Roman Church?

TH: On some levels, I sympathize with them. I absolutely
understand. But as a Roman Catholic, I would be obliged
to say that insofar as they see Vatican II as being wrong or

flee our Church in anxiety that the old ship will sink, then their Catholicism is at fault. They did not believe what a Catholic is supposed to believe. On the other hand, I would not quarrel with them for landing themselves in the Orthodox Church. But I would say, if they asked me first, "You know, you don't have to do what you are doing in order to stay with the true Church." But if a Catholic is convinced that an ecumenical council, which Catholics believe Vatican II was, if he believes that a council can go wrong, then he doesn't believe what a Catholic is supposed to believe anymore.

FS: You know, from the Orthodox point of view, all the Roman Catholic councils that did not include the Eastern bishops ...

TH: ... are not ecumenical.

FS: Right. I mean, they may have said something true, but they certainly don't have the authority to say they're speaking for the Church. In other words, it's no longer Peter saying, "It seems good to us and the Holy Spirit." It's Peter saying, "It seems good to me!"

TH: So every council after, whatever the seventh one was, Constantinople or whatever, from the Orthodox point of view is not really an ecumenical council and, therefore, does not have unqualified authority. But in the Roman Catholic Church—it's like the Petrine question—councils cannot err.

FS: Do you feel your journey is complete? Sometimes I meet Orthodox who knew you back a dozen years ago when you were considering both Orthodoxy and

Catholicism. They'll say to me, "Oh, you see Tom Howard from time to time. What's Tom doing? Is he going to come into the Orthodox Church at last? Is his journey continuing? Is he happy in the modernized Roman Church?" In your heart of hearts, Tom, do you feel that absolutely, unequivocally your journey is now complete, or could there ever be a scenario where you might say, "You know, my step to Catholicism was a part of the road to the Church in the same way my sojourn in the Episcopal Church was. That road now has to be followed to an Orthodox conclusion ..."

TH: ... That Rome is only halfway between Canterbury and Byzantium?

FS: Right, so why not head on to Byzantium?

TH: Whichever answer I give would be slightly amusing. Supposing I said, yes, my journey is going on. By that I would mean, of course, I hope I'm going to heaven. I hope I'm in the Ark. I hope that my life has as its motivation the getting on with this business of being configured to Christ. So the next step for me is death and, after that, the Beatific Vision, I hope. Ecclesiologically, I mean obviously I'm a mortal, I'm limited, I'm not omniscient. But no, I have dropped anchor, I am home. I would say that. I don't see Rome as halfway to Byzantium, obviously. And if we really put the edge on the question, and if you were to ask me how I see the whole, the truly ecumenical— not the Geneva World Council of Churches one—but the real ecumenical question, if Christ's Church were to come back together, what would it look like? Obviously you and I, fast and firm friends and allies that we are, would give a slightly different answer. I would see it as in some sense gathered under the bishop of Rome. Who knows what sort of form, whatever it might be. You would not attach the same Petrine plumb line as I would to that question, but there we are.